Preaching Your Way Out of a Mess

Preaching Your Way Out of a Mess

A Handbook for Preaching in a Crisis

Johnny Teague

WIPF & STOCK · Eugene, Oregon

PREACHING YOUR WAY OUT OF A MESS
A Handbook for Preaching in a Crisis

Copyright © 2019 Johnny Teague. All rights reserved. Except for brief quotations in critical publications or reviews, no part of this book may be reproduced in any manner without prior written permission from the publisher. Write: Permissions, Wipf and Stock Publishers, 199 W. 8th Ave., Suite 3, Eugene, OR 97401.

Wipf & Stock
An Imprint of Wipf and Stock Publishers
199 W. 8th Ave., Suite 3
Eugene, OR 97401

www.wipfandstock.com

PAPERBACK ISBN: 978-1-5326-7762-5
HARDCOVER ISBN: 978-1-5326-7763-2
EBOOK ISBN: 978-1-5326-7764-9

Manufactured in the U.S.A.

This book is dedicated first and foremost to our Heavenly Father who is love and who demonstrated that love by giving us His Son Jesus to leave His side and come and bring us forgiveness and eternal life through dying on a rugged cross and rising from His death out of a burial tomb.

This book is dedicated to my parents who taught me of His love, to my wife Lori who shows me His love every day, and to our girls Brittany and Kate whom He has given us to love.

Contents

1. **The Crisis**—This opening chapter describes candidly the need which is well known to so many pastors. It cites specific examples and statistics which will be familiar to many and alarming to all who read through this chapter. | 1

2. **The Call**—To keep a pastor in the battle, it is important for him to remember his call into the ministry. This chapter reminisces about the day when pastors surrender to the ministry, their idealism, and the clarity of their purpose. It also looks at the natural attributes that every pastor should notice in his identity. | 13

3. **The Adversity**—This chapter is the "so what happened" chapter. It bridges the gap between the crisis now faced and the call once so determined. This chapter covers the agents of discouragement which must be recognized by the pastor. | 21

4. **The Pastor's Struggles**—This chapter investigates the dynamics of depression, discouragement, family stress, and personal money issues, whereby the preacher may be considering discontinuation of his vocation. | 30

5. **Pastoral Error**—This chapter will delve into errors made by the pastor with regard to leadership, attitudes, interpersonal relationships, prejudice, temper, and the ability to accept criticism constructively. If left uncorrected, the pastor's ministry or the life of the church may be in jeopardy. | 43

6. **Staff Immorality**—This chapter covers those crises in a ministry when members of the staff are involved in sexual misconduct, inappropriate relationships, or integrity issues. These issues can disrupt the ministry and fellowship between the church and the church staff. | 59

CONTENTS

7. **Doctrinal Crises**—This chapter lays the groundwork for various doctrinal issues where one or more people within the church begin to follow, recruit, and/or teach a doctrine contrary to Scripture. These may cause many to stumble. Focus—Charismatic Movement. | 76

8. **Doctrinal Issues**—Focus—Calvinism misunderstandings. | 96

9. **The Sins of the Church**—This chapter will discuss cliquish groups, moral drifts, prejudice, economic class struggles, and immorality within the body (such as theft, affairs, gossip, hypocrisy, and unforgiveness). These may quench the Holy Spirit's work. | 111

10. **The Power Struggle**—This chapter includes issues, such as challenges to the pastoral authority, manipulation by older or younger member groups, dominance by deacons or elders, and obstructionism by prime financial supporters of the church. These prevent a united stride toward fulfilling the Great Commission. | 132

11. **The Unexpected**—This chapter will deal with financial deficits, shortages, or windfalls. In addition, they include things such as facility problems, civil interruptions, and unexpected staff resignations. These draw focus away from the purpose of the church. | 153

12. **The Dying Church**—This chapter will deal with attitudes and contributors to a church's decline in attendance, relevance, and witness in a given community. These rob the church of its ability to be a going-concern in the community. | 170

13. **Church in Strife**—This chapter will deal with churches, which have been through a crisis, and face a desperate need for healing and a resetting of mission. These bring defamation to the name of Christ when love is not easily recognized. | 178

14. **The Culture**—This chapter will consider the pressure which culture places on churches to adopt lifestyles contrary to Scripture, tolerance of other religions, Biblical illiteracy, and quieting the focus on Jesus Christ. These seek to place the light of the church "under a bowl." | 198

15. **The Charge**—This chapter deals with a final encouragement that no matter the crisis, the pastor can preach his way through every one. | 210

Bibliography | 213

Chapter 1: The Crisis

Personal Story

I remember it like it was yesterday. I stood up in our business meeting to announce that we were moving our youth program from Wednesday nights to Sunday nights so more kids could be involved. This was such an innocuous move. No big deal I thought. One of my deacons—the best prayer warrior in our church, the man I probably respected more than any of our other deacons—stood up and interrupted my next comment. He did not just speak; he screamed, "You will not move the youth program to Sunday night. You don't have the authority in this church to do anything!" "Wow!" I wondered "Where did that come from?" I told the deacon that it was not a big deal, and that I felt I had the right to lead our church and make such a decision. He said, "You don't have any rights." I looked at my other deacons for help, or some other church member, but no one said a word. The whole congregation just seemed in shock. One deacon even began to laugh. What a nightmare! The following Sunday I resigned from the church. I felt that if I could not carry out the pastoral duties and hold the authority even to make small decisions, then I could not continue to be their pastor.

Some history—I had been in seminary for just one semester when I saw the note on the seminary's "Opportunities Board." The note was from a little rural church seeking a "supply preacher." I loved to preach, and immediately was interested as long as "supply preacher" meant more than taking care of pencils, pens, and other supplies. I called them, and we visited. They were a little church of eight people meeting in a house. They explained their situation and asked if I was still interested in doing some preaching. I said, "Of course I would love to help." They asked me to preach on the second Sunday that May. After that Sunday, they asked me to return two Sundays later. Then they requested me to stay until July. In July, they asked me to stay until October. Then in October, they called me to be their pastor. Our church began to grow until we outgrew the house and moved into a caterer's complex. We then bought and renovated a Ford dealership, and our church was off and running.

Along the way, I had several little skirmishes in which the founding deacon and a couple of others met with me and asked questions like, "Who told you that you could run an advertisement in the newspaper for our church?" (an advertisement for which my family paid), or "Who said you could allow a local radio station to air our services?" Each time I was so disgusted. We were growing, people were getting saved, new members were being added, and visitors were always present. Several times, I thought of quitting. I even submitted a letter of resignation once, to which they quickly apologized and retreated. However, this last Sunday, after six and one-half years, to have the deacon I respected so much spell out that I had no authority just broke my back. My family and I had commuted ninety miles one way every week for that entire pastorate and I served bi-vocationally for most of that time ministering to these families and this community. I finally decided if this is how little they appreciate me, it is time to resign.

The Reality

Have you ever been in this spot? I have heard harrowing stories of preachers going on vacation, just to come home to their parsonage to discover their furniture and clothes thrown out into the yard in the rain and the locks to the parsonage changed. I have read of a church sending their pastor and his family on vacation, just to hurry to the church and vote him out and name his replacement while he was away. I have seen churches lock a pastor and staff out of the church, changing the church locks three and four times, including calling the police to keep the preacher away. These are rash, extreme cases. These events begin subtly, usually with flare-ups over silly things. Perhaps, you will recognize something familiar in the tiffs illustrated below:

- Before a Purpose Driven Life Campaign in one church, a widow took the time to handwrite invitations to all the church members. One of the deacons and his wife met her at night in her driveway where she lives alone—and yelled at her for including them in the invitations. "Does she actually think they are so immature to need such training?!"

- After a young lady was saved in their church, church members complained she had the nerve to show up the next Sunday not dressed "appropriately" (she was wearing jeans and not a dress), so they took it upon themselves to tell her how wrong she was. She never graced their congregation again.

- Others complained that some of the youth had the "audacity" to use their "good" tables to make posters for the youth car wash. Their

complaint was the tables might actually get dirty; then, they would have had to clean them—see the problem?
- A ministry team put "special" stuff in one of the cabinets in the fellowship hall, so they determined it had to be locked at all times even barring church staff from access! Can you say petty?
- At one point, a pastor decided to trade offices with the secretary (to make it more efficient), and one of his deacons called and asked why he did not ask permission first.[1]
- A pastor who had faced loud opposition concerning tearing down the old sanctuary and building a new one was called the night before the last service in the old facility and told that if he tore the church apart he would be killed.[2]

Or, have you seen any of these?

- A deacon's meeting ends in a fistfight.
- Two women get in an argument over the preacher eating one's meatloaf and not the other.
- A lady says, "We need more people in this church who are normal like us, not like those trailer-park kids!"
- A family loved their church, but hated their preacher so badly that they would be delightful in Sunday School, sing joyfully in worship, and then make a big production as the whole family would get up and leave just as the preacher approached the pulpit to preach.
- In another church, some would open newspapers while the preacher preached, and a few would make faces at him during the sermon.

These incidents will bless you, will they not? Is it any wonder, pastors have so little energy left to grow a church![3] This reminds me of W. A. Criswell's reply when asked how he could possibly know all 25,000 members at his church. His response was, "I know two groups of people in this church—all the key leaders and all the kooks."[4] There may be merit in Criswell's quip;

---

1. Byron Brown, senior pastor of a Texas Baptist church, interview with project leader via e-mail, March 30, 2008.

2. H. Beecher Hicks Jr., *Preaching Through a Storm* (Grand Rapids: Zondervan Publishing House, 1987), 72.

3. G. Lloyd Rediger, *Clergy Killers: Guidance for Pastors and Congregations Under Attack* (Louisville, KY: Westminster/John Knox Press, 1997), 15.

4. Marshall Shelley and Kevin Miller, "Fundamentally One: An Interview with Truman Dollar," *Leadership* 7, no. 4 (Fall 1986): 16.

one church expert ventured to guess that 10 percent of church members possess personality disorders.[5] When you read such things, you might gain some grasp for why a San Antonio columnist wrote at the start of the 2007 Southern Baptist Convention, "Southern Baptists Are Convening; Will Any Christians be with Them?"[6]

The Statistics

The building appears the same, the church billboard is updated, the activities continue, and every Sunday, the pastor takes to the pulpit. To the outside world and the adjacent neighborhood, all looks well inside the church. However, if one inspects closely, one will see a hurting smile on the pastor, an uneasy walk in the congregants.[7]

One survey states that over 1,500 pastors in Protestant evangelical churches leave their positions every month. Half of these leave the ministry altogether within five years. In a large study of 324,000 clergy from 6,900 congregations in Australia, it was noted that small churches seem more stressful than larger ones due to the added pressure of viability. Contributors to this struggle included: lack of support and/or conflict with denominational leaders, conflicting demands within the church, conflict between church and family, and conflict with staff.[8]

Another survey states that "every six minutes in the United States a pastor is fired. It is estimated that over one-fourth of all ministers have been forced out of one or more congregations."[9] Seemingly, a "fire-the-pastor" movement is spreading through our nation.[10] A *Leadership Magazine* study cited reasons why pastors were terminated: personality conflicts (43 percent), conflicting visions for the church (17 percent), financial strain in the church (7 percent), theological differences (5 percent), moral failure (5 percent), unrealistic expectations (5 percent), unrealized expectations (4 percent), and the remainder to lesser occurring reasons.[11]

---

5. Stephen Muse, "Clergy in Crisis: When Human Strength Isn't Enough," *Journal of Pastoral Care and Counseling* 61, no. 3 (Fall 2007): 185.

6. John R. Bisagno, *Inside Information: Worship Wars, Calvinism, Elder Rule & Much More* (Longwood, FL: Xulon Press, 2007), 11.

7. Rediger, *Clergy Killers*, 7.

8. Muse, "Clergy in Crisis," 184.

9. Rediger, *Clergy Killers*, 6.

10. James Qualben, *Peace in the Parish: How to Use Conflict Redemption, Principles, and Process* (San Antonio: Lang Marc Publishing, 1991), 112.

11. Rediger, *Clergy Killers*, 13.

Dr. John R. Bisagno, former senior pastor of Houston's First Baptist Church, currently serves as an author, an adjunct professor, a capital campaign fundraiser, and a revival preacher. He has been amazed that in all the duties he has carried since his retirement, none seem as prevalent as the calls he receives from churches in crisis. He says that seldom does a day go by where he does not get a call from a church, a pastor, or a staff-member who desperately plead with him for advice and help. One day, he received three such calls.[12] The ingredients for church crises often include: corrupt attitudes toward conflict, a collapsed purpose, the past running amok, deflected distress, shoot-out meetings, bombsite Biblicism, theological thuggery, Christian immaturity, selfishness, pride, cliques, immorality, hyper-dependency, and dominance by a handful of families; all of which spell disaster.[13]

The Preacher Run

The preachers realize the danger, often early into their first pastorates. They find the modern-day proverb true: "Leadership always puts the pastor at risk."[14] Before long, they are singing the words of a wise, experienced prominent preacher, "Crisis seems to follow me."[15] How pastors wish that such risk and insults were targeted solely at the pastor. Unfortunately, people often draw the pastor's family into the fray. Family stress increases, and the family's view of the church decreases. Sadly, 80 percent of ministers polled say that their ministries have had a negative impact on their families as a whole.[16]

Is it any wonder that the ministry has the highest fall-out rate of any profession? When entering the ministry (or as some would define, the "misery"), Bisagno's father-in-law told him that only one in ten men who enter the ministry at age twenty-one will still be in it at age sixty-five. Bisagno recorded in the back of his Bible the names of twenty-five of his contemporaries, friends who preached revivals or were pastoring churches at his age. Through the years, one by one, they fell, they quit. Now at age seventy-three, Bisagno says only five have endured to the end.[17]

12. Bisagno, *Inside Information*, 9.

13. Qualben, *Peace in the Parish*, 111.

14. James F. Jackson, senior pastor, Chapelwood Methodist Church, Houston, Texas; personal interview by project leader, June 11, 2008.

15. Paige Patterson, president, Southwestern Baptist Theological Seminary, Fort Worth, Texas; personal interview by project leader, April 22, 2008.

16. Muse, "Clergy in Crisis," 184.

17. Bisagno, *Inside Information*, 85-87.

Dr. David Allen states that many preachers go into churches with high hopes. Then they experience a problem, or face huge opposition, so they turn and run. They look for a new church, or they resign in the absence of God's leading.[18] Such running was never necessary, according to George Fraser of the Titus Task Force, a thirty-year-old ministry in California, whose goal is to minister to troubled churches throughout the United States. In their experience, the Titus Task Force has found that 80 percent of the pastors who left their churches during trials did not have to leave. They just bailed out to keep from standing up, facing discomfort, or to prevent hurting others. They did not have the fortitude to face a shoot-out, even when the situation warranted one.[19]

Too many preachers hide behind the virtue of "love conquers all," not realizing that sometimes love has to be tough, love has to discipline, and love has to sacrifice.[20] Statistics prove Fraser's research. A past *Leadership Magazine* survey found that 43 percent of all pastors were forced out by a faction of ten people or less.[21] That this statistic has lost its veracity today is doubtful. Dissent often starts with just one or two people who do not get their way, and who then begin to vocalize and are influential enough to build a bandwagon-appearance of disgruntlement. That so few people could drive so many away from God's will is hard to believe.

Sometimes pastors leave for a less acute reason—over time, they just get fed-up. Once they leave one church, leaving the next one becomes easier. They lose the tenacity and endurance to see the problem through to its solution. The more often a few powerful leaders run a church, the more often pastors leave because of lack of power. The more pastors leave for lack of power, the more they exacerbate the problem that caused the personal frustration in the first place. Let me tell you why.

When a congregation sees preachers come and preachers go (the average tenure of a Baptist pastor, for instance, is said to be twenty months),[22] they grow skeptical that decisions made by preachers will be seen to the end, and the church fears becoming strapped with the aftermath (i.e., at the commencement of his ministry, a preacher sells a building plan to his church, then leaves in the middle of the construction). Ultimately, the congregation

---

18. David Allen, Dean of the School of Theology, Southwestern Baptist Theological Seminary, 2008 Expository Preaching Workshop lecture, Fort Worth, Texas.

19. George Fraser, Titus Task Force, personal phone interview with project leader, 28 May 2008.

20. Rediger, *Clergy Killers*, 13.

21. Ibid.

22. Paul W. Powell, *Basic Bible Sermons on Handling Conflict* (Nashville: Broadman Press, 1992), 98.

will come to the realization that the only people, upon whom they can rely, are those men or women who have made up the church tapestry for a span of years. They will begin to give those men and women the power over the preacher, because a belief exists that the local leadership of the church will look after the well-being of the people and protect them from the mistakes of transient pastors. With this mindset, a natural occurrence is for the people to desire to follow the pastor, but always to hold in reserve their full support, giving in to the local leadership (regardless of how unbiblical) for the perceived survival of the church.

The Eternal Result

From the world's viewpoint, the church and its mission are dying. Of all the churches in the United States, 80 percent have plateaued or are experiencing decline. Another fraction, 19 percent are growing, because they are swapping church members. The final 1 percent is growing legitimately, because they are making new converts.[23] Without the strong Biblical leadership that God designed for it, the church becomes marked with the inability to fulfill its God-given mission, because the sinful nature has lost the restraint of its Biblical rudder. What follows is a church that is plagued by sexual immorality, impurity, idolatry, new age philosophy, false doctrine, hatred, discord, jealousy, rage, selfish ambitions, and divisions.[24] No real delineation is made between it and the lost world.

Speaking of the lost world, J. Robert White, executive director of the Georgia Baptist Convention, said it best. While the world is dying around the church, lost and condemned without Jesus Christ, Christians are shooting at each other.[25] *Newsweek* once reported that, on any given Sunday, only 18 million Americans are involved in Bible Study, while 13 million were attending weekly support groups.[26] *Time Magazine* reported that "there are 36 million Generation X-ers in America and 34 million have never been to church and aren't going."[27] Fearfully, without some change, this new offspring of church history could be called "Ichabod," for the glory has departed.[28]

---

23. Bisagno, *Inside Information*, 12.

24. Jerrien Gunnink, *Preaching for Recovery in a Strife-Torn Church* (Grand Rapids: Zondervan Publishing House, 1989), 38.

25. Bisagno, *Inside Information*, 9.

26. John R. Bisagno, *Letters to Timothy* (Nashville: Broadman & Holman Publishers, 2001), 250.

27. Ibid., 199.

28. Jerry Vines and Jim Shaddix, *Power in the Pulpit: How to Prepare and Deliver*

The Purpose of this Book

Prayerfully, this book will present a better view. This book's aim is to help pastors/preachers understand that staying in the fray is important. How can this be done? One must remember two key things. One, when someone is struggling with suicidal thoughts, the preacher comes to their aid with the Word of God. In that Word, they find life, comfort, strength, and hope. When a couple in the church is going through marital difficulties, the preacher brings them God's Word. In that Word, they find strength to stay together as one, and they find the counsel on how to make their marriage become the marriage it ought to be. When church members face temptation, the preacher turns to God's Word and quotes 2 Timothy 2:22 and 1 Corinthians 10:13. They look at Genesis 39, and they instruct the tempted on how to avoid temptation like Joseph. Reference is made to the Lord's prayer—"lead us not into temptation, but deliver us from evil." All these are found in God's Word.

Why is it, then, that when pastors face trouble in church, they do not rely on God's Word to get them through the pastoral crises? In his seminary lectures, Bisagno says that a healthy congregation is like a healthy body—it must be fed good food.[29] God's design is for men to stand up and preach the Word of God, the full Word. This may sound simplistic, but no better way exists to see a congregation change, to see people saved, to see problems solved, and to see the people's opinion of the preacher lifted. No better, legitimate way exists to garnish the authority from the people than from standing before them week-in, week-out, opening the Bible and proclaiming, "Thus saith the Lord."

Criswell began a series from Genesis all the way through Revelation. When he began the series, many came to him and told him that this would be the death-nail on the coffin of the church. Contrary to that warning, he believed in the Word of God. He believed that every verse, every chapter, and every book had something to say to his people. He even believed that, for that time in his church's life, the Bible—preached in order, could have a positive effect on the life of his congregation. Despite the naysayers, he did as God led. As the sermon series came to a close, beginning the last chapter of the last book of the Revelation, he shared some startling statistics with regard to what had happened in his church. The church had grown beyond belief. He addressed his congregation that Sunday and said,

---

Expository Sermons (Chicago: Moody Press, 1999), 17.

29. John Bisagno, retired pastor of First Baptist Church, Houston, TX, lecture in Pastoral Leadership class, Southwestern Baptist Theological Seminary, Houston, TX, Fall 2005.

"This is one of the largest church auditoriums in America, and for years our people have filled it three times every Sunday. Coming to hear what? The latest fancy, fad, notion, theory? Not at all, nor ever at all, but coming to listen to a man open the Bible and expound the words of the Living God."[30] The general health of the church depends on consistent proclamation of God's Word. For a sick body, nothing is better than the medicine of God applied by the servant of God.

Even when a body is generally healthy, some nagging injury or pain can exist. For instance, I just had a physical. I am in good shape, thanks to God's grace. However, I do have osteoarthritis of the knee. I have had several issues with both knees, primarily from years of football and jogging. As a result, I ride my bike to protect them. A body can be healthy generally speaking, but still have issues. An ailment in a body requires specific attention. Paul told Timothy, "Preach the word; be ready in season and out of season; reprove, rebuke, exhort, with great patience and instruction" (2 Timothy 4:2). God's Word is available for preachers to preach in order to correct errors in the church family, to rebuke when they are unwilling to adhere, and to encourage those who are walking with the Lord, pleading with them to continue this fight of faith for a Savior is present that loves them and is preparing a home for them. Notice, Paul instructed Timothy to do this with great patience. A preacher of the Word in any church must realize the outside spiritual forces at play. The preacher must remember the sinful nature of man. As a result, friction occurs. Obstacles prevent the Body from being what the Body ought to be. Paul did not say to quit after you do it. Paul said do so in season and out-of-season with great patience. The remainder of this book will deal with real-life preachers who have faced problems just as you face, but who have relied on God's Word and discovered victory and help.

The more time that passes, the more difficult it will be for the preacher of God's Word. Paul wrote an addition to the previous verse:

> For the time will come when they will not endure sound doctrine; but wanting to have their ears tickled, they will accumulate for themselves teachers in accordance to their own desires, and will turn away their ears from the truth and will turn aside to myths. But you, be sober in all things, endure hardship, do the work of an evangelist, fulfill your ministry (2 Timothy 4:3-5).

Not only will the preacher fight with the worldly and Satanic influences in his church, but he will be competing also against the "ticklers of itching

---

30. W. A. Criswell, *Expository Sermons on Revelation* (Grand Rapids: Zondervan Publishing House, 1962), 174.

ears" for the heart of the people. Such "ticklers" will see growth in their churches, which you may not experience.

Further, people in your church may assume something is wrong with their preacher, because their church is not growing like others. They will not realize that a cheap, counterfeit Gospel exists, which tells any who will listen that they are okay, that God does not judge anyone but the really bad people, and that God wants them to be wealthy, happy, and healthy. Because of this, God says to us, "But you, be sober in all things, endure hardship, do the work of an evangelist, fulfill your ministry" (2 Timothy 4:5). In this journey, Paul's guidance is as much applicable to today's preachers as it was to Timothy many years ago.

God calls on His mouthpieces to hold their ground in harrowing situations. Instead of quitting in the battle, endure it; stick to the duty to which God has called us. John Meador, pastor of First Baptist Euless, told of a time when he wondered if he really had experienced a call to his current church, or if he needed to leave. While working out, he remembered a word that God had spoken through the writer of Hebrews, "let us run with endurance the race that is set before us" (Hebrews 12:1). Meador responded to the call, stuck to the task, and never looked back.[31] Not only does God call His servants to discharge their duties, but also God's instruction to Ezekiel should give all pastors comfort that He will work in them.

Ezekiel was to proclaim God's words of judgment to a hard people. God told him,

> Yet the house of Israel will not be willing to listen to you, since they are not willing to listen to Me. Surely the whole house of Israel is stubborn and obstinate. "Behold, I have made your face as hard as their faces and your forehead as hard as their foreheads. Like emery harder than flint I have made your forehead. Do not be afraid of them or be dismayed before them, though they are a rebellious house (Ezekiel 3:7-9).

God made Ezekiel as hard-headed and determined to preach as his audience was not to listen. No matter how difficult the audience, God would give Ezekiel the resolve to discharge his duty, and He will do the same for preachers today. Often, God sends us to a hardened people, but we must be as hard with God's truth and not quit. Seemingly, God says further to Ezekiel that not to speak, not to stand for Him amongst the people, is the preacher's rebellion against God (Ezekiel 2:8).

---

31. John Meador, senior pastor, First Baptist Church Euless, Texas, personal interview by project leader, March 27, 2008.

The second thing to remember is that as we faithfully expound God's Word to our churches, in nearly every church crisis, only a few are voicing and causing opposition. Less are against us than we perceive. The word to Elisha's servant is true for us today in our churches, "Be strong and courageous, do not fear or be dismayed because of the king of Assyria nor because of all the horde that is with him; for the one with us is greater than the one with him" (2 Chronicles 32:7). This is most true in the spiritual reality. I love the painting of the preacher preaching with all the famous prophets and preachers from the past standing around him. This picture hangs in my office as a reminder. We are waging a spiritual battle in which God guarantees us we will win.

Beyond that, at the human, church level, as we expound God's Word faithfully, the majority of the church membership will be behind us. Should something come to a vote, we can have the confidence that we will win the day in most situations. It is so easy to hear the voice of one or two complainers and believe they are speaking for the whole congregation. When they say, "Everybody is against this preacher," what they really mean by "everybody" is "me and my brother-in-law."[32] I shudder to think how many preachers have run away from their churches in response to a couple of malcontents, leaving hundreds of other church members, who were being fed by God's Word, disheartened and discouraged with God, the church, and the preachers.

To wrap up the lesson from my initial story—looking back, I realize that I had been preaching God's Word faithfully for six and one-half years. God had blessed that time with growth and changed lives. I possessed the following of over 98 percent of the congregation. I let one voice, coupled with a couple of voices from the past, convince me that it was time to leave. I know now, I ran from a battle that God had already won. I possessed the capacity to lead this body by my faithful exposition of the text, and by the ascent of the mass-majority of the believers in that church. I should have stayed and used my God-given position to continue to facilitate that church to grow. I did not. As a result, I went to a church in worse shape than the one I left. I have faced many more trials in my current pastorate, but God has steadied my hand and led me through many more. I have stood on God's Word, spoken it from the pulpit, and God has moved my current church through trials that dwarf that first experience. I have found that God's Word comes with power and gives power when used according to His will.

---

32. John R. Bisagno, retired pastor of First Baptist Church, Houston, TX, interview with the project leader, Houston, TX, June, 2008.

Many people have used an old phrase for years to inform others of their inadequacies. There may be a guy who is weak and puny, but because of his temper, he always wants to fight. Unfortunately, because of his stature, he loses every fight. In a lighter moment, a friend might tell him, "You couldn't fight your way out of a wet paper bag." There may be a lady who is a poor salesperson, who may think she is good, but she can never close a deal. Her boss might tell her, "You couldn't sell your way out of a wet paper bag." Another may think they can sing, but the entire church knows they cannot hold a note, much less let it go. They might be told, "You couldn't sing your way out of a wet paper bag."

Perhaps in the fires of the pastorate, that is what you feel or hear right now. Perhaps an attitude has permeated your congregation that says, "You are so weak and anemic, you couldn't preach your way out of a wet paper bag." The purpose of this book is to let you know that, in any trial, hope exists. The reason for this optimism is that the Word of God has authority and is sufficient to deal with every issue in life. God has given this Word as an incredible instrument for one to handle through the gift of preaching to bring help and healing. God spoke the world into existence. He spoke and order reigned out of chaos. That same God can speak through the preacher and bring healing out of hurt. Buckle-up, and get ready. The following pages will inspire you with evidence of how God's Word proclaimed can give you victory where you are and where you are headed.

Chapter 2: The Call

At expensive restaurants, in between scrumptious courses of an elegant meal, the waiter sometimes will bring out a little bowl of sorbet. I always thought that was odd to have ice cream before dessert time. Additionally, I think it strange to call sherbet "sorbet" (though a technical difference does exist). I asked a waiter about this the first time I saw this occur. He explained that the sorbet was to clean the palate to prepare for the next course. According to a website, About.com, sorbet is served to give the diner a fresh perspective for the next course.[1] Perhaps, after the last chapter of seeing the ugliness of the ministry, one might need a little "sorbet," a fresh perspective before proceeding.

Perhaps a little sorbet is not what the troubled pastor envisions before proceeding. To him, an analogy of taking a bath after a hard day at a dirty job would fit better. When I was in college, I worked at the Texas Highway Department in the summers. The primary job of a summer employee is to scrape dead animals off the road. That is right! You don't think those dead animals just walk off the road, do you? The radio code for a dead animal is a 10-45. Assume a summer hand named Johnny is riding with a regular employee named Bill (a summer hand is not allowed to drive). The summer guy may hear on the radio, "Bill, I've got a 10-45 on Highway 67, take Johnny over and get it." Of course, the summer hand hates the thought of going, and he surely wishes the dispatcher would at least tell Bill what the animal is so that he can get his mind right. Nonetheless, the workers go; every animal is a surprise. He scrapes, throws the animal in the tall grass, and on down the road they go looking for more. This practice can be an all-day thing. One hardly has time to eat. He scrapes in between bites, washes his hands, and continues. He goes home that evening, cleans up, and goes to bed exhausted. The next morning, he is back out scraping dead animals again. Perhaps that is the vision a pastor forms when facing trial after trial, day after day.

---

1. Rebecca Franklin, "Traditional French Palate Cleansers," About.com [online]; accessed 29 August 2008; available from frenchfood.about.com/od/explore/frenchfood/a/palatecleanser.htm; Internet.

The Call

Now, put away that negativity! Let me take you back. Remember the dawn? Remember the call? The scene was Latham Springs Baptist Camp in the heart of Texas. I had been a Christian for about four years. After receiving the Lord, I began diligently to have a daily prayer time. I read my Bible and I was enamored by the Lord, His love, and His eternal security. I had two incredible pastors in my life—Bro. Bill Schibler and Bro. Bruce Wells. From a servant's heart, Bro. Bill taught me a love for people and a passion for people to know Jesus. Bro. Bruce taught me how to have a passion for Bible study, the power of fervent prayer, and the resulting effective proclamation of God's Word.

I suppose all these things were going through my mind as the Lord began to stir in my heart to serve him in full-time ministry after I arrived at my last youth camp. Near the end of the week, the camp evangelists called for those who would follow God's vocational call to come forward. I knew that was for me. I stood and, with joy and purpose, went forward acknowledging before God and all the campers that I would follow Him into ministry. Afterwards, I went home looking at college, knowing that at some point I would be a preacher, but not sure when. Do you remember your call?

The traits of a preacher were evident early on in my life, as I am sure they were in yours. The very first time I stood to challenge injustice was as a sixteen-year-old at Rainbow Baptist Church. The Vasquez family had been serving the Lord devoutly at our church for many years. God had given them the gift of serving. They used that gift in the weekly sacrifice of cleaning our church. The whole family was present every week taking part. The church would give them a little money for their effort. Though appreciated, this family never required wages. One day, a new professional family moved into our rural neighborhood and joined our church. A short while into their tenure with the church, they began to be active verbally in the monthly business meetings.

I will not forget the month that the moderator asked if anyone had any new business, and this family stood up. They said, "The church is not as clean as it should be, we should get the Vasquezes to improve or let them go." I could not believe my ears, nor could I believe the silence from the rest of our members. Here was a family doing a great job, but just not up to the expectations of one family. I stood up immediately (that is how you get into trouble). I reminded the church of the Vasquezes' incredible sacrifice; and additionally, what a discouragement such criticism could bring to their lives and their Christian walk. As a sixteen year-old member, I was not privy to what happened after that, but I was pleased to see the Vasquezes continue to clean our church, as well as be active in our body.

Another time, the superintendent of our public school retired and soon after graduated to be with the Lord. He had made a huge impact on my life, not to mention his positive impact on the school. In a post-1962 era, where the government began to restrict Christian influence in school, Mr. Gibbs continued to stand for the Lord in our school. He had two revival meetings per year in our school. He allowed prayer and Scripture memory to go on in the classroom at the teachers' discretion. He always stood for what was right. Soon after his death, the new school building was being built, and nothing had been done to honor Mr. Gibbs. I called the school board and requested an opportunity to speak. In front of many citizens and the whole school board, I requested they name the new high school after Mr. Gibbs. They said they would take it into consideration, but they never did name the school after him. I hated that, but what mattered was I had to speak up.

Dr. Paige Patterson felt the same drive. When he was eighteen years-old, his dad, who was well-loved at First Baptist Church in Beaumont, Texas, resigned to take another position. At that time, it was the sixth largest church in the convention. Dr. Patterson stayed behind to finish high school in Beaumont, where he remained active in his church. The church brought in Jaroy Weber in view of a call. Weber had a different approach and was more bombastic than Patterson's dad had been. Having lived under the eloquence of their former pastor, many were discontented when Weber made many grammatical errors in the sermon he preached in view of a call. Many violently spoke out against him in the ensuing business meeting. The meeting went back-and-forth for several hours. Young eighteen-year-old Paige Patterson was present the whole time, watching the church he loved and had grown-up in, tearing itself apart.

At the end of the meeting, Patterson went to the platform to speak. He spoke decisively against what was going on in the church, and called on the church to do the right thing. He said, "If there is a moral issue or a theological question, then bring it forth, otherwise this pastor deserves your support." No such issues existed, so the church voted to call Weber to be their pastor. The next day, Obadiah Sheeply, an English professor, wrote a poem with two stanzas each to Patterson's dad, the pulpit committee, Jaroy Weber, and then to Paige Patterson.[2] Even early in his life, Dr. Patterson was displaying the early traits of a preacher. Incidentally, some say that a term

---

2. Interview with Paige Patterson, president, Southwestern Baptist Theological Seminary, Fort Worth, Texas; personal interview by project leader, April 22, 2008.

exists for the preacher who follows a well-loved, long-tenured pastor. "If you follow a guy who has been in the pulpit and loved for over ten years, you may think you are the senior pastor, but in reality, you are the interim!"[3] That is a little cynical, mostly untrue, but still funny.

I did not immediately answer the call to become a pastor. I took a job working at Shell Pipe Line Corporation, then Pfizer Pharmaceuticals. While a pharmaceutical representative in Beaumont, Texas, I ran into a great Christian man, who was an incredible doctor. His name was Dr. Bonnie B. Westbrook. I will not forget our first encounter. I expected a lady with this name, but that was *his* name, and actually, *he* was Dr. Bonnie B. Westbrook Jr. He made me sit on the examining table, and I was not even sick. I said I want to share some information about my product. He said you will have time to do that, but right now, I want to learn a little about you. I told him a little, and he asked for more. Somewhere down the line, he gathered that I had been called to preach. He asked why I was not pursuing it. I gave him many reasons, but none were valid. He said, "You were called to be a preacher and you need to be a preacher. I am going to get you into seminary." Surely enough, he did. At age thirty-five, I was back in school. I will never forget that man. Dr. Westbrook graduated to be with the Lord a few years back, and I cannot wait to see him again in the presence of our Lord.

I have already shared how I accepted my first pastorate at Calvary Baptist Church in Weimar, Texas, beginning as a supply preacher. What I did not tell you was what you already know if you are a pastor. First, I could not believe anyone would pay me to preach. That boggled my mind. When they called me to be their full-time pastor, I remember exactly where I was, and exactly what I did. I was living at 9902 Elm Meadow Trail in Houston, Texas. After I received the offer, I walked onto my back porch and began to sing and praise God that He would allow me to pastor a church. I could not get over it. To be honest, I still cannot. I called my best friends and let them know. I could hardly sleep all night.

Adrian Rogers remembered. He was filled with awe that God would call him to preach. He prayed over and over, "God, I want You to use me." One night, he knelt before God and repeated, "God, I want You to use me." Kneeling did not seem good enough or humble enough, so he lay prostrate in the grass and said, "Father I want You to use me." That did not seem humble enough, so he took his finger and made a hole in the dirt and put his nose down in that hole. He called out, "Lord, I am as low as I know how to get. I want You to use me."[4] Do you remember that feel-

---

3. Jackson, interview.
4. Joyce Rogers, *Love Worth Finding: The Life of Adrian Rogers and His Philosophy*

ing? Being a preacher is a privilege. It is said that God had only one Son, and He made Him a preacher. Jesus said, "Let us go somewhere else—to the nearby villages—so I can preach there also. That is why I have come" (Mark 1:38).[5] What an honor that God would entrust his flock with mortal men. Herschel Hobbs, who pastored First Baptist Church of Oklahoma City for thirty years, said, "If I had 10,000 lives to live over, I should want to be a pastor in each of them. [6]

What the Preacher First Pictures in His Mind

Many things go through a preacher's mind at the point of His call. All the planets seem to fit in the right order. Life makes sense, and purpose simply overwhelms the minister. All-consuming love for God exists. That is the number one motivation to a preacher that Jesus gave. Jesus did not ask Peter, "Do you love sheep?" He did not ask Peter, "Do you love feeding sheep?" He asked Peter, "Do you love Me?" The reason a preacher preaches is he loves Jesus.[7]

As a preacher, that awe of God's Word is present. This comes when he realizes that what a preacher holds in His hand is Divine, and that it makes a difference in the now and in the eternity for every man who will respond. The preacher is zealous, for he realizes what George W. Truett once said, "Jesus meets the three tests of life: thetest of life, the test of death, and the test of eternity." He helps men live, to die, and to live throughout eternity.[8] In the freshly called preacher, a hunger to proclaim God's Word with every moment of life right up to one's last breath occurs. Truett's granddad did just that. When the doctor said he only had a few moments to live, he asked to be propped up in bed, asked that the neighbors be called in, and then he died sharing with them the Word, the Gospel of Jesus Christ.[9] That is the way to go!

The preacher begins not only with a love for God, for Jesus Christ, and for God's Word; additionally, he has a love for people. He longs to be a model of the Christian walk to them, to enable them to walk that same way

---

of Preaching (Nashville: Broadman & Holman Publishers, 2005), 156.

5. John Bisagno, *Letters to Timothy* (Nashville: Broadman & Holman Publishers, 2001), 154.

6. Ibid., 13.

7. Rogers, *Love Worth Finding*, 188.

8. Joe W. Burton, *Prince of the Pulpit: A Pen Picture of George W. Truett at* Work (Grand Rapids: Zondervan Publishing House, 1946), 16.

9. Ibid., 15.

and better. He longs for them to learn more about God. The preacher desires his people to fall madly in love with the Lord Jesus Christ and sacrificially serve Him where they live.

This thought captivated Gordon MacDonald as he watched his preacher dad every Sunday morning before the service began. His dad would walk down the aisle of the sanctuary to the front of the church. He would go to the pulpit, kneel down before all the people, and silently begin to pray for all the people on his knees.[10] God challenged the preachers through Peter, "Be shepherds of God's flock that is under your care, serving as overseers—not because you must, but because you are willing, as God wants you to be" (1 Pet 5:2). When the sheep see the preacher as their shepherd, one who loves them, they will follow him as he follows God.[11] He will long to stay and be with them. Because he loves them, he will feed them, water them, lead them, serve them, discipline them, and defend them.[12]

This longing is present in the selfless pastor, in the idealistic pastor, to serve a church for their whole ministry much like John Fawcett did in Yorkshire England. In the first part of the nineteenth century, his salary was the equivalent of two hundred dollars per year. He was asked to pastor another church with a much larger salary in London. He accepted, packed up his family, and was ready to go. When he came out that day of departure, he found a crowd of his church members at his door. They came to send him off, but they could not contain their weeping in deep sorrow at their loss. They had shared their lives with him, and he with them. He shared their love and grief so much, that he ordered his family's things unloaded, and declared that he was staying.[13]

At the preacher's call, a drive is present to make a difference, to bring transformation to those he pastors. Bonhoffer said that a vocation is the place where one's deep gladness meets the world's need.[14] The preacher envisions a church functioning like the one in the book of Acts. He sees himself leading a people empowered by God, devoted to God's teaching, to prayer, to singing and worship, to fellowship, and to having everything in

---

10. Gordon MacDonald, "Behind the Curtain: When Things Get Ugly," *Leadership Magazine*, Spring 2007, 52.

11. E. Glenn Wagner, "Preaching from Down Under," *Great Preaching—Practical Advice from Powerful Preachers*, ed. Paul Woods (Loveland, CO: Group Publishing, 2003), 133.

12. Ibid., 135.

13. Powell, *Basic Bible Sermons*, 71.

14. Muse, "Clergy in Crisis," 187.

common. He envisions his church daily having more people join the ranks of the saved and the membership.[15]

The people have entrusted the preacher with the capacity to speak as God leads.[16] They come to hear from God through the mouth of the preacher. In the preacher's purest mind, he is holding to the prophetic call. He believes what God's Word says, the mandate that he is to stand up and cry out when things are not right. He is to be the vessel by which God sets things straight and points to an everlasting hope.[17] The preacher knows that it does not matter what the people may think, or what the church may think, or what the denomination may think, he must preach the Word of God courageously. He realizes the preaching is vital because one day he will stand and give an account before Jesus.[18] No matter what, he has the assurance that God has called him to preach and that God has called him to preach in this particular church setting.[19] Naturally then, an expectation exists of some difficulties.

No doubt, in answering the call to be a pastor, someone came to you at some point and laughingly said, "Now you know, if you want an easy, quiet life, this is not the job for you!"[20] You chuckled back, but deep inside, you knew you loved God, loved Jesus, loved His Word, and loved His people. You probably told them that you appreciated the concern. You probably further replied that you would be cautious, and that your eyes were wide open. Do you wish now you would have paid greater heed to those words of that well-meaning friend?

As a man who loves God's Word, he recognizes that the church is not perfect. He realizes that Jesus is purifying His Church through His Word. He realizes the Holy Spirit's part in the mix. The preacher is to speak the truth, but the Holy Spirit imparts it.[21] The minister should be able to recite times in the church when trouble was present. He will remember that all seven churches in the Revelation had challenges. He will remember the friction between Paul and Barnabas, between Euodia and Syntyche, between Paul and Peter, and between John and Diotrophes. Definitely, the preacher

---

15. Mac Brunson and Ergun Caner, *Why Churches Die: Diagnosing Lethal Poisons in the Body of Christ* (Nashville: Broadman & Holman Publishers, 2005), 9.

16. William H. Willimon, *Preaching About Conflict in the Local Church* (Philadelphia: Westminster Press, 1987), 54.

17. Ibid., 55.

18. Rogers, *Love Worth Finding*, 174.

19. Hicks, *Preaching Through a Storm*, 16.

20. Charles Haddon Spurgeon, *Lectures to My Students* (Grand Rapids: Zondervan Publishing House, 1954), 162.

21. Rogers, *Love Worth Finding*, 155.

will be able to recite the struggles at Corinth and Galatia.[22] Thus, in the preacher's expectations, he has room for the fact that trials will be present. Most celebrate that fact. Why? Because it provides a chance to fulfill the mission of the preacher—to see lives changed.

The pastor understands that the make-up of his church inherently will bring divisions and struggles. He is not pastoring all mature believers who are serving the Lord with every ounce of their being. Prayerfully, some of those will be present in the congregation, but more of the members will be those who have good and bad days. Some will serve the Lord greatly at times, but then trials come and they pull back. Some come to church selfishly to get what they can. Some are lost, but are inquiring about the Lord. Some are lost and are drug into the church by a family member. Some are those whose life goals have not been achieved, so they try to find fulfillment through an organization in which they can have more freedom and control—the church. Others are those who are well-meaning believers who have been drawn innocently into some poor doctrine, while

still others are babies in the faith.[23] The preacher will be glad to have each of these in his congregation, willingly accepting the tension, because this is his mission field. Above all that, Jesus stated that this would be the case. He warned that wheat and tares would be present, and that they would grow up together. The beauty to the preacher is these are *his* wheat and tares, and he celebrates the opportunity God has given him.

---

22. Austin B. Tucker, *A Primer for Pastors* (Grand Rapids: Kregel Publications, 2004), 94-95.

23. B. Clayton Bell, "Preaching and Conflict," *Handbook of Contemporary Preaching*, ed. Michael Duduit (Nashville: Broadman Press, 1992), 530.

Chapter 3: **The Adversity**

So who cut you off, who hindered you?
—The Enemy among us!

A line is drawn between chapter 1's difficulties and chapter 2's idealism. The preacher who is called into this beautiful vocation of chapter 2 believes that with God, he can lick the world. The preacher under the heavy burden of conflict and crisis of chapter 1 is ready to hang it up and start in a new, fresh direction. What caused the difference? That is what this chapter hopes to reveal. Even in the righteous, pristine setting of Church, a challenge exists to incorporate people of diverse backgrounds into a united Body of Christ, a loving church community. The preacher, in working to this end, faces inevitable tensions. Even in communities that are homogeneous on the surface, beneath are coalitions of interest groups unknowingly or unintentionally working against each other.[1]

Paul realized that elements existed that would seek to escalate hostilities and explode unity and function. In Galatians 5, Paul was speaking to Christians who had committed themselves to the truth of Jesus Christ, but had taken a detour because some in their midst were trying to recommit them to legalism rather than to grace for salvation. Paul realized that enemies in the church were causing trouble for the believer. In the same way, the preacher faces enemies in his church who are trying to force him to make a detour away from obedience to the Lord's call and His Word. This will occur when a preacher is attempting to be faithful to living by and proclaiming the whole truth of Jesus Christ.

Preaching

A way exists to avoid this conflict altogether. A pastor of forty years was asked how he could stay at one church so long. His reply was, "I never preached on

---

1. James W. Thompson, "Preaching to Philippians, *Interpretation Magazine* (July 2007): 309.

a controversial subject."² This may be a nice way to avoid conflict, but this is not the Lord's will for His servants. If it were, Stephen would have lived a good long life, as would have Isaiah, Paul, Peter, and many others. The requirement of the prophet or preacher is to stand against what is wrong. Additionally, a beckoning for repentance is required. The preacher is to challenge people to change their ways. Good preaching will provoke strong resistance. When Jesus preached in His hometown of Nazareth, He was run out of town. Why? Not because He was a bad preacher, but because good preaching pleads for people to repent, to change.³ Repentance is difficult. The natural man's inclination is against change, to go with the world's direction. Thus, the call of a preacher is opposite the call of a pied-piper.⁴

If the preacher persuades people to change, how can they change? Changes occur by the Holy Spirit's use of the Scripture, the full counsel of God. It is this point that gets the preacher into trouble today. Many preachers are calling for change. Unfortunately, they are calling for people to change themselves, to get a right attitude, to practice the right habits, to think the right thoughts, and to be positive. These are the Dr. Phil's of the pulpit, and they can sure load a church with people. The pressure then comes within the non-megachurch members. They want *their* churches to grow like that. They begin to look at the preacher. They believe that if the preacher will change his preaching style to the cotton-candy sermon then the church will grow. They could be right, but is that the call God has for your life? God's Word says that no man is righteous. God's Word says the heart is wicked in *all* its ways. God says mankind *cannot* clean up his or her act. Cleaning up one's act requires divine intervention, which arrives through the blood of Christ and His sanctifying work.

The premise of the soft-Gospel preacher is "I'm O.K., you're O.K., and God wants to bless you." I have a friend who is a trainer at a local workout studio. Pretend his name is Dan. Dan is a muscle-bound man, who trains professional athletes as well as the general public. He is a strong Christian and is witnessing constantly to those who come to his gym. One day, Dan began training two girls in his gym. They were dedicated to their physical appearance and were faithful in their workouts. The more he got to know them, the more he discovered about them. They revealed to him that they were exotic dancers at a local men's club. My friend began to witness to them. They said they appreciated Dan's witness, but that it was unnecessary. They divulged that they were Christians and members of such-and-such

---

2. Tucker, *Primer for Preachers*, 103.
3. Willimon, *Preaching About Conflict*, 64.
4. Spurgeon, *Lectures to My Students*, 87.

church. When he asked how they could dance naked day-in and day-out and not be convicted as Christians, they said it was their understanding from their preacher's sermons each Sunday that God does not mind. He loves them just as they are.

The Gospel these girls have been taught skims over Scripture and works with positive-thinking psychology. David Jeremiah believes that, in many of the church-growth movements and seeker-sensitive churches, preachers who once felt they were to preach the depth of God's Word have caved to the cultural pressure to be "relevant" and cute. In doing so, Jeremiah says the sermons are so topical that not enough Bible exists in the message to recognize it as a sermon.[5]

R. Albert Mohler Jr., president of Southern Baptist Theological Seminary, says the line of work in which a preacher finds himself is a nasty way of getting into trouble. The more a preacher is faithful to preaching God's Word, the more trouble he will encounter.[6] The reader may catch the contradiction with this statement and the title of this book. If a preacher preaches God's Word and can get into deep trouble, then how can a preacher preach God's Word and get out of trouble? It is God's design. The foolishness of preaching offends and brings trouble, because it convicts and calls for change. The preacher is not the one who is saying the things that offend. The preacher's opinion is not that which is rubbing the listener the wrong way; God's Word is. God loves the listening audience too much to leave them in the destructive life of sin and the eternal torture of Hell. The foolishness of preaching, if done in God's Spirit, is to bring a healing hurt. God's Word brings a full message to these two exotic-dancer girls, telling them that their life is going to hurt them now and forever. However, God's Word does not leave them there. His Word says forgiveness is available, and joy and an incredible life are ahead if only they will believe.

Those who are offended have a real problem with God and not the preacher. The one offended cannot lash out at God as readily as he can at the preacher. As a result, one may bring strife to the preacher, but God's Word is available to defend the preacher. That same Word of God can be preached to get through the crises in churches, because that Word has power. No human, no entity, and no other power can refute God's Word or overcome it. As a result, the title of the book still holds. The preacher in crisis can know this truth. The crisis the preacher faces may be the crisis that the church must face for God's glory. This should bring you comfort.

5. David Jeremiah, "Preaching Through Pain," *Preaching* 18, no. 5 (March/April 2003): 19.

6. R. Albert Mohler Jr., "The Preacher as Servant of the Word," *Preaching Magazine* (September 2002): 9.

Satan

Who is behind most of these troubles and crises that have the preacher thinking he cannot make it? Or, as Paul might ask, "Who's cutting you off?" Paul is obviously saying someone is. In Galatians, false teachers were present, but behind the false teachers is the usual suspect—the devil. He is active in your church, just as he is active in my church. One of my favorite classmates in seminary was Nathan Lino. Nathan brought a sermon out of Ephesians on the spiritual forces at work. He personalized it more clearly than I had ever heard before. He said, "The devil wants my church. The devil wants my wife. The devil wants my daughter." How much more personal can that be? Satan's practices have not changed over the years.

When Jesus began His ministry, as recorded in the very first chapter of the Gospel of Mark, He went into the synagogue in Capernaum and began to teach. The Bible says that the people were amazed, because He taught with such authority. Mark 1:23 says, "Just then there was a man in their synagogue with an unclean spirit; and he cried out." Jesus immediately told the evil spirit to "be quiet." Jesus commanded "Come out of him," and, immediately it did. The devil is the adversary to the preacher of the Word of God. When the preacher preaches God's truth in the authority of the Holy Spirit, the demons will stir, distract, drown out, and try to discredit the messenger. Understand, adversary number one is Satan himself. Paul said, "For our struggle is not against flesh and blood, but against the rulers, against the powers, against the world forces of this darkness, against the spiritual forces of wickedness in the heavenly places" (Ephesians 6:12).

The preaching of God's Word brings trouble. However, the preaching of God's Word also brings victory over that trouble. In the demonic realm, preaching is not seen as foolish. In Acts 8, when Philip was in Samaria preaching the message of Jesus Christ, the demons shrieked and fled. By this preaching, demons fled out of many people.[7] In 2 Corinthians 10:4, we are told "the weapons of our warfare are not of the flesh, but divinely powerful for the destruction of fortresses". Rick Warren holds to this power in his preaching. He says that the preacher's weapon of God's Word has the power to pull down every argument and every pretense.[8]

The devil is expected to be active in the Bible-believing, Bible-preaching church. In later chapters, one can see how he acts out in individual crises in church. To use a favorite old phrase, Peter "wasn't just whistling Dixie"

---

7. Wayne Grudem, *Systematic Theology: An Introduction to Biblical Doctrine* (Grand Rapids: Zondervan Publishing House, 1994), 433.

8. Rick Warren, "It's OK to Preach Repentance," *Leadership Magazine*, Winter 2004, 59.

when he said in 1 Peter 5:8 that "the devil, prowls around like a roaring lion, seeking someone to devour". Jesus said in Matthew 16:18, "upon this rock I will build My church; and the gates of Hades will not overpower it". He was not being allegorical, nor was He seeking to use some fear factor to motivate His church. An old preacher once said that at times, he sees more evidence of the devil than any other thing.

Satan's handiwork is being revealed in beliefs held in the United States as reflected in the " U.S. Religious Landscape Survey" conducted by the Pew Forum on Religion and Public Life. He has permeated the culture with his lies so much so that now 70 percent of Americans believe that many religions can lead them to salvation. Even 57 percent of Evangelical Protestants hold to that belief. In reverence to the Dr. Phil mentality, one theological professor stated that people now shop for churches as they shop for restaurants.[9] In a Barna Update, 80 percent of those polled claimed to be Christians, and yet almost 60 percent reject the existence of Satan.[10]

For the preacher to forget his formidable opponent is easy with this prevalent cultural denial. Because Satan hates God and hates what God loves, he strives against the church. Subtly, he is discounting all that God's Word testifies is true. Without notice, Satan can sneak in as a wolf in sheep's clothing to disrupt the good that a church can do. He will bring damage to the church and horrible hurt to the people, even those in the pastor's family. This is why Paul urged believers in Corinth to forgive one another and be reconciled because, otherwise, the devil will be able to work his schemes (2 Corinthians 2:11).[11] Paul urges the Ephesians to guard against their anger, giving the devil a foothold (Ephesians 4:27). If for no other reason then, a pastor should stay in the church combating every crisis because of his hatred for the enemy of God, not willing to let the devil win one inch in his church or his ministry. The preacher definitely possesses the weapons to win.

Sinful Man

With this realization, one must be cautious to not look for the devil behind every bush or try to blame him for every trial. Sinful humanity left alone

---

9. Barbara Karkabi, "On God, Religion and . . . Texas," *Houston Chronicle*, 24 June 2008, 1 (A).

10. Barna Update, "Americans Draw Theological Beliefs from Diverse Points of View" (October 8, 2002) [on-line]; accessed 27 July 2008; available from http://www.barna.org/FlexPage.aspx?Page=Barna Update&BarnaUpdateID=122; Internet.

11. Powell, *Basic Bible Sermons*, 14.

can bring enough trouble. James explains why strife exists in church—it is because of man's selfish desires that manifest themselves even in the best-intentioned believer. The selfish mentality says "serve me." Pastors are instructed to be servant leaders, but the selfish man wants more than the pastor can perform. In the pool of fallen humanity, anyone in that congregation at any given moment can step out of God's will and bring persecution on their Christian leader. Surprisingly, the older deacon whom I loved the most was the one who threw the fit that day when I was changing the youth night from Wednesday night to Sunday night.

Another problem in sinful man is that he cannot stand to be given mandates. When the preacher tells the world it must repent and trust Christ as Savior, the world screams as if greatly offended. The world holds a mindset that rejects any "you-must" statement.[12] Every man desires to do what is right in his own eyes. He does not want another to tell him what is right, even if that person is God Himself. Some of the most painful adversaries who struggle with mandates are staff members. These are those whom the pastor has loved, cared for, and helped. Pride often weighs in, and a staff member begins to second-guess the pastor, feeling he or she could do a better job, or simply resists taking orders. The aftermath leaves the pastor feeling worse than in any other conflict, because he feels betrayed by a friend. The sinful nature is not restricted to the everyday congregant, but also extends to the staff.

Some parishioners relish being the "employer" of the pastor. They want a report on what is going on, and want to give approval for every move. Accountability is a one-way street in many church relationships. Church members often see themselves as stockholders and the preacher as the CEO. He is the hired hand. If the church is not growing, then a change in pastor needs to occur. This is the baseball strategy. In major league baseball, if a team is not winning, they fire the manager because firing the whole team is too hard. (This is the beauty of the Titus Task Force strategy in troubled churches. They put every member, deacon, and pastor on probation and see how they measure up to God's Word.[13]) Some church members, usually the most vocal ones, want the pastor to be the chief bottlewasher, the diaper-changer, the administrator, the head of staff, the counselor, the hospital visitor, the theologian, the preacher, the accountant, the outreach coordinator, the activities director, the family man, and the whipping boy. This heavy load is what birthed the role of the deacons in the very beginning. Unfortunately,

---

12. Calvin Pearson, "Sheep, Serpents and Doves: Using Argumentation Theory in a World Hostile to Truth," *Preaching* 42, no. 1 (July/August 2008): 17.

13. George Fraser, Titus Task Force, personal phone interview with project leader, May 28, 2008.

most do not realize that each member of the church family, along with the pastor, has responsibilities that they themselves must carry.

Some congregants have huge personal issues that crop up and the pastor is on the front line to combat or to assist. Sadly, this puts the pastor in a precarious situation. When these issues surface, the pastor faces the opportunity and the sad tragedy to be called. In his book, *Primer for Pastors*, Austin Tucker gives a perfect illustration to describe the saddest of tragedies. A married couple had been fighting, and the husband threatened to kill himself. The wife phoned for the pastor to come immediately. He responded, and was able to bring calm to the situation. Unfortunately, in the family's mind, their embarrassing moment was now known by the pastor. Every time they saw him, they wondered if he thought less of them, or if that traumatic moment crossed his mind. One would think the family would be grateful eternally; but instead, as long as the pastor was at that church and knew their deep, dark secret, they felt their conflict was not resolved. As a result, to the pastor's dismay, when opposition was mustered against the pastor, this couple joined the opposition. Have you been there? I have. Every person in ministry must recognize the sad fact that sometimes the pastor becomes the garbage man. He is to provide a vital service to the community, but afterward, they would like him to take out the garbage and leave.[14]

An outsider will say, "Church people should not act that way." They are correct, but everyone should rejoice that these are in church. A pastor should be elated with every sinful man or woman who comes through his church's door. They bring the mission field to him. They bring the wood on which to carve. They bring the stone on which God can sculpt. Some of the worst enemies I have ever faced in the ministry, have with God's Spirit and His Word, become my greatest allies as their walk with the Lord became real. Jesus died for each of these. They come to church to be loved, to be consoled, to be assured, to be guided, to be guarded; and even though like a child they might not want it, they come to be disciplined.[15]

Sinful Pastor

One can be his own enemy. Look at function. Preaching will cause problems; but thankfully, preaching faithfully to God's Word will bring the right kind of problems. Not preaching God's Word will bring different problems. George Fraser's experience with the Titus Task Force of dealing with churches in turmoil frequently finds this to be the case. He says, "If you do teaching

14. Tucker, *Primer for Pastors*, 99-100.
15. Hicks, *Preaching Through a Storm*, 60.

without preaching, there will be strife. Teaching just brings information to the members but no conviction."[16] One pastor believed that before covering a controversial issue, he should ask a few members beforehand to get a feel of the congregation's reaction. He felt he should test the congregation's temperature before preaching on the subject.[17]

While this pastor has great tips in how to deal with controversy, this recommendation can be taken too far very quickly. The pastor should not be more concerned about self-preservation than he is about carrying out his God-given duty.[18] In addition, he should not err too much in the other direction. Many use the pulpit to bully their people. They constantly scold their people, saying things to them that they would never say one-on-one. As a result, some have labeled the pulpit the "coward's castle."[19]

The pastor must look inside. Some get so caught up in their position that they cease to have their quiet time with the Lord. They stand as a man of God, but they have drifted far from Him. When a kid goes swimming in the ocean, he gets so wrapped up in the fun that he never notices that he has drifted well beyond his swimming ability. He does not realize the danger until it is too late. Christian ministers can do the same. When a pastor strays from the Lord, his own moral failure can bring almost insurmountable adversity. Further, preachers can find so much authority in preaching God's Word in the pulpit, that they begin to think the authority is their very own. They become autocratic. They begin to think that if they feel strongly about something, then so does God. They even can get defensive over the little things. A minister may preach a strong sermon on Sunday. Monday comes, and he tells the secretary to order one thousand paperclips. She says that they do not need that many. The preacher thinks, "How dare you question me?"[20] Inadvertently, he has misperceived God's authority as his own.

Additionally, the preacher may misuse the gifts God has given him. He may try to win every battle with his gift of debate or speech and wind up producing his own crisis. He may win a verbal battle, but cause and lose a war.[21] Furthermore, a preacher can expect too much too soon from the congregation, especially respect. By demanding it too early, they drive others

---

16. Fraser, interview.

17. Louis Lotz, "Preaching on Controversial Issues: Keeping the Peace vs. Keeping the Purity," *Preaching* 16, no. 2 (September/October 2000): 40.

18. Willimon, *Preaching About Conflict*, 59.

19. Spurgeon, *Lectures to My Students*, 88.

20. Shelley and Miller, "Fundamentally One," 17.

21. Ibid., 20.

away. Not all church members will love the pastor equally at once. Love and respect must be earned over time.

Summation

Usually, not just one adversary sparks a feeling of hopelessness in the pastor. Generally, a combination of all the adversity above sparks the feeling of hopelessness. Even the strongest of stones will be worn away by constant dripping.[22] Thus, it is the same for the preacher. After constant multiple attacks, a change occurs. The pastor who once was an idealist, now finds himself wanting to bag it and leave. He starts feeling the deacons are against him unanimously, that every member is ungrateful, that none are warm to his family members. He feels virtually that the whole world is against him.[23]

Before the preacher gets too down, he needs to remember that Jesus said that people hated Him, so they will hate His followers. Jesus warned that in this world, the Christian will have troubles; but take heart, He has overcome the world. The field is ripe and the workers are few. Over one million attorneys are in the United States, along with six hundred thousand doctors, five hundred thousand police officers, and only three hundred thousand clergy.[24] Jesus has commissioned the preacher to a needed work, and that work he must do.

In times like this, a preacher must have the confidence that God's Word can "defang and declaw every evil attack."[25] The following chapters will show exactly this confidence placed in action. A pastor faces many crises. After reading and studying numerous surveys and conducting many in-depth interviews, the ten crises that follow appear to be the most common. These chapters begin from the inside struggles and move to the outside, analyzing how each can be dealt with from the pulpit. You will be comforted by the understanding that truly "nothing is new under the sun." You will find amazement as you read the actual accounts of pastors like you facing tremendous opposition. You will find strength as you read their sermons which they preached into the storm. You will find hope when you read how things worked out afterwards. The belief exists that, just as Jesus spoke into the storm and calmness came, the preacher with God's Word can find that same power at work through the Holy Spirit in his own church.

---

22. Spurgeon, *Lecture to My Students*, 163.
23. Ibid., 162.
24. Rediger, *Clergy Killers*, 49.
25. Allen, personal interview.

Chapter 4: The Pastor's Struggles

I could not believe the call. My preacher friend wanted to have lunch. As we visited on the phone, I could tell something was wrong. He seldom came into Houston. When I asked why he was in town, he said he was going to a psychiatrist. "A psychiatrist?", I asked. He said he would tell me about it at lunch. Needless to say, I began to pray for him immediately and was anxious to meet with him to make sure he was alright. Lunchtime came, and there he was. Maybe it was my imagination, or maybe it was reality, but he looked different. He looked older than me, even though he is a few months younger. He seemed heavy. His eyes seemed very moist like from a recent cry. We sat and exchanged pleasantries, but he could wait no longer, nor could I.

He said, "I have been horribly down." "Why?", I asked. He said that he could not put a finger on it. His marriage was great. His children were excelling. His church just finished a new building and was thriving. No internal church struggles, his last one had been some ten years before. He was just overwhelmed with depression. Never in his life, and I have known him since childhood, had he been so down. He was the wittiest guy in school, not to mention the most popular. Beyond that, he was one of the most Godly men I have ever known. My own challenge for prayer and witnessing came from his example.

Preachers carry deep struggles inside. Some days he knows what is wrong. A preacher can get down from the constant drips of opposition over time. He can get down when a program is not producing, a staff member is not living righteously, or a building project has not gotten off the ground. He can sometimes feel discouraged looking at the lives of people in his church and wondering, "Is the Holy Spirit using me to change these people at all, or are they simply coming because they like me and my stories?"[1]

He can be upset when his family is under attack. John Goss, still pastoring after twenty-five years, said the biggest trial in his pastorate was when his son got hooked on drugs, and he had to watch his beloved son live an

---

1. Mark Labberton, "Our Daunting Hope: Can Preaching Really Change Anyone?" *Leadership* 26, no. 3 (Summer 2005): 31.

out-of-control life.² Jim Cymbala faced a similar struggle with his daughter. Nothing would seem harder than to enter the pulpit and bring a Biblical message for others, with the knowledge that the foundation of your own home is crumbling.

On other days, the pastor cannot put a finger on his emotional depth. It may be just a one or two day funk that comes and then leaves. He may be suffering from an unidentified internal torment. The pastor is sad, but he does not know why he's sad. No matter what he tries, he just cannot break free of it. He does not want to minister. He does not want to study. He does not want to fellowship. The last thing he wants to do is enter a pulpit, but that is his job. How does he face his people? How does one carry that into the pulpit?

It may sound self-serving, but there is comfort in knowing that others have been here before. King David was down and struggled greatly. Sure he faced bouts of depression when Saul sought to kill him, and when Absalom rebelled against him. He faced greater internal struggles as a result of his personal sins. No doubt he found times of depression when he was anointed king at a young age, but had to wait many years to take the throne and; even then, he had to fight to obtain it. Elijah found himself depressed at the oddest moment, after victory over the prophets of Baal, one of the greatest victories in the history of God's people. Peter grew troubled by his denials. Timothy became down over his youth and self-perceived ineffectiveness.

Paul got down over the lack of progress in some of his churches. Further, he got down over the "thorn in his side." From Romans 7, it appears Paul was devastated also by the inner struggle of sin that continued to grieve him. Even the "Prince of Preachers," Charles Spurgeon, knew this feeling all too well. In his *Lectures to My Students*, he said that fits of depression come on most of God's servants. He said the strong are not always strong. The wise are not always wise. The joyful are not always joyful.³ Does this surprise God? Psalm 103 says that God remembers that we are dust. When a Christian reads that God's Word is designed to complete them, the inference is present that the Christian, in some sense, is incomplete.⁴ This includes the pastor.

The work of the preacher is not a 9-5 job where one draws a paycheck and the only care is that work will exist tomorrow. The preacher's work is heart work, naturally opening the pastor to attacks of depression. He feels

  2. John Goss, senior pastor, Central Baptist Church, Crockett, TX, personal interview with project leader, February 13, 2008.

  3. Spurgeon, *Lectures to My Students*, 154.

  4. Bryan Chapell, "The Fallen-Condition and the Purpose of the Sermon," *Preaching Magazine*, May/June 2005, 29.

defeated when the hopeful turn away, when the professor teaches a different doctrine, when the faithful member leaves in a fuss, or when the sinner grows harder right under his nose. He is left gasping for air when a most relied upon friend and brother turns in vicious attack.[5] He finds himself walking with his head down, questioning if any reason exists to continue.

Can any virtue come from such bouts? David Jeremiah asked the same question when he was diagnosed with cancer. His question was even more fervent as he began treatment. His answer came in many forms. He found that when he preached about suffering and challenges in life, he did so not just because they were in the Bible, but because he had experienced them himself. He found that because of his ordeal of cancer, his spirit grew tender and his heart became softer toward others in their predicaments. He found that spending all that time in the hospital, where looking up at the white ceiling was all he could do, allowed him to become more in tuned with God.[6]

After Jeremiah's diagnosis was made public, several people listening to his radio broadcasts commented about how his preaching of God's Word seemed to possess much more passion. He thought that was funny, considering the sermons to which they were listening had been preached before he had even been sick. He was not preaching differently; they were listening differently.[7] Spurgeon said that Christians are promised tribulation, and a pastor may expect a larger share of them than other Christians. Through them all, he concluded that these trials enable the preacher to pastor a flock that is ailing.[8]

The people in the flock listen better to that preacher, because they see a man who truly can empathize with what they are facing or feeling. They hear experienced credibility in the preacher's words. God can enable a minister to care for people going through particular trials that he has never experienced himself because God's Word is ever relevant. However, the pastor who has faced some of these trials forms an emotional tie to the church member. He no longer speaks some platitude nonchalantly and moves down the road. He stops and sighs and provides the shoulder on which the hurting can lean. Suddenly, the hurting people recognize that the message which the preacher shares may be the same one he has been sharing for years, but it is different too. It is different because they know and feel he has walked that path himself.[9]

---

5. Spurgeon, *Lectures to My Students*, 156.
6. Jeremiah, "Preaching Through Pain," 18.
7. Ibid., 15.
8. Spurgeon, *Lectures to My Students*, 156.
9. Jeremiah, "Preaching Through Pain," 18.

So, how do you preach through a trial or a storm in your life? God's servants can be cast down and still bring God glory. In their trials, they can still bring something from God's Word. Even if the enemy's foot is on the preacher's neck, by God's power, the preacher can rise up and cast off the evil one.[10] David Jeremiah had leaned on the Psalms throughout his long ordeal with cancer. When he returned to the pulpit, he wondered what he could preach. He decided to preach ten of the Psalms that had meant the most to him during his time of trial, and his people responded.

H. Beecher Hicks's mom had died. He loved her very much. She had been his support much of his life. Then, right in the midst of other pressures, she graduated to be with the Lord. He went into the pulpit hurting. He decided that covering it up was not the answer. He preached a sermon, "How Long the Night" from Psalm 30:5. He wept throughout the whole sermon. He felt that many probably were in the pews that day who thought to themselves, "I have troubles of my own, I don't need to be here for him to selfishly share his. He needs to minister to me."[11] Even though perhaps some in his congregation felt this, Hicks realized more had compassion on him and saw in their preacher their own grief.[12] His transparency had a healing effect.

Situation

Dr. Jim Jackson is an incredible preacher at Chapelwood Methodist Church in Houston, Texas. Currently, his church is thriving in a growing community. Though his membership would be considered upscale by most standards, their focus is on ministry to the needy. Always, the needy have been his passion. He has had struggles in his past—alcoholism, budgetary crises, church disputes, and the like. God has given him grace through every one. He has held true to his call and preached God's Word faithfully his whole ministry. Looking at him, the success he has had, the size of his church, and the way people respond to him, you would think he would not have a care in the world. Then two Sundays before Christmas a few years ago, things came crashing down—on the inside—a darkness he had never known.

Jackson was preaching a Christmas series, "Banishing the darkness and seeing the light." That particular Sunday, he was going to deal with the issue of depression. The whole week, he had himself been struggling with depression. He got up that Sunday morning and could not preach. Unsuccessfully, he attempted to work his way through the dark emotion. He finally

---

10. Spurgeon, *Lectures to My Students*, 164.
11. Hicks, *Preaching Through a Storm*, 22-34.
12. Ibid., 34.

called his assistant pastor, requesting him to preach. He told him that he hated to do this to him on such short notice, but he was on the wrong side of depression and could not preach. Jackson felt he would be spreading darkness if he were to step into the pulpit.

The following week, things got a little better. He planned to preach that Sunday, but he debated what to preach. His normal practice was to preach pretty close to where he was living. As a result, he took the pulpit that next Sunday and delivered this message:

Sermon

James F. Jackson

"The Promise of Light"

(Isaiah 9:1-7; Matthew 4:12-17; John 3:19-2)

Now and then I'll hear someone say, "Gosh, I sure wish I could have been a prophet a long time ago," and I'll know right away this is someone who has never read the Bible. This is someone who is incredibly naïve. One of the things you would never want to be is a prophet. If God ever comes to you and says, "I want to make you a prophet to speak my word," say, "Oh, no!" God has this way of feeling at perfect liberty to jerk His prophets through a knothole any time He wants to. It is a terrible thing to have to see the future and speak it. I'm not saying that everything about the future is bad. There are going to be wonderful things that happen to you in your future. There is joy, and there is contentment, and there is exhilaration, but unfortunately it won't all be good. If you could see the future, some of you would see sickness, sorrow, death. A few of you would see that things will turn the wrong way for you financially. Maybe somebody in this room would see divorce.

It's sometimes better not to see the future. That's part of the reason why the prophets were all weepers; they cried. They saw the future, and they wept. Did you ever wonder why Jesus wept on Palm Sunday? Everyone else was singing, and waving palm branches, and taking off their cloaks and throwing them down, and shouting, "Hosanna!" Jesus rides in on that donkey. He leaves Bethany where He has spent the night, and He comes over the crest of the hill. He looks at the city for the first time on that Palm Sunday, and He starts to cry. This is what He said: "How often would I have told you the things that make for peace?

How many times would I have gathered you as a hen gathers her brood, but you would not come?" And He cries. Do you know why He is crying? Because He sees the future.

He sees the year 70 A.D. when the Roman soldiers would lay siege to the city of Jerusalem, not for a week or two, but for years, choking off all the sources of life, choking away the food so that they got so hungry that when people died of starvation, the others ate their flesh. He saw the Roman soldiers breaking the wall down; not only breaching it, but tearing it down, moving immediately to the temple, doing unthinkable things there, and then tearing it all down until there was not one stone on top of another, then torching the city and burning everything that was left to the ground. So much blood was present from the murder of people who remained that Josephus, the Jewish historian, said that they had to relight the fire three times, because the blood of the people all over the streets kept putting the fire out. He saw that. Everyone was celebrating. Everyone was feeling joy. Everyone was saying, "Whoopee!" Jesus was crying, and that's why.

Isaiah is seeing doom himself. You know, I wish we had about an hour or an hour-and-a-half. I could go through chapter eight and chapter nine of Isaiah. It's dark. The prophets saw things that were unthinkable. Isaiah wept. He saw the destruction of the ten Northern Tribes. He saw what happened in the eighth-century B.C. when the Assyrians swept down on them and destroyed them—the ten lost tribes we call them. He saw what would happen in the next century when the Babylonians swept in on the Southern Kingdom and took them off into captivity. We know their stories from Daniel, Shadrach, Meshach and Abednego, and Ezekiel, and all the others. Then he saw darkness set in; darkness was everywhere.

When people are in the dark, they will do anything to find light. Anything that looks like light, they will follow. It's true in our world. The very same truth is true in our world. They turn to mediums, witches, and people who were a part of the occult, conjuring up people who were dead. Anytime you see the occult begin to grow in our world, it is because people are chasing light, and they think it is light. The only problem is that things appear to be light out there that drive you into a deeper darkness. So these people who are experiencing this deep, sick darkness, it says, begin to curse God and the darkness and the anguish set in on them. I'm not referring to physical darkness, but rather emotional, spiritual, and relational darkness. It's pervasive. It's all around us. Do you realize the darkness that is around you every day? I buried a woman last Monday. Her family might be here this morning. A Godly woman, Martha joined our church about a year ago, I guess. They lived out in Fulshear. They lived thirty-five miles from here, something like that, I don't know. They lived in a gated community—not just a community with a gate; people actually man it. They broke in on her and stabbed her fourteen times with her own butcher knives. That's darkness!

An emotional darkness exists. There's an ethical darkness where we don't know what's right and what's wrong, and we can't figure it out; light is darkness, and darkness is light. We start practicing what I call statistical morality: if enough people do it, it must be O.K. Darkness is everywhere. I'm going to put a scene on the screen from one of my favorite movies called "Scent of a Woman." It's a story about this man who was a colonel, a retired colonel, and he had gotten involved in something and he had had an accident. It was his own fault, but he was blind, and he decided he didn't want to live anymore. He had one big fling before he died, and he went to New York City, where he was going to do all the things that were really important to him; then he was going to kill himself, just bail out. The darkness was too much for him. He couldn't go alone, so he found a young fellow who was from an un-affluent background, who was involved in one of these boarding schools where rich people go. The Colonel talked him into going with him, offered to pay him some money, and did all these wonderful things, then sent him on an errand in hopes that he could kill himself before the young man came back. But the young man figured it out and came back and stopped him. They wrestled. This is part of the scene at the end of that wrestling match. "Get out of your life, would you? It's my life. I got no life. I'm in the dark here. Do you understand? I'm in the dark."

If you could live with me, and go with me, as I do what I call ministry, you would see that there are people in the dark all around you, thick darkness. They don't know how to get out. They think it is permanent. They think it will never, ever, go away. This is their life. Christmas is maybe the worst time of all. Not only is it the darkest time of the year physically, the sun goes down earlier, right now, than any other time of the year. It's that way in other ways.

Christmas is when we experience so intensely the fact that this person is not sitting at the table anymore. It's when we become aware of how bad those relationships are. It's when we have to be with people whom we detest. We hate being with them, but we have to because it's Christmas. See, we put on a happy face, and we act like everything is O.K., but it's not O.K. Let me tell you something, friends. If you could know the truth, if people who are sitting around you today could tell you the truth, people are here who would say exactly what that man on the screen said: "I'm in the dark. I'm in the dark. I want to bail out," while holding on for dear life, hoping, treading water, weary, tired; they're in the dark.

That's when Christmas happens. That's the scene. Darkness everywhere, pervasive darkness. It a thick darkness. Look at the scene. Look at where Jesus grew up. Read what Isaiah said (let me put back on the screen what Isaiah said); these are verses one and two: "But there will be no more gloom for those who are in anguish." I love that word, that power, that's more powerful, anguish. "In the former times you brought into contempt the land of Zebulun and the land of Naphtali." Do you know what those are? Do you know when the children of Israel came in with Joshua, and the twelve tribes came in and they were assigned certain territories, and they were told, "Now you go here, and you conquer the people there."

The tribes of Zebulun and Naphtali were given the territory that we call the Galilees. In other words, the people who settled in the Galilees were those two tribes, but notice they're in contempt. Why are they in contempt? They're in contempt, because they didn't do what God told them to do. They were told, "Go and conquer the people of Caanan who live there," and they decided not to do that. It's in the Bible. It's in the nineteenth chapter of Joshua. They decided not to do that. They decided, "Well, let's go along to get along." So they just lived with them, you know? So the truth is the people who lived in Galilee were notoriously irreligious. Not only that, but later on the Assyrians came down and conquered the ten lost tribes, carried most of them away, but some of them they left, and they just kind of intermarried with them. So these guys were not real good Jews. They were just different.

Remember when Jesus was on trial, and Peter was warming his hands over the fire and talking, "He's from Galilee. We can tell by the way He talks. They even talk different. They even have a different dialect." These are not very religious people. They lived in the land (let me show the next slide) . . . the way of the sea. Do you see that? This is where they lived. They lived in the way of the sea. In other words, this is the trading route. A trading route ran from Syria down to Egypt, from Damascus all the way to Cairo, and the trading route came right through the Galilees. What that meant was, it didn't go through Jerusalem.

It came through the Galilees. In other words, because it came that way, it was a very cosmopolitan place. People from all over the world came to visit. A lot of money floated through, a lot of power floated through.

Look what else it says: "The land beyond the Jordan, the Galilee of the nations." Notice in Matthew's Gospel, it's translated—I think more correctly—the Galilee of the Gentiles. The nations are the Gentiles. The Galilee of the Gentiles. Now, what I recall is that this is the prophet Isaiah talking. What's he saying? In other words, people who lived up in the Galilees just went along to get along. They were not too religious. It was the Galilee of Gentiles, all up in there around the Galilees where Jesus was raised.

In fact, right outside the city of Nazareth, a Roman Legion was camped permanently. In fact, Nazareth was considered a red-light district. When you wanted wine, women, and song, Nazareth was the place you went. It was a low-class town. One of Jesus' disciples in the first chapter of John's Gospel, says they told him He was the Messiah and He was from Nazareth, and the disciple said, "Can anything good come out of Nazareth?" Nazareth was a place of moral disrepute, a place where good people didn't hang out. Nobody good lived in Nazareth. In fact, it was true of all the Galilees. In the seventh chapter of John's Gospel, someone said to the group, "Jesus is the Messiah, and He's from Galilee." They said, "No. Messiahs don't come from Galilee." This is the Galilee of the Gentiles.

In fact, when reading the eighth chapter of John's Gospel, a very interesting criticism, they are talking to Jesus and they say, "Well, at least we're not illegitimate." Do you know what's going on? There's an accusation during Jesus' lifetime that Mary was not a virgin; there was a soldier who did that to her. You see, the Old Testament law was pretty clear. If your birth was illegitimate, they wouldn't allow you in the Temple or the synagogue. You were just bad. And that's the context! We're talking darkness, friends, the people who walked in darkness. This is the least likely place in the world from which to have a Messiah come. These are from bad people, people who are of ill repute, people who have been condemned, people who didn't do the right thing, people who intermarried and hung out with Gentiles, people who cavorted with them; He's from a bad town. And the light comes and chases away the darkness. It's always that way. It's always that way.

We want to go through the Christmas season, and we want to pass out toys and think that's all that it is. We miss Christmas. Christmas is all about realizing that you are in the dark and stepping into the light. As long as you stand around saying, "I'm O.K. You're O.K. Everything's O.K. How are you? I'm fine. Everything's great," you don't experience the light. You can't understand the light unless you've experienced the dark, and you see, darkness is the absence of light. It is only when we realize that something is missing, something is wrong, that we understand our need for light, that we want to come to the light. We don't experience Christmas when we stand around saying, "Everything's fine with me. How are you?" "Fine. Great." It's not true. I've been trying to tell you that all fall about the darkness. I haven't been doing that because I want you to experience darkness.

I want you to experience light, but you don't experience light unless you come to terms with the darkness in you. Let me put up for you some of the things I've talked about: grief, addiction, disappointment, dissatisfaction, jealousy, perfectionism, pain . . . man, we could have gone on and on. There are some more I thought about preaching about. I mean, to be honest with you, I could have gone on forever.

Bless Bob Johnson's heart! Last Sunday, he preached and I'll tell you why he preached. I couldn't preach. I met with the staff, and I told them the truth. I said, "I'm experiencing depression. I don't know how to preach about depression." I can describe it for you. I can tell you about it. I can describe it so graphically I will cast darkness all over this place. Through most of the fall I've been holding on for dear life. I've been treading water. I've been struggling. It's easy to say, "I'm fine. How are you?" "I'm fine." "Great, just great." So we never experience the light. You don't experience the light until you come into the light from the darkness. You realize this is not O.K.

It's interesting to me that so much of the time Jesus is described as light. "I am the light of the world," He said. Zacharias said this wonderful thing about Jesus. Zacharias was the father of John the Baptist. He said this before Jesus was born. He said, "When He comes, He is going to be the dayspring from on high." Some of the translations call it "the dawn". That's just such a powerful image—the dayspring from on high, the source of the day that creates the day, the source of life that creates the dawn, which calls forth life into the world, which chases away the darkness. That's what He is like. The Book of Revelation calls Him the bright and morning star. The Book of Revelation says that when we get to Heaven, we won't see Jesus looking like the little pictures we were taught in Sunday School. What we're going to experience is light, and there won't be any sun, and there won't be any moon because Jesus will be the light, and you don't experience that light if you're holding on to the darkness and saying, "I'm O.K., I'm O.K." We go through Christmas lying to one another, to ourselves, and we are self-deceived: "I'm O.K. You're O.K."

How do you come to the light? You don't do it by figuring it all out academically. I'm not saying you don't put your best foot forward. We're to love God with all of our hearts and all of our minds. We're not to check our head at the door. We use our minds. But let me tell you, if the only way you can experience the light of God is through intellect, then the people who are a part of our circle of friends don't have a chance. And I say, "No." If you really want to experience what it means to be alive in Christ, go to one of their meetings. It's not even about serving. I mean, serving is wonderful; we ought to serve. But you can deliver manna to families all day long and never get in the light. You can just cover up your darkness.

You can say, "I'm O.K. Look at what I've done for God." You've got to be humble. You've got to say, "O.K., I'm willing for the Spirit of God to point out to me the truth, and I'm willing to admit it. I'm willing to intentionally step into His light. I want the Sun of righteousness to rise with healing in his wings over my life. I want the dawn to break over the horizon, the dayspring from on high to break over the horizon of my life and chase away the darkness. You've got to want it. You've got to choose it. The writer of John's Gospel, the opening chapter, says this: "He came to His own people, and His own people said, 'No, thanks.'" The most amazing thing in the world—the light that enlightens every one of us had come into the world, and they said, "No thanks!" But all who received Him, who believed on His name, He gave them power to become children of God, who are born, not of blood nor the will of the flesh nor the will of human beings, but of God.

You can carry on the charade if you want to, but you'll miss Christmas. In John's Gospel in the third chapter, there's that famous verse, "God so loved the world that He gave His own Son, that whoever believed in Him will not perish but have everlasting life." The nineteenth verse of that same chapter says this: "This is the problem. Light has come into the world but people prefer the darkness to the light." The light had shined, and people chose to stay in their darkness rather than stepping in the light. That's amazing! But it's true. You've done it before, haven't you? I've done it before, but not this year.

Would you bow your head and close your eyes? Would you allow the Holy Spirit to work in your life right now in your heart, and just bring up gently, but graphically, the darkness that you've been afraid to give up? The darkness to which you've been holding on? The darkness that you use to define yourself? What is it? Now, would you step into the light, would you choose to believe, would you choose to receive, would you allow the Dayspring of on high to rise over the darkness of your life and call into existence new life and new hope and new meaning and new joy. Would you choose that today? Oh, Lord, would You give us an astonishing joy? Would You cause us to want to come and worship Him, adore Him, because of what He has done in our lives today? Oh, God, may Your Son be born in our hearts today for it is in His name that we pray. Amen.[13]

Lessons

Jackson discovered that what he was facing at that moment in the Christmas season was what thousands were facing all over the city of Houston. Some were out of work. Some had family who would not be home for Christmas. Some had loved ones who had just died. Some had sons in the war and who were in harm's way that holiday season. Because of these heartaches, Jackson believed God led him to address his hurt before the body of Christ experientially. He believes that, as preachers, "Everything doesn't have to make us look good. Like it or not, we are on the record with our struggles."

Jackson's candor brought an incredible response. People responded with love, new-found respect, and a new-found freedom. They realized that even men close to God hurt. What a relief! Many think that if they face such feelings, something is wrong with them. They feel isolated, doubting their salvation. Then, they see a man so close to God who struggles, admits it, and leans on the God he preaches. They begin to lean on God all the more. Jackson lived out the goal that he had set for his congregation. He wanted his church to be a place where people can be honest. He said, "If you've got to fake it to be here, then how will our church ever connect and help others walk in the light."

Dr. Jackson exemplified the Biblical form of worship, which is to live for God's glory. In his storm, he said that he knew more than anything he had

---

13. James F. Jackson, "The Promise of Light," from the Series "Naming the Darkness, Seeing the Light (Isaiah 9:1-7; Matthew 4:12-17; John 3:19-2)," 23 December 2007.

to be faithful to God. He said, "If things work out well for me, that's good. If things don't, that's good too."[14] May God be glorified in it all!

This pastor, having gone through a horrible storm, did not make this sermon about himself. His sermon was not a venting session or a pity party. He spoke about his experience, which added heart-felt emotion to his sermon. He acknowledged toward the end of the sermon, his own struggle to which most of his congregation had no idea. He used it to extend to his congregation the implied statement, "I am not just preaching to you, I am pulling up a pew next to you and hearing what God is saying to both of us."

One last thing exists of which a preacher must take note. Dr. Jim Jackson's trial came at the exact time he was dealing with the Scripture on that topic. As the real life dramas continue to unfold in the next few chapters, notice how often this occurs. A collision occurs at the intersection of time. At just the right time, God's Word collides with man's trial to bring relief, grow faith, and transform the believer more into the image of Christ.

---

14. Jackson, interview.

Chapter 5: **Pastoral Error**

Surprisingly, with all the crises that pastors face, they still carry a pretty high opinion of their own abilities. A Barna Update found that in ten of the eleven common pastoral activities, a majority of Protestant senior pastors rated themselves as doing either an excellent or a good job. This was true for pastors in both large and small churches. Of those polled, 90 percent believed they did an excellent or good job in preaching, 85 percent said they did an excellent to good job of encouraging people, and 82 percent said they did an excellent to good job of pastoring. The primary gift that these pastors believed they had was the gift of preaching.[1] Opinions like these make it difficult for many pastors to see their own errors in church crisis. This is understandable when the nature of man is to focus on the speck in another's eye.

Routinely, preachers in the 1950s were at the top of the lists of the most respected men in the community. Today, the preacher falls consistently to eleventh or twelfth.[2] Perhaps the reason for this drop can be explained in Scripture. Paul noticed a chink in the armor of preachers over two thousand years ago. Paul saw people preaching in his day to serve their own appetites (Romans 16:17-18), because of selfish ambition and vanity (Philippians 2:3), and out of envy and strife (Philippians 1:15). Further, Peter saw people preaching out of greed and a thirst for power (1 Peter 5:24).

Jesus noticed that the Pharisees sought lofty positions, because they loved honor, the chief seats, and people calling them "rabbi" in the streets, drawing accolades from those around (Matthew 23:5). Proverbs, written a thousand years before, pointed out that many just love to hear themselves talk, to air their own opinions (Proverbs 18:2). Things have not changed in all that time. Regardless how righteous a preacher may be, any preacher's

---

1. Barna Update, "Pastors Rate Themselves Highly, Especially as Teachers" (January 7, 2002) [on-line]; accessed 27 July 2008; available from http://www.barna.org/FlexPage.aspx?Page=BarnaUpdate &BarnaUpdateID=104; Internet.

2. John R. Bisagno, *Inside Information: Worship Wars, Calvinism, Elder Rule & Much More* (Longwood, FL: Xulon Press, 2007), 85.

motives, actions, and attitudes can stray into one of these sinful categories. When they do, look out! Trouble lies ahead.

One witnesses this repeatedly. On a Monday morning, after a Sunday of preaching God's Word, I once saw a preacher at seminary buy Houston Rocket tickets from a fellow seminary student with a wad of cash from his pocket. He paid over two hundred dollars for tickets with ones, fives, and ten dollar bills. Another person asked where he got all that cash. His reply was, "from the offering plate, of course," as if pulling cash from the offerings of the church for his selfish purposes was a natural thing for the pastor. Not knowing the situation at his church, his actions may have been completely innocent, but it sure did not appear right. The seeming reflection was that his motive for preaching was to satisfy his personal appetites.

People view gross immorality, such as viewing pornography, soliciting prostitutes, embezzling church money, having a drug addiction, and spousal abuse as gigantic pastoral errors. The writer will examine these more closely in the next chapter. While moral issues are the ones which make the headlines and quite probably do the most to shape public opinion, this chapter deals with the more subtle errors as those executed from the pulpit, in church business, in leadership, and in interactions with church members.

Perhaps the church believes the pastor is selfish, plays too much, shirks his responsibility to prepare for sermons, or does not respond to the hurts of the people adequately. They feel he is too preoccupied in other things, or he is simply not attempting to improve in his vocation.[3] These complaints may not make the headlines, but they can be just as detrimental as the tabloid-type sins. To put a label on these perceived failings is difficult, but Jerrien Gunnink's personal survey grouped these together with the phrase "pastoral incompetence." The respondents to his survey blamed as much as 75 percent of their church conflicts on what they deemed pastoral incompetence.[4] This seems high when compared to G. Lloyd Rediger's findings that attribute 2 to 4 percent of church conflict to pastoral incompetence.[5] Easily, one could conclude that the first survey was of church members, and the second survey was from the pastor's point-of-view. This could be a fine example of each seeing the speck in the other's eye. Regardless, pastors definitely can cause strife in a church. The cause may be pastoral brutality, selfishness, laziness, or personality disorders. The end result is still strife, which can lead to a church crisis.

3. Tucker, *Primer for Pastors*, 100.

4. Interview with Jerrien Gunnink, former pastor and author, personal interview with project leader, May 27, 2008.

5. Rediger, *Clergy Killers*, 105.

CHAPTER 5: PASTORAL ERROR

A tendency exists for preachers to run head-on into the rut of "I-thou" preaching.[6] They start to believe that somehow what they say from the pulpit applies to the people, but not to themselves. When a preacher does this, he finds that his preaching of Biblical mandates in his smug, self-righteous way moves no one.[7] The people know the truth. Gary Preston found his church embroiled in a war of words over a building project. The congregants said many ugly things about other congregants. Preston preached a sermon out of James 3 concerning taming the tongue.

After the sermon, many came forward in repentance. They promised to mend fences and to sacrifice their own feelings and work for the unity of the church. He was thrilled about the response. At a men's fellowship the following Tuesday, he was beaming over how great Sunday had gone. Then one of the men of his church looked Preston in the eye and asked if that message meant that he, the preacher, would make amends with the people with whom he had confronted and criticized openly. Preston felt the guilt rush over him. God's words that he preached applied to him too.[8] Pastors have to avoid the "I-thou" preaching in another way. One witnesses a side manifestation of this attitude when a pastor comes before the congregation and lobbies for his own selfish wants such as higher pay, pet projects, and issues that stroke his ego.[9] He may even be unaware that these things relate to "me" not "we."

Some pastors refuse to consider the benefits of criticism. Joe Dempsey, a conflict consultant for the Presbyterian Church, says that one of the causes of trauma in church is the inability of the pastor to accept criticism.[10] Some clergy take to the pulpit with the intent to berate members for every negative comment that they receive. Pastors who do this soon are looking for work. They may depart, but the church they leave becomes more protective and less willing to release authority to the next guy.

The pastor's opinions are not the ones that count, so one should not speak of them as the infallible Word of God. People come to church to hear from the preacher what Jesus has to say on an issue. His Word is the only authoritative word. Too many times, the preacher begins to think his words are naturally God-inspired. Congregants do not help when they view certain religious leaders' words as being equal to Scripture. When the

---

6. Shelley and Miller, "Fundamentally One," 17.

7. Adam Hamilton, "Opening Closed Minds," 25, no. 2 *Leadership* (Spring 2004): 38.

8. Gary Preston, *Pastors in Pain: How to Grow in Times of Conflict* (Grand Rapids: Baker Books, 2005), 81.

9. Willimon, *Preaching About Conflict*, 11.

10. Gunnink, *Preaching for Recovery*, 25.

preacher is told what a great preacher he is, or what a great message that was, and especially when the preacher hears members tell him how their life has changed since coming to his church, he begins to feel that his own words are the source of transformation. Proverbs 27:21 says that "each is tested by the praise accorded him".

To be so zealous on an issue that the preacher forgets to retreat back to God's Word is easy. I am very much against drinking. I would love to say drinking is a sin. In fact, in the past, I have stated that drinking is a sin, but God has convicted me. I cannot find clear Scriptural evidence to support my opinion. The Bible speaks of drunkenness as a sin. The Bible details the dangerous effects of liquor, but it does not say it is a sin. Paul even instructed Timothy to drink a little for his stomach ailments. Just because people come to listen and the preacher moves them, it is easy to take the message one step further and say "here's what I think." A former pastor of mine once said that the preacher sees all the glory going to Christ, and he starts to want just a little bit for himself. This is a big mistake.

The experience of every pastor is to have members question issues or stands made in a Sunday message. Sometimes it is through a phone call, sometimes a sidebar question after church, and sometimes through an e-mail or text. The pastor's first response often is defensive, "How dare they question me!" He fumes thinking, "I have been in the Bible all week. I have studied and worked and prayed. I have even been to seminary! They need to listen and search the Scriptures more." How pompous! Does the preacher have the monopoly on understanding God's Word? Even more so, can one man think they have somehow mastered all that God has revealed?

I was preaching on sin habits one Sunday and began to enumerate several Biblical characters and their apparent sin struggles. Some were prominent, and some were obscure. On one that was obscure, I named Elijah's sin as depression. A Godly woman in my church sweetly e-mailed me to ask if I was intimating that depression is a sin. She spoke of many great Christians who have struggled with depression (see the previous chapter), and added that many in our church struggled with depression. She said I gave the impression, when I preached, that depression was a sin.

She was correct. I do not think depression is a sin, and I never have. What I meant was that sometimes depression is a result of faithlessness. I meant to emphasize that man cannot please God without faith. I meant that one should never doubt God. Unfortunately, what preachers say, and what preachers mean often are two different things. After a private clarification with her and asking her to forgive me, I went to the pulpit the next Sunday, and before I began my sermon, I apologized to the congregation and clarified the Bible's stand. That was hard, but necessary nonetheless.

Situation

That pastors make mistakes is clear. That the errors made by pastors can affect the whole body and that one sometimes can pass them on to the church is true also. How can one address them best? W. A. Criswell gave all preachers a perfect example. Dr. James Bryant of Criswell College had the privilege to serve as Criswell's associate pastor for several years. When interviewed about church crises, he related from a social point-of-view, the greatest crisis that First Baptist Dallas faced in Criswell's tenure as pastor - the integration crisis.

Criswell was a staunch supporter of segregation, and even preached a sermon in South Carolina for Strom Thurmond on the curse of Ham. He had a reputation on this issue. His attitude attracted racists to his church. One of the richest men in the world at that time was one of the first billionaires, H. L. Hunt. Because of Criswell's stand on segregation, Hunt left the Methodist church and received baptism at First Baptist Church, Dallas. Because of this stand, Bryant almost did not go to work for the church. Part of the reason Bryant accepted the position was the hope that God could use him to lead this precious pastor away from this prejudice.

When the Civil Rights Act passed in 1954, churches placed deacons in the doorways to turn blacks away. Baptists confessed this in the year 2000. Over many years, God was working on Criswell's prejudice. One can imagine how often in his prayer life, and in Scripture reading, he felt internal tension that something in his heart was not right. In June of 1968, that tension came to a head. God convicted Criswell and, though not documented, he confessed this to the Lord and sought forgiveness and change. After this, he went to his deacons and confessed his racism. With weeping, he declared it was a sin, his sin, and he asked those men to forgive him. I am sure he wondered if the deacons would protest, criticize, or revolt. Instead, the deacons met his brokenness with their own brokenness. The deacons began to weep and said to him, "God needs to forgive us too." What a glorious moment in the life of this fine church! On June 9, 1968, Criswell went before the church and preached from Revelation 3:7-8, "The Church of the Open Door." The reader will be shocked early in the sermon at the national setting in which the preacher preached this message.[11]

---

11. James Bryant, senior professor of pastoral theology, Criswell College, Dallas, TX, personal phone interview with project leader, April 21, 2008.

Sermon

W. A. Criswell

"The Church of the Open Door"

REVELATION 3:7-8

On the radio, you are sharing the services of the First Baptist Church in Dallas. This is the pastor bringing the message entitled, "The Church of the Open Door." Before I bring the word of the Lord, from God's Book and the message the Lord has laid on my heart, I would like to mention two things.

The first—the president of the United States has appointed today as a national day of mourning, and in keeping with that appointment by the chief executive of our nation, all of us would extend to the family of Senator Kennedy our remembrance in prayer and our sympathy in the tragic loss of husband and father and friend. We would take this occasion as a time of rededication to an ordered society, seeking in every means at our command to encourage our people and to demand of our citizens, obedience to the law and respect for authority, and above all, under God, a prayer that we shall come to reverence human life, which is a gift of God. In next Sunday's sermon, I hope that I may speak of some of these things at a much deeper and more lengthy and meaningful extent.

The second preliminary word concerns an exigency that has been placed upon me, for which I importune the sympathies and remembrance of our dear church. A few weeks ago, the representatives of our publication society of the Southern Baptist Convention, the Broadman Press, came to me and asked me to write a certain book. I have gathered the material for that book, and it must now be written. To show you the exigency of this hour, I have never written a book in under a year, and some of them I have taken two years to write. I must write this book in three weeks. What heretofore, I have done in a year, I must do in three weeks. Thus, you will understand if the pastor is consumed day and night and night and day in this assignment. Then, after three weeks, why, we shall see what other fires the pastor will fall into, but right now, I'm in that one. So understand, I'll be hibernating all of the moments that I can possibly command, writing this book.

Now, to the message—in the third chapter of the Book of the Revelation, beginning at verse 7: "And to the angel of the church in Philadelphia write. . . ." Now, verse 8: "Behold, I have

CHAPTER 5: PASTORAL ERROR

set before thee an open door." This message is in no wise, or in any part, an exposition of the text or of the passage in God's Word in which the words are found. It is a name for a sermon that God has sent me here at this hour to deliver. "Behold, I have set before thee an open door." Thus, the title of the message is "The Church of the Open Door."

One of the questions asked me again and again, both in press conferences and by individual representatives of the press, and by an innumerable host of interested friends and leaders of our convention, "Why is it that in these years past, you have always declined the nomination to this highest place of leadership in our denomination, but now, you accept it? What has happened? Why have you changed? Why did you reject it heretofore and why do you accept it now?" There are three reasons why in the years past I have declined such a nomination.

First, I never felt that it was God's will for me to do it. Nor could I quite describe all of those convictions that entered into that feeling in my soul. My classmates and men, whom I have known intimately through the years, have accepted such a place of responsibility. And I have loved them for it, and prayed for them in it. But I never felt it was God's will for me.

The second reason—I never felt worthy to assume so tremendous an assignment. This is not false or cheap humility. I am just telling you why it is that, in years past, I never accepted such a proffer. I never felt worthy in my soul for such a tremendous assignment from God.

The third reason was you, our dear church, and there were two reasons in our dear church. First, I had watched the churches of men who assumed this great far-flung mandate, and their churches suffered. This church, Dr. Truett was ambassador plenipotentiary to the whole world, and the church greatly suffered. Dr. Truett was gone most of the time, and such a prospect for me and our church hurt my soul. And one of the things that I resolved when I came to be pastor of the church was that I would accept it as my chief and primary assignment. Whatever else I did, my first work under God would be this pastoral ministry, and for years, I never accepted a revival meeting. For years, I never left the church. I stayed here, every week, every Sunday. When finally, I did begin to accept revival invitations, they were never more than two. I would accept one in the spring. I would accept one in the fall, and I stayed here through the years, trying to be a good shepherd for God's flock. So I refused, because I did not want to hurt our church, and being gone hurts the church.

The second thing I staggered with before was this question of race. What would be involved in our church if I were to receive an assignment such as the presidency of the Southern Baptist Convention, what it would mean to this church in the violent turmoil that has engulfed and convulsed our nation in these racial crises. I am just telling you why it is, the best I know how to say it, that in these years past, I have refused even to consider such an assignment.

"Then why is it now that you have accepted it?" Why? For all three of those reasons that heretofore I have refused it. First, as the days pass, and in the exigencies and fortunes and vicissitudes and turns of life, ten thousand things entered into it. I finally came to the deep conclusion and persuasion that this was something God wanted me and called me to do. My wife, Mrs. Criswell, greatly objected to it. All through these days, she sought to dissuade me from it. Some of the friends, who love me most and pray for me the deepest, sought to dissuade me from it. But as the days passed, and as the turns and fortunes and incidents of life would come, they increasingly pressed upon my soul the conviction that this was something God called me to do. It was God's will for me.

Second was my feeling of unworthiness. I laid it before God the humblest, the most meaningful, the sincerest that I knew how, and there came into my life that feeling that I had when I was a boy. In the days now so long ago, as a child and as a teenager and as a youth and as a young man, when I felt God's call to be a pastor, a preacher, in those days, now so long ago; as a child in the grammar school, I consecrated my life in preparation for that work. As I look back now in age to those childhood days, I cannot imagine such a thing could be. Yet, as sincerely and as deeply as I know, did I then give myself in preparation for this ministry. As a child, as a teenager, as a youth, and as a young man; I have done it all over again in these days. I have recommitted and reconsecrated my life to God.

Now, the third, what of the church? First, being gone—what of that? There is no doubt, nor should we hide our faces from the fact that there will be many, many more times that I shall be away than in these days and years past. What of that? And, what of the church? This was a conviction that I came to about you. I believe there is also in the church such a like spirit of dedication and consecration, that we shall be more faithful to God's work than we have ever been before. We shall assume for ourselves also a contingent, component, constructive, consecrated part of this ministry. Our deacons will be more faithful now than they've ever been before, and our teachers will be more faithful. Our leaders will be more devoted. Our choir will be more faithful. Our membership will be more faithful, and our staff will be more committed than we have ever been before.

Wouldn't it be an incomparable gift to offer to God that, in these next coming immediate two years, we had our greatest advance? Oh, if God would just give to us. And instead of the church waning and lessening and ebbing and staggering and stumbling, that in these immediate two years that lie ahead, we should offer to God our finest achievements, and I have felt it could be done. If we would each one in his place, resolve that now, in this time and in this hour, I shall be doubly committed to my task and to my assignment.

Then what of race? The First Baptist Church and the racial tension and turmoil that we witness all around us, what of our church and race? If we had hours and hours, we could hardly enter into all that lies back of the message delivered this morning by the pastor. I have been asked countless numbers of times: How is it that there has never been an ugly, bitter, racial incident in your church? All through the length and the breadth of this land, those bitter, ugly incidents have taken place in the churches. And the churches have been torn apart and they've been decimated. And some of them have almost been destroyed by that bitter conflict and confusion. Yet in the First Baptist Church in Dallas, there has never been even an approach to such an ugly incident. Yet, you would think that out of all of the churches of the Southern Baptist Convention, that our church would be the prime target. And you would think that of all of the pastors of the Southern Baptist Convention, that your pastor would be the first and primary target. Yet in the years and the years, and they've been many years, more than we realize now since this racial tension has been heightened in America, yet in our church there has never been even an approach or an approximation of any ugly racial incident. Why?

And I have answered. I have never had any fear, never. There has never been any fear in my heart regarding this church and any ugly racial incident. I took it to God years ago. And I had an answer to prayer and an assurance from Heaven that such an ugly incident would never come to pass, would never be seen in this congregation. And through these years, I have walked and preached unafraid. My heart has been quiet. I felt I had an answer from God. We will never have such bitterness in our church.

Then, through the years, I have watched our congregation. We have been in the years gone by, a church of Philadelphia—the Philadelphian church of the open door. And I have watched it and watched it, and prayerfully watched it through the years and the years. I have seen Japanese come down these aisles, loved and welcomed by our people. I have seen the Chinese come down these aisles, loved and welcomed by the people. I have seen the Indian, the American Indian, the Indian from India walk down these aisles, loved and welcomed by the people. I have seen Mexican families and children and young people walk down these aisles, loved and welcomed by the people. And as I watch you, and the fabric of our church, I began to see colored people walk down these aisles, loved and welcomed by the church.

What do you mean "colored people"? I mean dark people with Negro blood in them. A pressman talking to me, I asked him, "Is Adam Clayton Powell a Negro?" "Yes," he said. I said, "What part Negro? He looks like a white man to me?" Coming down these aisles, I have seen them—Mexican and Negro-colored people. Finally, I saw a Central American come down these aisles. He was black—loved and received by the people. And finally, I saw a Nigerian come down these aisles—loved and received by the people. Through these years, as they have continued, I have seen our church with an open heart and a compassionate spirit, welcoming into the kingdom and into the body of Christ these whose pigmentation might be different from yours and mine.

Then, a few days ago, I received a letter from a man whom I loved and admired so much—a leader of great dedication in our Convention, in our state, and a loved fellow elder in this church. And out of the deepest love of his heart, he wrote me the sweetest letter. And in that letter, he said, "Pastor, I awakened in the night in South Carolina with a burden on my heart, I cannot escape. It is about you. And it is about our church. And as this presidency of the Convention is being pressed upon you, I have a burden, I am afraid designedly there will be those who will try to destroy you and destroy the church."

I, at that time, this was just a few days ago, had fully made up my mind, I would not accept such a proffer. I happened to mention it inadvertently without plan or forethought, I happened to mention that letter and my decision that I would not be pressed into such an assignment as the leadership of our Southern Baptist Churches. I happened to mention it to the finance committee that is getting ready to launch our church in a multimillion dollar building and expansion program. I happened to mention it. And I said, among other things, "On account of race, I will not respond to that appeal."

And those men, you can look at their names, they have been printed, you'll see them. Those men answered as though they had been thinking about this a hundred years. They said, "Pastor, the time has come for us to face this now and forever." Well, I said, "I don't want to do it now. It would be as though the pressure from others concerning the presidency of this convention had precipitated such a discussion in our church." They said, "Pastor, the presidency of the Convention does not enter into this one way or another. Some time, somewhere, this has to be faced and now is the time to do it. We're going to do it now." So Mr. Cantrell, who was there, called a meeting of the deacons Tuesday of a week ago. And after the business of the session was done, they said, "Now, Pastor, stand up here and bare your heart." So I stood there and for an hour, I bared my soul.

What is this thing that obtains in our people and among our churches? This is what obtains. I turned my face toward the Buckner Home, and the Buckner Home has in it all kinds of children—yellow, black, white, and red. And when the time came that they discussed the bringing of those children to the First Baptist Church in Dallas, as many of them are here this morning, one of the leaders came to me and said, "But Pastor, some of our children are colored, maybe we ought not to come." I replied, "It would be unthinkable that our First Baptist Church in Dallas would refuse the Buckner Home and their ministries, because you have in your love and compassionate concern, a colored child. Welcome. Come." And the Buckner children have been brought these years to our dear church.

Then I turned to look at Dallas Baptist College. I went out to speak at their chapel service, and all through Dallas Baptist College, are colored young men and young women—our Dallas Baptist College. Then I turned to look at our Baylor School of Nursing, and in the Baylor School of Nursing are colored young women. And I walked up and down the halls of Baylor University Hospital and there, you will see all races and all colors—our hospital seeking to minister to them all. And when we began our retarded children's ministry, one of the sweetest in the earth, they brought down here retarded children from one of the homes in the city of Dallas. And a part of them were colored. They came to me and said, "Shall we close the door?" I said, "Close the door to these retarded children because some of them are colored? No! No!" And they've been coming.

As I looked through the length and breadth of our institutions, everywhere, everywhere there is that open door. And there are those hands outstretched and arms of welcome. I have said a thousand times with regard to tax money for church institutions, I have said this sentence: "You cannot separate a church from its institutions." And to give tax support to an institution owned and operated by a church is to give tax support to the church itself. And I have found myself in this congregation with our Buckner Home and our Baptist College and our nursing school and our hospital with an announced policy of one way and no announcement from our church of any way.

Finally, as I spoke to my brethren and compeers in the church, our deacons, I said, "And I bare my personal soul to you. I cannot describe and I have come to feel the weight of it and the burden of it. I cannot describe to you how I feel when I preach the gospel of the Son of God and call men to faith and to repentance, and then stand there afraid that somebody might respond who has a different pigment from mine. It is though I were living a denial of the faith, to preach and be afraid that somebody might respond." What if there came down the aisle a Buckner child who was colored? How would I explain to that child? In a ten thousand years, I couldn't explain to that child. I couldn't do it. But that's not so much the point, how can I explain to God? You tell me how. You give me the words. What do I return to say to God? "This child, Lord, out here at the Buckner Home found Jesus today." What would I say?

I think of Patrick Henry who assumed the defense of the three Baptist preachers who were placed in jail for preaching the Gospel of the Son of God. And in the court, the great, eloquent Patrick Henry held the indictment and waved it above his head and asked, "What does this indictment say? These men are accused of preaching the Gospel of the Son of God. Great God! Great God!" And this indictment, this is the pastor who preaches the Gospel of the Son of God and somebody responded, and he refused. Great God! Great God!

When the hour was done, our deacons had intended, I think, to discuss it, and to speak it. But when I sat down, one of the deacons stood up immediately and said, "Every man here stand to his feet." And the deacons stood up just like that—all of them. And, Chairman Cantrell called them to the front—a hundred and eighty or more of them to fall on their faces and ask our deacon missionary to Nigeria, Dr. Wayne Logan to lead in the prayer. And this was without fanfare. It was without dramatics. It was just the simple announcement that as you walk up and down the streets, as you visit the Buckner Home, as you look at those retarded children, this is just the plain, simple, unadorned announcement that the First Baptist Church in Dallas is like the Philadelphian church of the Book of the Revelation. It is a church of the open door. And when the pastor preaches, as he quotes Isaiah 55:1: "Ho, everyone that thirsteth, come ye to the water. Yea, come buy and eat without money and without price"—everyone in it. As Jesus said, in Matthew 11:28: "Come unto me all ye that labor and are heavy-laden and I will give you rest"—anyone, everyone. As Simon Peter wrote in 2 Peter 3:9: "God wills that all should come to repentance and that none should perish." As the Book closes, in Revelation 22:17: "And the Spirit and the bride say: Come. And let him that heareth say: Come. And let him that is athirst come. And whosoever will, anybody, you, let him take the water of life freely." Come. Come. Come. God bless us and God attend in the way as you come.

Now, we're past our time. We must sing our song of appeal. And while we sing it, a family you, a couple you, one somebody you, as the Spirit of Jesus shall press the appeal to your heart, make it now. Come now. Do it now. And bless you as you come in Jesus' name, welcome. While we stand and while we sing.[12]

Lessons

Did you catch it? Two days before, Robert F. Kennedy had been gunned down. Two months before that, Martin Luther King Jr. had been assassinated. Dr. Criswell was preaching into a heated conflict. God was changing our nation, and God was changing the hearts of Christians everywhere. At the intersection of time, God brings a collision between His Word and the situation. Into that conflict, a man stood up, and admitted he was wrong. He admitted the prejudice he had, hoping that one of a different pigment would not come forward to pray with him for salvation. One could not describe the depth of this prejudice adequately, but then God interrupted. Between the planning and the sermon preparation, a time comes when God interrupts and calls on the preacher to draw a sermon from Scripture to address a need in a life or a church. Criswell admitted in the sermon that this message was different. He would not be doing an exposition of

---

12. W. A. Criswell, "The Church of the Open Door (Revelation 3:7-8)," preached 9 June 1968, Criswell Sermon Library [on-line]; accessed 8 August 2008; available from http://www.wacriswell.com/ index.cfm/FuseAction/Search.Transcripts/ sermon/1589.cfm; Internet.

the text, but rather delivering a message God gave him from a passage that speaks of a church with the right attitude.

The results of this sermon were immediate and long-term. Dr. Bryant said that, from the day of this sermon forward, First Baptist Church Dallas would be a church for all. They held to the tenet that "You can't kneel down beside a man and put your arm around him and lead him to Christ if you are prejudiced." Billionaire H. L. Hunt, in opposition to this new stand, left the church, and did not return. With him, thirty more members left. People will always be present in a church who, when confronted with their sin, will not change. Those who refuse to change will leave, or they will stay and cause torment to the church and the pastor. What strife they bring matters not, what matters is being true to God, His love, and His Word.

In strife, a preacher must be courageous and humble. If he is courageous without being humble, then he becomes a bully. If he is humble but not courageous, he is a wimp.[13] The balance pleases the Lord and impacts the people. A pastor must be humble enough to realize his sins, and courageous enough to admit them before his people. He must always realize that the people in his congregation and area of ministry hold him to a higher standard. That is all right, because God also holds him to a higher standard.

A pastor needs a healthy approach to criticism. With each critic, the pastor must consider the source, but even if that source is not extremely credible, he must still search the comment for truth.[14] If more than one person brings the same criticism, the pastor should consider their relationship. If they are coming from two different walks-of-life, he should consider the comment for truth. If more than two, the pastor needs to sit down and really grapple with the comments. In conflict, he must ask himself, "Am I the reason for this conflict?" "Am I right on this issue?" Or, he should ask, "Am I negligent in some duty?"[15]

Scripture is replete with the value of criticism, rebuke, and instruction. The writer of Proverbs 9:8-9, "Do not reprove a scoffer, or he will hate you, reprove a wise man and he will love you. Give instruction to a wise man and he will be still wiser, teach a righteous man and he will increase his learning". God uses criticism to show the Christian where he needs to grow.[16] General Dwight D. Eisenhower once said that he would not make a tactical decision

---

13. Rogers, *Love Worth Finding*, 175.
14. Tucker, *Primer for Pastors*, 101.
15. Bell, "Preaching and Conflict," 531.
16. Ken Sande, "What Are Three Ways Leaders Can Deal with Difficult Congregants?," BuildingChurchLeaders.com (2008) [on-line]; accessed 18 August 2008; available from http://www. buildingchurchleaders.com/help/asktheexperts/kensande/q1.html; Internet.

CHAPTER 5: PASTORAL ERROR

until he found someone who would oppose it. By defending his stand, he could see and think through the weaknesses in his decision.[17]

A preacher does not have to be the complete repository of truth. He can admit to his congregation that he has been wrong, that he has made mistakes.[18] Often when a pastor is queried whether he has made mistakes, he volunteers information from way back in his ministry and, of course, at a different church. That way is always safer. If a preacher does not stay current with his flock, they will know it. Since they know it, the preaching moment is so much more effective when the people perceive their pastor is up-to-date in his confessions, speaking God's Word with a clear conscience. In this way, the preacher is a model of Christ for his people to follow.[19] This is the exemplification of what Jesus said when He called on Christians to die to themselves, to take up their crosses, and to follow Him.

Relationships with church members are essential for the vitality of a preaching ministry. In relationship, the people will be more prone to extend mercy to the pastor. The pastor will find it easier to admit his mistakes. To have this relationship, though the pastor is to spend time in prayer and Bible study, he also must step out into the lives of his people. He must visit them at work, stop by their homes, and demonstrate that he is present when they are struggling.[20] He will come across as less aloof, and God's Word will quicken the listener in the sermon moment. The most effective preachers are the ones who have striven, barring compromise, to have great relationships with their members.[21]

Prayer life and personal time alone with God's Word enable the pastor to deal rightly with whatever he is facing. This time works to calm fears, cool tempers, and soothe hurts. Further, this time is when the pastor is most apt to be convicted of sins in his own life. Would it not be better for God to winnow out one's faults, rather than have church members point them out, before they lead to a cataclysmic explosion?

God is faithful. David came to the Lord and asked Him to search his heart and see if any wicked ways were present in him. Thus, the preacher must do the same. Though Criswell elaborated on a weakness of Truett, he was used mightily by God. They said the secret to George W. Truett's effectiveness in ministry was that he lived close to God, and because his oneness with the God of the universe allowed him to win many souls for

---

17. Powell, *Basic Bible Sermons*, 55.
18. Shelley and Miller, "Fundamentally One," 20.
19. Ibid.
20. Jeremiah, "Preaching Through Pain," 20.
21. Willimon, *Preaching About Conflict*, 35.

Christ.[22] This was evident in Criswell, and, likewise, it can be evident in you. Romans 6:13 implores the Christian to be an instrument of righteousness, not an instrument of wickedness.

---

22. Burton, *Prince of the Pulpit*, 57.

Chapter 6: **Staff Immorality**

I was just out of college. I moved to Houston, Texas and began working as an accountant for Shell Pipe Line Corporation. I was in between the time of my call and my surrender to the pastorate. My first order of business was to find a church home. One of my co-workers invited me to his church, but it was not the type of service to which I was accustomed. Another friend and co-worker then invited me to his church. His church had just called a new pastor, and this friend was excited about having him at their church. My first Sunday to attend was the new pastor's first Sunday. I fell in love with him and the church immediately. Hearing this preacher preach thrilled my soul. Anytime he was absent from the pulpit, I was disappointed. It was not that God could not speak through another man, it was just that I enjoyed hearing God speak through our regular pastor. The church grew, added a vibrant associate pastor, and then a dynamic youth minister. The church was really making an impact. The day I changed jobs and had to move to Beaumont was a sad day. I could not stand leaving this beloved church and pastor behind.

A couple of years passed, and I was in Houston for a meeting and decided to meet with some of my old friends from this precious church. We had a great meal, but then I felt sick to my stomach. The food had nothing to do with this feeling. My friends shared with me the tragedy that had hit the church in the last few months. The associate pastor had been caught having an affair with one of the ladies from the choir. He resigned, and a week or two later, the senior pastor, my favorite preacher, was caught having an affair with another lady in the church. Both were out of the ministry. One left his family, while the other was seeking reconciliation. The church was left in the aftermath, crumbling at the seams. I could not believe it. Never in my life had I heard of such things occurring in the ministry.

In this culture, that sounds naïve. Since then, I have become much more aware of this epidemic. A church in Beaumont lost their pastor due to his obsession with internet pornography. A local church in Houston struggled with three consecutive senior pastors who fell to sexual immorality. Even as I type this page, I can name three churches that I know that currently are facing similar situations. Is it any wonder an old adage used in my hometown said, "The two professions which get the most women are preachers and butane salesmen." The most respected Christians can fall. Jim Bakker and Jimmy Swaggert were two preachers of notoriety who fell.

Eugene Robinson of the Atlanta Falcons was another. Noted for his righteous lifestyle and Godly example, he played safety for the Atlanta Falcons in the 1999 Super Bowl XXXIII against the Denver Broncos. The morning before the Super Bowl, he was given the Bart Starr Award by the Christian group "Athletes in Action". After considering all other NFL players that year, this award was given to Robinson for being a person who displays "high moral character." Later that evening, he was arrested for soliciting a prostitute. Robinson was devastated by his own actions, as was his family. He quoted a true statement afterward, "Confession is good for the soul, but bad for the reputation."[1] What this Godly man discovered was how quickly any of us can fall.

In an interview with former Southern Baptist Convention president Johnny Hunt, I asked him some questions concerning his church ministry to pastors who have struggled in previous pastorates. One question concerned the reasons cited for pastors losing their churches. The second and third reasons he gave were moral failure and moral indiscretions.[2] John Bisagno was asked what challenges does he see being most problematic for the preachers of today. His third concern had to deal with staff morality issues.[3] Statistics support this. *Leadership Magazine* found in one poll that 38 percent of pastors say they struggle with the temptation of internet pornography. Of the average 19,200 pastors who are required to leave the ministry each year, up to 12 percent confessed to inappropriate physical involvement outside of marriage. The Titus Task Force found in their ministry that the third most prevalent cause of church crisis is the issue of immorality.[4] Jerrien Gunnink's survey of 480 pastors found that 36 percent of major church trauma comes from immoral behavior of a pastor or church member.[5]

---

1. "Sorrowful Time: Falcons' Robinson Gives Postgame Apology," *Sports Illustrated* (February 1, 1999) [on-line]; accessed 28 July 2008; available from http://sportsillustrated.cnn.com/football/nfl/1998/ playoffs/news/ 1999/01/30/robinsonarrested/ index.html; Internet.

2. Johnny Hunt, president, Southern Baptist Convention, interview via e-mail to writer, June 27, 2008.

3. John R. Bisagno, retired pastor of First Baptist Church, Houston, TX, lecture in Pastoral Leadership class, Southwestern Baptist Theological Seminary, Houston, TX, Fall 2005.

4. Fraser, interview.

5. Gunnink, interview.

CHAPTER 6: STAFF IMMORALITY

As referenced in the first chapter of this book, Bisagno was challenged to see how many of his preaching friends would stay in the ministry throughout their lives. Of the twenty-five that Bisagno wrote down, twenty of them left the ministry. Some left for the love of money, some because they grew liberal in their theology, and some left because they were disillusioned with never reaching the success they envisioned. The majority, however, left because of sexual impurity.[6] When one discusses immorality within the staff or in the pastor, sexual dalliances are not the only source. Pastors make immoral choices in the realm of theft, unpaid bills, income tax evasions, hot-checks, homosexual behavior, improper remarks, lies, theft, and broken contracts.[7] While all these are serious offenses, this chapter looks specifically at sexual sin, which tends to be the most prominent. Whether the sin is of a sexual nature or some other moral failure, the healing comes through a common path—God's Word and preaching.

How does this struggle come upon a man of God? The answer can be found in a guy named David, who with idle time looked out at a woman bathing at a neighboring home. The choice to sin can begin so innocently. Many pastors, in an effort to minister to all members in their congregations, may find themselves counseling a female alone in their offices. In her emotional state, she sees the pastor as a "white knight." In his position of helping her, he is flattered to be found attractive. One does not have to fill in the blanks. Seeking to be safe, a pastor may choose a public meeting such as over a meal, so some built-in accountability safeguards are in place. Unfortunately, a meal with a person of the opposite sex is considered by some as one of the most intimate of all meetings.

In the land where "Sex in the City," "Desperate Housewives," "Modern Family," and different forms of music glorify sexual freedom, even Godly men and women can be influenced and find themselves vulnerable. They see billboards, commercials, and radio advertisements that excite. They see entreating advertisements in the newspapers. Virtually every movie has suggestive content and gratuitous sexual material. One goes into a store to buy a soda, and they see the adult magazine covers and stand-up cut-outs of scantily clad females. Promotion of sexual help-aids like Viagra and Cialis are ever-present. Additionally, such marketing also targets women. They cannot help but spot a young man in a provocative pose as they scan their favorite ladies' magazine.

Paul's viewpoint, and God's, is that the corporate narrative for the Christian community should be one that is pure and blameless, ethically

---

6. Bisagno, *Inside Information*, 87.
7. Gunnink, *Preaching for Recovery*, 26.

transformed, filled with love, and able to know what is best.[8] Billy Graham and Chuck Colson have both spoken openly and written widely on the extreme efforts they took to avoid sexual indiscretion and even perceived sexual indiscretion. Job's advice is more applicable today than ever before as stated in Job 31:1, "I have made a covenant with my eyes; How then could I gaze at a virgin?" No victimless or harmless exposure exists. Thankfully, God's Word is available to help. Proverbs 6:23-28 says, "For the commandment is a lamp and the teaching is light; and reproofs for discipline are the way of life to keep you from the evil woman, from the smooth tongue of the adulteress. Do not desire her beauty in your heart, nor let her capture you with her eyelids. For on account of a harlot one is reduced to a loaf of bread, and an adulteress hunts for the precious life. Can a man take fire in his bosom and his clothes not be burned? Or can a man walk on hot coals and his feet not be scorched?"

As opposed to the rest of the situations of crisis, this is one through which a preacher who is guilty of such sin will have difficulty preaching. Confession from the pulpit would be very helpful, but at that moment, sermonizing may find a deaf ear, and rightly so. A need exists for repentance and evaluation, along with counseling. A need exists for making things right with others, for working on one's family and one's own weaknesses. The Methodist church does an incredible job helping such pastors in these matters. I believe a pastor who falls has the opportunity for restoration, but this is another issue whose complexity goes beyond the scope of this book. The focus here is "Preaching your way out. . . ." The preaching moment that one must consider is when a church is harmed by the sexual sin of a staff member or church member, which becomes public. Such immoral failures rip the church and often cause some to take theological and personal sides. At this point, the issue cannot be ignored. Direct and indirect victims are involved. How can a preacher deal with this from the pulpit?

The first strategy is to do so proactively, before the fact. Brian Newman is lead pastor of Crossroads International Church in Amsterdam, The Netherlands. He preached a seven-week series called "Sex and the City" to a congregation in a city famous for sex. His stand brings recall of the great stand that Paul made to the churches in promiscuous Corinth and Ephesus. In Holland, where Newman preaches, 80 percent of people live together before marriage. Each Sunday, he addresses congregants who favor this lifestyle. In this arena, Newman presented to his whole congregation, without apology, a couple from three thousand years ago who, in a rampant promiscuous society, sought in a radical manner to be pure. His congregation was challenged,

---

8. Thompson, "Preaching to Philippians," 298.

and many responded.⁹ Such a sermon puts on display what God desires for His children. The Scripture never differentiates between the congregation and the paid staff. The scriptural mandate is for both.

Situation

The second way to deal with sexual or immoral issues is reactively. Reactive dealing with the issue is the least favorite, but the most repetitive experience. Bruce Wells has led an exciting church in North Texas. He is a man who believes preaching and prayer must be the majors of every pastor. His fruitful history proves their merit, and his church and staff have agreed wholeheartedly. A great shock occurred when he discovered two sexual scandals in his church. One was between two church members. No sooner did his church get through this, a staff member fell to sexual immorality. The church was crushed. No way was available to avoid the issue. The issue had to be addressed. Thus, Bro. Bruce mounted the pulpit with a heavy heart, knowing his church needed a word from God.

Sermon

Bruce Wells

"State of the Church Address"

GALATIANS 6:1-2

Once a year, we try to take a time to at least remind ourselves of who we are—as a church, as a particular local congregation, or you who are members. For you who are visiting with us, at least you will get some idea of maybe who we are, or from where we come. We will take just a brief minute reviewing what we feel to be God's call upon this particular church, and we will look to the Word of God prayerfully for a word to us as we face a new church year.

Let me begin with our motto, our slogan, our purpose statement. Our motto is found in the simple words of "To the glory of God alone." This tells what we are about. This motto makes a statement that we are seeking to be a God-centered church. Our primary concern is not what people might think, but what God thinks—that it is not about us, that it is about Him. By seeking

---

9. Brian Newman, "License to Thrill," *Leadership* 27, no. 1 (Winter 2006): 48.

to direct ourselves with the thought of the glory of God alone—that means whatever we do, we would desire that it would be pleasing to Him. This thought should direct everything this church does and give it guidance. That is where we start, and that is our primary statement of our purpose. Reformers had a Latin phrase—it was "*Solo deo Gloria*," meaning the very same thing, "For the Glory of God alone." That is why we are here. God be glorified and honored and praised.

Second, we believe the Lord has set this particular congregation to be a lighthouse on the west side of Gregg County, to be a light on the hill that shines for Christ in our worship, in the lives that we live in community. We believe that the Lord will desire this church to be a beacon of hope and of rest and of peace and of life and of salvation through which the hurting and needy and lost might come our way.

Third, we believe that the Lord has called this church particularly to be a house of prayer. We would think every church should be a house of prayer, but we believe that God has placed on this church particularly the calling to be a house of prayer. That is why you will notice on the back of your bulletin that numerous prayer meetings are listed, particularly the one on Saturday night. The one not listed, but that you are invited to, is on Wednesday mornings at nine o'clock in our conference room. The staff of this church and the secretaries gather, and you are invited—any of you—to come and join us in prayer. We believe prayer is vital, and although we have a long way to go in this area, we believe this is God's call for us.

Finally, we believe the Lord has called us to be a mission-minded church—both in the community in which the Lord has placed us and around the world. This mission will involve our praying for a mission, our giving financially to missions, and our going out in mission. For this particular congregation, several places exist in the world in which God particularly has placed us at this time at least. An interesting story is behind every one of them.

We are connected with a little mission in the jungles of Bolivia—a place called Renqal del Tiqua. We have a connection with the Mesi in Tanzania, Africa. Mexico, how could we leave that out, where the last seven years I believe, we sent teams of youth and adults to a particular church in San Guiana Ventura, Mexico. Thailand, where we have faithful missionaries that serve and some of you in this congregation this morning have gone to that Asian country as part of the mission work in which we are involved. There are others, in fact we might say on the front burners of our church. Right now preparation is being made to send a team from our worship ministry to New York State to minister to mission churches and help those people in a place where church life is very difficult. We just believe that the Lord has called us both here, where we are, and also to reach out into a dark world and not be limited. As God has the world in his heart, so we seek to have. Thus, we believe God has called us to be a mission-minded church.

This Baptist Church of Liberty City is not a perfect church. As you well know, we have had failures in the past, and we have weaknesses in the present. Wherever we might have come that is in a positive and good way, we realize it is by the grace of God alone that we are where we are. This is not a church, obviously, that is a fancy church—if I might use that terminology. We are not seeking to be a megachurch or on the cutting edge of anything. We truthfully are very simple—plodding might be a good word for how we go about it, just trying to be people that we feel God has called us to be. I wish more things were of a dramatic order, but that's just—that wouldn't be us, would it? It is a very plain, simple people that God has placed here in the middle of a rural area of East Texas to let our light shine. We must trust and depend upon Him.

This day, many things are on my heart as your pastor. I would like for us to turn now to an emphasis for our church for this coming year, but not just for a year, because we find in the Scripture the will of God expressed in the Word of God to be our goal for all of our existence. Would you open your Bibles with me this morning as we seek to hear the Lord's voice? In Galatians—the Book of Galatians, chapter 6 and the first two verses. I hope that we might, from this Scripture, address a great need. Let me read it for us, "Brethren, if a man is overtaken in any trespass, you who are spiritual restore such a one in a spirit of gentleness considering yourselves, lest you also be tempted. Bear one another's burdens and so fulfill the law of Christ." As we look at these verses, let us begin first with the sad reality, and that sad reality is this—Christians do sin, though they have a new nature, though their lives are changing due to the work of the Holy Spirit, and though they seek to lay aside the vices of their past life and gain Christian virtues. Nonetheless, true, genuine, regenerate Christians in this life are not perfect and, sadly—as everyone here that is a believer can bear testimony—sadly Christians do fall into sin and sometimes into very serious sin.

Our passage says that if a person is overtaken in any trespass, the person who is involved is a Christian person.

That's the topic, that's what we're talking about, Christians that are overtaken in any trespass. The word "trespass" is one of the words in the New Testament that is used to describe sin. Trespass means literally falling aside or a false step. You might tread if you could—someone walking through one of those English marshes or bogs or whatever they call them and there's a trail through there and off of this trail is some type of marshy vegetation growing. Quick sand pools exist hither and yon and you need to stay on the path. The picture here is of a Christian brother who, as he goes through the marsh of life, has gotten off the path. He's in a dangerous area. He's been overtaken by a trespass. He's stepped aside.

Our Scripture says he's been overtaken in a trespass. The idea is that he's been mugged by sin, if you would like that term. He's fallen into a sin. This was not a habitual pattern of his life, but as he went along the Christian way, something happened to him and he fell into sin. It doesn't tell us what caused him to fall into sin. It would make a very interesting story for all of us to consider the many causes that might work in an individual Christian's life, that along the Christian journey, they somehow become misdirected and fall into grievous sin. Seems to me that this falling into sin, in the context of these verses at least, is talking primarily about sins that are serious. Now, degrees of sin exist, some more serious than others, though all sin is serious. All sin comes from the same root of selfishness and rebellion against God, yet some obviously are more serious than others, and this seems to be that which is described in this context—someone has fallen into a very hurtful and grievous type of sin. Although our text says that if a brother is overtaken in any trespass—that's a very large scope here—but I think primarily we're talking about those serious sins, but certainly all sin is hurtful and destructive and bears disastrous consequences.

When I was a boy—and I don't want to date myself into absolute oblivion—but when I was a boy, I would listen to radio programs—every week serials were played—have you ever heard of anything like that, some of you younger people? You would sit by the radio, and it would come on at a certain time, and I listened to several programs. We didn't have a television. Thus, I'd listen to these radio programs. One of the programs was a crime-fighting super hero-type of thing called *The Shadow*, and it was always introduced by this kind of creepy voice that my dad always liked to try to imitate. The voice went like this; it says, "The weed of crime bears bitter fruit, *The Shadow* knows." Now, this guy—he could become invisible, and only his shadow would appear, but anyway, I'm here to tell you today that the root of sin bears bitter fruit.

The weed of sin bears a bitter fruit. Sin has its pleasures for a season, and it does not matter who you are, when you fall into sin, a bitter fruit is present. It's hurtful to you. It is hurtful to others. It can be hurtful to your church. Do you not remember the story of Achan from the Book of Joshua? It tells how the sin of one single individual, unknown to the rest, caused defeat of the whole army of Israel. Yes, your sin or the sin of a few, can affect the many when we're in a congregation, a body of Christ like this. Of course, it can harm the name of Christ, which a Christian bears.

Our church here at First Baptist, Liberty City, has had our share of Christians falling into sin. In fact, in the last three or four years, we have had some of our church leaders fall into very serious sin. I'm thankful for our elders—they were so helpful in trying to deal with these circumstances in a Biblical and Godly way. There are things as I look back—I wish in some areas that I would have done things differently. One thing I wish we would have done—because obviously these things are very hurtful to a church—I have shed many a tear as you have.

This has been years ago, but I still think of dear Brother Woodard and how he fell, even with his great gift of teaching and theological knowledge. He knew more than I did, but I wish—one thing I wish to have done that we didn't do, would have been to have given this congregation an opportunity to weep and mourn together in a corporate way and to confess our own sins, because we are a body. I think this would have helped us to move through all that more easily. I am thankful for Dave Tyler, that when he fell, he submitted himself to church leadership and resisted the great urge to abandon this congregation. Now many years since, he has stayed faithful and has given us a chance to try to do what the church should do in these circumstances. In light of some of these things and others (obviously, this weighs heavy upon my heart in these areas), we now turn to look at the Christian responsibility to those who have fallen in sin.

What is the Christian's responsibility in these situations? They happen here; no use trying to hide that. They happen here, and I suppose moral failure happens everywhere. So, what is the Christian's responsibility to that brother who falls in sin? The Christian's responsibility is marked by the word "restore"—the word means literally, put in order; to restore to a former condition. In ancient times in the Greek language, the term was used in medical terms for setting a broken bone—putting it back into place, restoring it. I cannot help but think of a time in Tanzania—when the Masai young man (they were all men playing around as men still do) got his shoulder out-of-joint, and it just hung in a terrible position. Masai warriors, which he was, are taught not to complain, but he was in a lot of pain.

Where we were, you just did not stop and go to the hospital. No hospitals were anywhere around, and here was this poor guy, and we just stood there. His arm was all out-of-joint. Anyway, the missionary, Kim Tidenberg, as many of you know, pulled out this book entitled something along the lines, "Medicine in the Bush," and looked up the injury. He had this guy lay down on the ground—it was a terrible situation. He put his foot underneath his arm, right under here, and grabbed his arm and pulled—I don't know what else he did—and the thing popped right back into place. He stood up, and it was back where it belonged. I'm sure it was still painful, but it wasn't painful like it was, and in a few days, he was practically well. Something was out-of-place, and it needed to be restored. Even in this church, the cause of moral sin might be inflicting pain, and a need exists for it to be restored.

Another way that the word was used in ancient times was to mend nets—that's used in the New Testament—that's the very same word used in Matthew 4:21 when Jesus passed by. These disciples were sitting on the seashore mending their nets. These were the large fishing nets that they used. In the midst of fishing, there's inevitably going to be times when the nets are torn and you pick up debris, so before the next fishing, you need to clean things up and patch the holes, and that's what they were doing. They were taking those nets that were torn and damaged and restoring them to usefulness. They didn't patch those nets to be put on the shelf. No, they patched them, because they were going to need them the next night. That tells us something of the purpose of restoration of this Christian who has fallen into sin. They're not to be put upon the shelf just because they failed and because they've sinned. The purpose of the church is to take a fallen sinner and restore him or her, to redeem him or her into a relationship with God and to the fellowship, and eventually so that he or she might go back into Christian service. Occasions occur when they can't always do the things they've done before because of the nature of their sin. God's purpose is that they be *restored*, and they come back into effective service for the Lord. The sin had rendered them ineffective. The church's role is to bring them back into effective service. That's the purpose; that's the goal.

Now, who is to do this ministry of *restoring* the Christian that has fallen into sin? Well, according to this text of Scripture, it is individual Christians. The task is not given to the pastor only. The task is not given to the elders, except for the part that they themselves are individual members of the congregation. It goes to individual Christians like you who are to be involved in this ministry of restoration. Now, you notice it says, you who are spiritual *restore* such a one. Now, all Christians—all true Christians have the Holy Spirit of God working in their heart and lives. We use the term indwelt by the Holy Spirit, but we mean God's Holy Spirit is at work actively in a life. That is true of every Christian.

Sadly, all Christians are not completely yielded to the Holy Spirit's work. The context of our passage that is before us, verse 25 says, "If we live in the Spirit, let us also walk in the Spirit." Living in the spirit, having the Holy Spirit at work in our lives, that's our position. Now the imperative comes—better translated, I think—since we live in the Spirit, here's what we need to do—walk in the Spirit. In other words, be led and be empowered and be controlled by God's Holy Spirit to such a degree that the fruits of the Spirit, as listed in the passage above it, become more and more evident in our lives. Different degrees of spiritual maturity exist, but any Christian can be empowered by God's Spirit and moved by his Spirit and led by the Spirit and come under the Holy Spirit's mighty sway in their lives. Because not all walk in the Spirit, Paul designates that those who are spiritual minister to those who fall, because not all Christians are walking spiritually in the Spirit.

I hope you do not jump upon this as an excuse for you not to be involved in the ministry of restoration saying, "Well, I can't do that. I can't go to someone who has fallen into sin and say anything to them. I'm not spiritual." Well, that in itself is a great concern. Not being spiritual is an abnormal condition. God expects all His people to be spiritual people, walking in the spirit, and if you're not spiritual, then something is dreadfully wrong, and you have a lot to be concerned about.

I would urge you, if you honestly look at yourself as not being a spiritual person, I would urge you to fall upon your face and begin to ask the Lord to be your helper and give you a full measure of the Spirit's power in your life and to help you. I would do things like getting into the Word of God and reading it regularly and to take up a prayer life and to get among the people of God so that God graciously might work in your heart that you might be a spiritual person like you should. It is not a very good cop-out to say, "Well, I can't do that. I'm not spiritual." This is a terrible thing to say really. In the ideal situation, all of you would be spiritual; all of you would fear this command for yourself. Thus, it is not prideful to say, "I'm one of those spiritual ones." That is what you should be, that is just the normal condition of a Christian.

Now, we are not told how to go about this work of restoring the fellow brethren who have fallen into sin. We might get some ideas from Matthew, chapter 18, verse 15, where the Lord Jesus says, "If your brother sins against you. . . ." This passage before us is a bit larger than the one Jesus was addressing in Matthew 18. This passage is broader. If you find one that has fallen, been overtaken by a trespass, you restore them, period. This Matthew 18 passage pertains to someone offending you personally, but we get from it some idea of what to do. Jesus says that you go to them privately, face-to-face, and you share with them the difficulty and if they repent, you have gained a brother. What Paul would say is that you have restored a brother. We gather that it should be done in the same way when you see a brother, a fellow Christian, fall into some sin; you are to go to them privately and share with them and seek to restore them. Do not report it to the pastor. You go.

Now, we do have before us the manner in which this restoration is to be done. The restoration is to be done—and you just follow your Scripture—in the spirit of gentleness. This is the very same word that we find in chapter 5, verse 23, one of the fruits of the Spirit, "gentleness." This is what the Holy Spirit of God is doing in the life of a Christian—he is making you gentle. And this work of *restoration* is a delicate work and needs a *gentle spirit*. This does not mean the Christian cannot be forthright in his speaking, that he cannot be tough when it needs to be done, but the attitude needs to be a gentle attitude.

Often a rebuke is a poor tool when a man is down. Thus, we come with a gentle spirit. Let me read what Martin Luther, commenting on this verse, said. He said, "Run into him and reaching out your hands, raise him up again. Comfort him with sweet words and embrace him with motherly arms." We generally do not find much of that, do we? That is the point. What is needed on their part is true repentance of their sins. We are not to condone their sin or failure in any way, but we are to approach them with a gentle and a loving heart to try to help them.

The second attitude we need in dealing with these people is *humility*. Notice our verse, "Considering yourselves lest you also be tempted." That means we come in the awareness of our own weakness and liability to sin and fragility. We come with the attitude to say, but for the grace of God that would be me. And if all the truth were known, I'd probably be a lot worse than they are. Do you really think about that when you address those that have fallen into sin? It is pretty easy to be judgmental and look down and condemning to someone who has sinned, because we have a tendency to think that we would never do such a thing as that. The needful attitude is to realize our own potential for falling into grievous sin and, but for the grace of God, every one of us in here would have fallen.

Let me remind you of the words of a Godly man, Murray McShane, from Scotland who lived a couple of centuries ago. I think about it a lot. He made the statement, "I have discovered that the seed of every sin known to man dwells in my heart." This statement kind of makes you think. In this ministry of *restoring the fallen believers*, plenty of Christians, in some way or another, fall into a sin, and they have the great need for Christians to seek to *restore* them and get them off of the dangerous way and back on the right path. They need someone to help them into repentance and back to service for the Lord. Someone must go to them in *humility* and *gentleness* and *truthfulness* and *forthrightness* and *share* with them. I would think this morning that much sorrow and pain could have been avoided in many a life, if Christians had the courage and the strength to do as the Lord commands us in these verses and go to brothers and sisters and try to help them before it is too late. On some occasions, people will not listen. We know that. That is dealt with in other ways. This is a first start for any time we see a brother or sister in sin. What a vital work it is, how we need it here.

Finally, let us consider just a moment the continuing ministry, and in light of all that, heed what verse 2 says, "Bear one another's burdens." I call it *continued ministry*, because the word *bear* is in the present imperative. Continually bear. This is a continual ministry of bearing one another's burdens. Some burdens in life the Lord does not expect you to bear alone. Burdens come, but how do you handle them? The first thing is that you cast your burdens upon the Lord, and He will sustain you. That is the first thing you do. But God's way and God's method in answering your prayers is to have other Christian people bear them with you.

Then there is this reciprocal ministry of *bearing* one another's burdens. Now, you will notice in verse 5 of this passage, "Each one is to bear his own burden" or "bear his own load" as the New King James says. Well, responsibility exists that no one can take. It is yours alone for your own actions. But there is another sense with which others can help you bear your burdens. A certain translation or a paraphrase is called, "The Good News for Modern Man." It has all these stick figures that picture the stories in the Bible. The one about this particular verse always sticks in my mind. It shows this line of people, and every one of them has a tremendous sack upon their back that is their burden, their load. They are carrying their own load, and behind each one was a brother—now, he's got a load himself, but he's got one hand holding his own load, but the other hand is reaching out holding, helping the other one in front of him to bear his load. So, he's bearing somebody's load, and there's somebody behind helping him bear his own load. And that's what we're called to do as Christian brothers and sisters in the fallen world of woe where burdens are on every hand; we are called to bear one another's burdens—to help them with the woe, to care for them and encourage them and pray for them and pray with them in whatever way we can to help them bear the burden of life that has come their way.

Bear one of those burdens, and so fulfill the law of Christ. We are not told what the law of Christ is exactly. I do not think we have to go far. Chapter 5, verse 14 of Galatians says, "For the law is fulfilled in one word, even this you shall love your neighbor as yourself." We recall the words of Jesus from the fifteenth chapter of John, "This is my commandment that you love one another as I have loved you." I think we are going to be on pretty safe ground when we say the law of Christ is that law of love, which we are called to love one another. You see, you fulfill the law of love when you bear burdens, because if you really love somebody and really care for them and you see them burdened down, you will help them. You see them fall into sin; if you really love them and care for them, then you will go to them and try to restore them. That is part of the burden I think that is included here in verse 2.

Our problem, obviously, is that we do not really care for one another as we should. We do not really love one another and, therefore, we are not involved in bearing burdens. We are not involved in trying to restore the brethren that have fallen into sin. Here is where we really need to start, that God would grant us a heart for His people. How can we love a lost world if we do not love our fellow Christians? I am very concerned about loving the lost world, but how is it going to be done if we do not love one another? So, here's where we start. As we learn to love each other, and the world sees us loving each other, then we are able to reach out and love them with the love of Christ too.

This thing of burden-bearing—by nature calls you to be near somebody. How can you bear their burdens if you are not close enough even to see what the burdens are? It involves you coming side-by-side with them. We are going to have to lay off some of our ideas of isolation Christianity and just get in here beside people—not only for our own good, but for the good of others. It is imperative here for us to bear one another's burdens in the situation that God has placed us. Some hurting people are going to come your way. Love them, care for them, and bear their burdens.

As your pastor (and of course the Lord gives pastor's hearts to pastors, you hope), I would love to just reach out, in Christ, to every single one of you and help you bear your burdens. Obviously, I cannot do that. One, I have some burdens of my own that limit me. Number two, there are just too many. There are just too many. I just can't. One person can't do it. So, I'm calling, I'm pleading with you today that you will hear the Word of the Lord for the good of His church, that you will take it to your heart, and say, "I will be one of those who will bear others' burdens. When God brings it to my attention, a brother or sister who is straying from the way, I will, out of great love and care for their soul, go to them and speak to them. I will put off this idea, that I don't want to butt into somebody's business, or I don't want to be involved, or I don't have time." Just lay aside those things. Do what the Lord has called His church to do. I'm pleading with you. Help me with my burden for this church. I am calling you today, you hear the Word of the Lord, put yourself in a place where you can do what God has commanded you to do.

We have got a lot—God gives us days and time, we have got a lot to do before our Lord comes again. Today's the day to start. I call you, in the name of the Lord, to hear His call to you. Your circumstance is going to be different from maybe all of us. May God speak to your heart and in your life this morning. We are going to take a few moments and call upon the Lord's name as is our custom. This altar's going to be open. I invite you to come and bow down here and pray and renew and commit yourself and repent of your sins or whatever you might need to do. I will be at the front to pray, minister, and help you in any way that I can. As we stand together, let us call upon the Lord in these few moments and look unto Him.[10]

---

10. Bruce Wells, senior pastor, Liberty City, Texas, "State of the Church Address

Lessons

With the backdrop of a church leader's sin, Bro. Bruce Wells laid out his church's mission and purpose statement for all to remember. It spelled out the Biblical goal agreed upon by this church. The goal called for all members to strive to adhere to God's standard. His church chooses to live for the glory of God. By God's standard, man is measured, not by the cultural morality of the day. All sin and actions are seen in light of God's Word with the awareness of their impact on the people around them.

He, as all pastors should be, was firm in admitting that everyone in the church commits sin and struggles with sin. Newman commented to his church that just about everyone has a sordid story. Most, if honest, would admit that they have messed up at some point in their lives.[11] He says that, though all sin is equally wrong, degrees of sin are based on its impact on the sinner, others, and the name of Christ. This statement automatically caused his members to lower their defenses. Using Galatians 6 as his text, he pointed out the fact that every Christian has the capacity to be tempted and to fall, that not one person is exempt from the temptation of any particular sin.

This brings Wells to the crux of the message for his people facing the crisis of staff immorality. The church is to work to restore the fallen Christian. He makes it clear in his illustration of mending nets, that repairing nets is not so they can be put away, but so that they can be used again. Thus it is for every preacher to encourage his church to work to this end. When given the Scriptural support, no Bible-believing church should let a morality lapse prohibit unity and continued growth and vitality. The church deals with it, loves the one who has fallen, restores them, and continues forward in their ministry. In dealing with moral crisis, the church and the pastor should begin with love of one another as Christ loves without condition. True love corrects, and true love restores also. Wells' church responded, and healing and growth continues.

He made a very important statement. In essence, he said that for a church to be salt and light for the community, they must first love one another. This love for one another enables them to love those outside the church. Further, this love will be the greatest billboard for the dying world around them.

My former senior pastor, who I described in the introduction to this chapter, left the ministry and began doing capital campaigns for churches. After a few years of being a pastor myself, I decided to hold an "Old-Time Revival." I called some of my favorite old preachers to preach on a certain

---

(Gal 6:1-2)," September 9, 2007.

11. Newman, "License to Thrill," 50.

night. I had never quit praying and loving my former Houston pastor who had fallen to adultery. I searched for him, and finally found him living back in Houston. After a great phone conversation, and then a lunch together, I was overjoyed to see him repentant and humble. God had restored his marriage, and he was serving the Lord as a layman in a new church, teaching children in Vacation Bible School. When I asked him to preach one night in our revival, he was very appreciative. The invitations had been few and far between. That night when he preached, he made an impact that could only be made by a fallen man restored by God's grace. Our church had no idea of his past. I wanted them to hear God's Word through him without prejudice. His preaching at our church was as fervent as I remembered, and then he surprised me with his closing illustration. He told a riveting story of a pastor who had fallen to infidelity and all the damage it had done to his ministry and his family. He closed the sermon by saying "that preacher was me." You could have heard a pin drop. God's Spirit moved among that little congregation through the vessel of a broken man restored.

Chapter 7: Doctrinal Crisis— The Charismatic Movement

The old church in the small town once thrived. Many Biblically faithful pastors had led the church. Then the new pastor arrived. He was from a conservative, Bible-based seminary. He said all the right things with regard to doctrine. He was kind and winsome. The vote was highly favorable to call him to be the next pastor of this historic church. The first few years went well, and then he began to contradict denominational doctrine. The members were fine in questioning their denominational doctrine as long as Scripture was the standard. The more he preached, the more the Berean-like believers studied. The more they studied, the more they found the dogma from the pulpit to be contrary to Scripture.

By the time they felt they were on firm enough ground to object, the church had grown with new members holding to the same theology as that of their erring pastor. Debate led to argument. Argument led to a vote. The vote led to the expelling of those who questioned the pastor. Further, the vote led to this church leaving the denomination and starting one of their own. Those who remained said those who left just did not believe the whole Bible. What they meant was, the believers who had searched the Scripture believed in holding to the expressed Word of God over some new "revelation."

Doctrinal issues are the most fervently defended of all arguments. Each side holds to the belief that they are on the right side. A minister at a Lincoln White House dinner once closed his prayer piously proclaiming, "The Lord is on our side." After the prayer, someone at the dinner table asked President Lincoln, "Don't you believe, Mr. President, that the Lord is always on the side of the right?" Lincoln replied, "We know that the Lord is always on the side of right. My concern is that I and this nation should be on the Lord's side."[1] Every church member embroiled in a dispute should pull back from the fray and reaffirm what is the Lord's will, for it is certain that the Lord desires unity, but

---

1. Alex Ayres, ed., *The Wit and Wisdom of Abraham Lincoln* (New York: Penguin Group Publishers, 1992), 86.

CHAPTER 7: DOCTRINAL CRISIS—THE CHARISMATIC MOVEMENT

He also desires truth and adherence to His Word. A wise saying that should govern all attitudes of disagreement in church life is, "In essentials, unity; in non-essentials, liberty; in all things, charity."[2]

Many of the struggles in churches today are over things that are of no real eternal significance. Someone asked Bill Schibler, "What are the major crises you have faced in your many years as a pastor?" Bro. Bill, my childhood preacher, responded that he never really had any major crises. The only one to come to his mind was the day that a lady from my hometown church attended a business meeting to discuss the remodeling of the old sanctuary. When it came to the kind of carpet, she emphatically demanded that it be the same type carpet that she had in her bedroom. The debate got so ugly that no one had the courage to put it to a vote. As a result, the church remodeled the sanctuary, but the old carpet remained as it was. It took six or seven more years for the church to reach an agreement on the carpet for that place.[3] Needless to say, that was a debate in which Bro. Bill would not waste his energy.

After almost fifty years of ministry, Dr. John Bisagno says, "If a preacher gets involved in every brush fire, fights every battle, and worries about every little problem, he will use up his leadership and not have it when he needs it. Do not go to war over the small issues."[4] A funny way to put this truth is, "A bulldog can whip a skunk any day, but it's just not worth it."[5]

Churches have split over cutting down an old tree to make room for more parking. Other churches have argued that the youth were destroying the pretty yard. The first church I pastored was in the planning stages of a new building. The church held a meeting to discuss the style of building the church desired. Most members were present because of the overwhelming excitement that the church was moving in a bold new direction. One particular family was present. This family was loving, caring, and for the first time really growing in the Lord. They had seen church squabbles in the past, and were devastated to see people they loved become enemies, acting in completely un-Christ-like manners.

For the purpose of illustration, we will call them the Baker family. Regretfully, the Bakers attended the meeting. Two of the founding families of the church got into a heated argument over the building style. The argument was silly; no real difference existed between the two styles, but to each

---

2. Powell, *Basic Bible Sermons*, 88.

3. Bill Schibler, pastor, personal interview by project leader, Hico, TX, March 10, 2008.

4. Bisagno, *Letters to Timothy*, 129.

5. Powell, *Basic Bible Sermons*, 53.

family their preference was at stake. Mr. Baker spoke up, saying that this was no way for people who love each other to talk. One of the founding families told him to "shut-up," and the arguing resumed. The Baker family quietly got up, left that night, and never returned. How tragic!

Doctrinal issues are viewed as more important than the color of carpet, the style of a building, or the permanence of a tree. With that said, a church should address doctrinal issues, and some should not be of great concern. Points of disagreement over the Millennium or the time of the rapture are worthy studies and provide for some intriguing preaching, but they do not carry as much weight as some other topics.[6] Music and worship style disagreements often escalate to crisis levels. Discussion and compromise on these type issues should occur, but by no means is this a point to break fellowship. I have heard it said that God has given His children great lyrics as found in Scripture, but God never gave sheets of music to the church. His desire is for believers to worship Him and for every culture to worship him in a way that is truly worshipful for them. Seemingly, with regard to diversity in worship, congregations are becoming more and more flexible as long as something in the worship set fits each group's preferred style. They do not seem to care if it all meets their preferences, just as long as a portion does. That is fair.

Some doctrines are central, while some are peripheral.[7] The central doctrines are those proclaimed clearly in the Bible and those that believers must stand upon and defend, no matter the cost—not because of the importance to the advocate, but because of the importance to God. Debate can occur over when Jesus will return, but His return is non-debatable. Jesus said He is returning. The illustration that best describes the Trinity can be discussed, but the existence of the Trinity, the Triune God is beyond any discussion. The Old Testament thoughts on whether the Angel of the Lord is Jesus is an intriguing topic, but the fact that Jesus is eternal and is God stands beyond any question.

One can study and research the meaning of a Biblical passage, but no doubt can exist that the Bible is the inerrant Word of the Living God. The Bible is God's Word, all-sufficient, and is the sole text of inspiration, not needing any additions or subtractions. To preach on key doctrinal issues such as faith, grace, mercy, holiness, the Atonement, the Holy Spirit, sanctification, and the like are always valid.[8] Such preaching helps to deepen

---

6. Gunnink, *Preaching for Recovery*, 104.
7. Clayton, "Preaching and Conflict," 530.
8. Tucker, *Primer for Preachers*, 78.

CHAPTER 7: DOCTRINAL CRISIS—THE CHARISMATIC MOVEMENT

the Christian and give them the ability to describe to others the hope that is within them.

To teach the non-negotiables is necessary, and one should never back away from their defense. Dr. Bisagno faced a doctrinal crisis at Houston's First Baptist Church when his personal banker, a member of his church, began to listen to a man named Herbert W. Armstrong, host of the radio program "The World Tomorrow." (Incidentally, Garner Ted Armstrong is Herbert W. Armstrong's son.) This member began to purchase Armstrong's material and study it.

Armstrong taught in this material "British Israelism," which said that the twelve tribes or part of the twelve tribes of Israel migrated to Great Britain, making Britain part of the new Israel. Further, the material contained a call for a very legalistic lifestyle. Armstrong taught that one could obtain salvation by keeping the Ten Commandments, a contradiction to the very Biblical tenet that salvation can never be earned. Another heresy taught by Armstrong was the denial of the Deity of Christ. The more this church member read, the more enamored he was with this false teaching. Several times he came to Bisagno's office to debate the Deity of Christ and salvation through the Cross.

One Sunday, after church, as the members left the service, they found pamphlets on their car rejecting the Deity of Christ. Bisagno knew who did it, so he called the man and confronted him. He told that member that he had two choices. He could come next Sunday before the church, apologize for the pamphlets, disavow those doctrines, and ask the church to forgive him. His other choice was to have Dr. Bisagno call for a vote to vote him out of the church. The member told Bisagno to remove his name from the church roll. They did. Dr. Bisagno said, "I have a lot of grace in my heart, but the Deity of Christ is a non-negotiable in this church."[9]

Truman Dollar called these non-negotiables the "irreducible minimum," which includes the Gospel message, the redemptive work of Christ, and the inspiration of Scripture. Dollar said that, on these battles, he is willing to split the church.[10] Holding firm to the essentials of the Christian faith is a command repeated over and over. Paul told Titus in Titus 1:9, "holding fast the faithful word which is in accordance with the teaching, so that he will be able both to exhort in sound doctrine and to refute those who contradict". Paul told Timothy and the church in Thessalonica the same message. The writer of Hebrews repeats the same message. The preacher's call is to be the defender and teacher of the faith.

9. Bisagno, class lecture.
10. Shelley and Miller, "Fundamentally One," 18.

Some points of conflict in the Christian church place respected and noted Christian theologians on different sides. Two of the primary debates concern Charismatic Theology and Calvinism. Often, a church is composed of people at different levels of the belief spectrum in these two areas. When someone asked Jerry Vines his opinion of the biggest challenges preachers will face in the coming years, he echoed the opinions of many scholars and preachers interviewed. He believed Calvinism would be a threat, as well as the Charismatic movement.[11]

To debate the validity of each side of these arguments is beyond the scope of this book. The purpose is for the preacher to understand that, in such doctrinal crises, the preacher must be sensitive to what is going on and realize that he must reach for the Bible to bring resolution. The Bible provides the most appropriate material to handle these issues. Every side can quote Scripture to support their stands through the art of prooftexting. What is most important in the preaching is that it should come from God's full revelation on the subject. When it comes to the doctrine of election, no doubt exists that God elects, but the Bible shows also that man has free choice. The preacher must be true to the text and see what the balanced view of Scripture says. At times, the preacher has to be honest and admit that some issues are mysteries to man, but beautiful in God's plan. An awesome thing is to know that the Christian serves a God whose ways and thoughts are higher than his own.

Unfortunately, when theological interpretations become movements, they bring incredible strife to a church. Crusaders begin to demand that all participants adhere to their pet theology.[12] With regard to the understanding of the Holy Spirit and spiritual gifts, Paul saw much debate, disagreement, and abuse in the church of Corinth. Paul handled this question by shedding light on God's plan, man's selfishness, and the need for order and unity.[13] A church will reach a point where they need to hear something from the pastor. At this point, Bisagno says that the preacher must admit, "I may not be the best preacher in the world, but I am the only one you got. It is my job to articulate the doctrine of this church. If it's not my job, whose is it?"[14] Prayerfully, the pastor is devoted enough to prayer, to God's Word, and its study that he will discern God's will on the subject in his church. When

---

11. Jerry Vines, retired pastor, First Baptist Church Jacksonville, personal interview by project leader, 2008 Expository Preaching Workshop, Southwestern Baptist Theological Seminary, Fort Worth, TX.

12. Rediger, *Clergy Killers*, 49.

13. Gunnink, *Preaching for Recovery*, 107.

14. Bisagno, class lecture.

covering the concern from the pulpit, the preacher must realize that he is about to dropkick a hornet's nest.[15]

Situation

A man named Milton Green started making big inroads into Houston. He had an obsession with demonism and a charismatic philosophy contrary to Scripture. Some of Houston's First Baptist members began to buy his tapes and became enthralled by his teachings on healing, tongues, and obsession, along with exorcism. The members began going to Green's meetings, having him in their homes, having Bible studies among themselves with his material, and bringing this doctrine into their Sunday morning Bible study classes at church. Ten of his deacons, who were fine men, got wrapped up in it themselves. They had a meeting with Dr. Bisagno in one of their homes, where they debated with him for over three-and-a-half hours.

Bisagno admitted that he was not the world's greatest theologian, but he knew what Scripture taught on such things and how Green's teachings did not adhere to God's Word. He told them not to teach that anymore. They called for a second meeting and, again, after much discussion, he told them not to teach this anymore at church. They did not change, but instead became less aggressive. The matter surfaced to the forefront again in church, so Bisagno knew he had to address it from the pulpit with the only ultimate source of authority he had—the Word of God.[16]

Sermon

John R. Bisagno

"The Unity of Faith"

EPHESIANS 4:11-13

Will you open your Bibles this morning to the book of Ephesians, chapter 4, verse 11? I want you particularly to mark and note the first part of the thirteenth verse in this passage. We should begin with Ephesians chapter 4, verse 11. Do keep your Bible at hand. We are going to turn throughout the New Testament and consider more passages, perhaps, than on any other Sunday. Maybe someone there in your family is more familiar

15. Lotz, "Controversial Issues," 40.
16. Bisagno, class lecture.

with the location of the books, and you can look together. As we move along, do so as quickly as possible. In Ephesians chapter 4, verse 11, the Apostle Paul is telling us about some of the gifts God has given to His Body, the Church.

"And he gave some, apostles; and some, prophets; and some, evangelists; and some, pastors and teachers." This is what I am—a pastor/teacher. Here follows the best definition in the New Testament of the ministry of the pastor/teacher over the flock of God. He has placed him to pastor, to shepherd, and to teach. "For the perfecting of the saints, for the work of the ministry, for the edifying of the body of Christ." For what purpose? "till we all come in the unity of the faith." Until we are all in the unity of the faith.

> And of the knowledge of the Son of God, unto a perfect man, unto the measure of the stature of the fullness of Christ: that we henceforth be no more children, tossed to and fro, and carried about with every wind of doctrine, by the sleight of men, and cunning craftiness, whereby they lie in wait to deceive; but speaking the truth in love, may grow up into him in all things, which is the head, even Christ.

The Scripture instructs the pastor/teacher to mature the congregation to a point that unity exists in the faith. This he does by correcting every new doctrine that comes along, by which humans are tossed to-and-fro, and exhorting them to the Scriptures. He does so firmly, speaking the truth, but he does so in love.

Our Father, we ask Thee that this message today may be the truth in love for the purpose of the maturing of the body to the unity of the faith as You have so clearly directed the office of pastor/teacher in the New Testament. Let the words of my mouth and the meditations of my heart in love and in honesty and in truth be acceptable in Thy sight, Oh God, my Lord, and my Redeemer, in Jesus' name, Amen.

When I retire as your pastor some years from now, if Jesus tarries and the Lord allows me to stay on, as is my intent and desire, someone might—for some strange reason—decide to write a little memoir about my efforts here. I would hope that as I had suggested a few Sundays ago, that they might say one of the main things that I contributed to the life of our Church was to keep calling us back constantly to the center of the road of the purpose of our existence and the doctrine for getting to that place. In

CHAPTER 7: DOCTRINAL CRISIS—THE CHARISMATIC MOVEMENT

recent years, many doctrines and theologies, many movements and ideas and practices and priorities have crept into the life of the Church with which we have tried firmly, and in love, to deal and call the congregation again into unity.

The charismatic issue places emphases on healing and the atonement and the speaking in tongues, new wine, the health-and-wealth movement, the name-it-and-claim-it theology, the doctrine of positive confession, and the emphasis of social action without evangelism. By the way, our evangelism is equally dangerous without social action. Going off on tangents on parades and demonstrations on issues such as abortions, homosexuality, and Christian politics have been just a few of the issues with which we have dealt, matured through, and come to unity. In our congregation, at this time, yet another concern of mine is present. Ninety-nine percent of you will not know about that of which I am speaking. Our Singles ministries, in our Young Married ministries, in particular our Young Married Adult Division and Singles, much of the teaching of what is called the Deliverance Ministry is afloat. My purpose primarily for you this morning is to give you insight about what the Deliverance Ministry, and those who espouse it, primarily teach and believe. The Deliverance Ministry teaching is contrary to what First Baptist Church has taught for 145 years and what those who espouse the Baptist persuasion have believed for some 2,000 years. The teaching primarily is that one goes to a deliverance counselor, who, after a few hours identifies certain demons that are supposed to have invaded the life of the believer. After a process of hours of efforts and ministry, they exorcize, cast out, and deliver the person from demons. That person, now free because of their actions, can walk in Christian victory.

This teaching is confusing, and this teaching is divisive in this congregation. I have addressed it in some degree for some time, and I will, this morning, sum it all up and speak as explicitly clear as I know how. I want to say about eleven or twelve things about what they believe generally, and what Baptists believe, and what this Church believes.

Number one is that they tend to believe that the pursuit of victory in the Christian life is primarily external—primarily fighting a supposed constant barrage and onslaught of demonic attacks on Christians. This church, along with Baptists and great Christian writers, has believed for hundreds of years that this emphasis is incorrect. The struggle is not on the outside, but is on the inside. The struggle is between the old man and the new. The struggle is internal and not external. The struggle is between the flesh and the spirit. The struggle is between the carnal man and the spiritual man.

This is contrary to the deliverance mentality that every problem, ultimately, comes down to a matter of fighting the demons externally. The Christian Church has agreed for 2,000 years that the most authoritative and conclusive passage of Scripture ever written on the subject of maturity and victory in the Christian faith is Romans 5-8. Not a word of demons is mentioned in this passage. The Bible is explicitly clear that the problems that keep us from being the kind of Christians we desire to be, the problems that we must crucify and find victory over through the finished work of Christ in the flesh and on the cross is imbedded in the human heart.

I would like you to turn in your Bibles first to Matthew, chapter 15, where no less an authority than Jesus Himself is speaking. We shall look at several verses, and I urge you to turn very quickly please and try to stay up, and you will probably get ahead of me, which will be very embarrassing. Matthew chapter 15, verse 19, Jesus says, "Out of the heart proceeds evil thoughts, murders, adulteries, fornications, thefts, false witnesses and blasphemies." From where do these constant problems come? From demons? No. They come from out of the heart of man, the human nature forgiven, but not eradicated of the old nature with which we still have to deal. They are internal and not external. Galatians chapter 5 is another classic picture and passage on the nature of the struggle of the flesh and the spirit. Verse 16 of Galatians 5 says, "This I say then, walk in the spirit and you will not fulfill the lust of the flesh." Fight demons and you will not fulfill the lust of the flesh? No. Walk in the spirit. For demons lust against the spirit? No. Verse 17, for the flesh lusts against the spirit and this spirit is contrary to the flesh. Now, verse 19, the works of demons are these? No. "The works of the flesh are these, which are manifest. These are works of the flesh adultery, fornication, uncleanness, lasciviousness, idolatry, witchcraft, hatred, variance, emulation, wrath, strife, sedition, heresies, envyings, murders, drunkenness, revelings and the like."

Now I would like you to turn if you will, please, to James chapter 1. James was no less an authority as the half-brother of our Lord Jesus Christ, another son of Mary, whose father was Joseph. James chapter 1, verse 13, "Let no man say when he is tempted, I am tempted of God. For God cannot be tempted with evil neither tempt He any man." Now let us pause there. He is saying no trial, no temptation to sin comes from God. I spoke to someone in the Deliverance Ministry only a few days ago, and this person said that nothing comes from God that is sin; therefore it is all demonic. The conclusion is not so. They rush from a premise to a conclusion with no intermediate logic. Listen to what the Bible says. It is not from the demonic, it is not from God, but every man is tempted, verse 14, when he is drawn away of what, of the demons? No. He is drawn of his own lust and entice.

James chapter 4 continues over to verse 1 and says, "From whence come wars and fightings among you." Now this is not internal dissention within the church, church member fighting church member. It is the division and "ism" and spiritual schizophrenia of human personality. "Are they not even of the lust that wore in your member?" The first proposition that folks sometimes are making is that the priority with the Christian life is an obsession that one must constantly be aware of fighting demonic attacks in the believers. It is the position of this Church, of Baptists for centuries, and Christian theologians, as law, that such an emphasis is relatively insignificant in comparison to the primary struggle for the victory of the Christian life that is from within, not external. The emphasis is on the spirit versus the flesh—internal and not external.

Number two is that they believe that victory, therefore, may be achieved by submitting to someone's counsel or ministry. They believe that going through a kind of experience or an act of a few hours can cause one to be delivered, gaining victory in the Christian life. The position of this church is that the process of sanctification, growing to full measure in Christ is not a one-time act or a one-afternoon experience. It is a lifetime process. From conversion, justification, to Heaven, glorification, the lifelong process of sanctification follows. Ephesians 5:18, you need not turn, "Be ye filled with the spirit" is a verb tense, which does not mean a one-time act. It is constantly "BE YE BEING FILLED WITH THE SPIRIT." One young man in our church, who had gone through this non-biblical charismatic teaching, as so many have of getting caught up in it just to finally see the error in it, came to me. He said, "I sat in on such a session. It was obvious that the person did not need demons cast out of them. They simply needed to be disciplined."

Number three is that they teach that the believer needs to be delivered from demons. The First Baptist Church of Houston believes we do not need to be delivered, because we have already been delivered. Colossians chapter 1, verses 12 through 13. We believe no such process, no such experience need occur to receive something we already have. Colossians 1:12,

"Giving thanks unto the Father which hath made us worthy to be partakers of the inheritance of the saints in light who hath delivered us from the power of darkness and hath translated us into the kingdom of His dear Son." I am in the Kingdom of His dear Son. I am obsessed with the Kingdom of Light, not with a struggle against a kingdom of darkness. If I have been set free from the law of sin and death, how is it that I need to be freed from the law of sin and death. If I have been converted, how is it that I have to be converted. If I have been delivered, how is it that I have to be delivered. We do not believe in the Deliverance Ministry, because we believe the Christian is delivered already and simply need acknowledge and appropriate what is already his in the state of light in which he now stands as a delivered child of God.

Number four is that they believe that a Christian can be demon-possessed and that the Christian needs to have the demons exorcized. The First Baptist Church believes that no such teaching exists in the New Testament, and I challenge anyone under the sound of my voice to bring me a verse in the New Testament that teaches that Christians need to have demons exorcized from them.

Number five is that they believe that there was one example of a Christian woman who had a demon exorcized in the Bible. The position of First Baptist Church is that the woman to whom they refer in Luke 13 was obviously not a Christian. I want you to turn to Luke chapter 13, verse 10, and this is the only prooftext they try to use to point out someone who is a Christian who was delivered. Luke chapter 13, verse number 10,

> And He was teaching in one of the synagogues on the Sabbath. And, behold, there was a woman which had a spirit of infirmity eighteen years, and was bowed together, and could in no wise lift up herself. And when Jesus saw her, He called her to him, and said unto her, "Woman, thou art loosed from thine infirmity." And he laid his hands on her: and immediately she was made straight, and glorified God. And the ruler of the synagogue answered with indignation, because that Jesus had healed on the Sabbath day, and said unto the people, "There are six days in which men ought to work: in them therefore come and be healed, and not on the Sabbath day." The Lord then answered him, and said, "Thou hypocrite, doth not each one of you on the Sabbath loose his ox or his ass from the stall, and lead

him away to watering? And ought not this woman, being a daughter of Abraham, whom Satan hath bound, lo, these eighteen years, be loosed from this bond on the Sabbath day?"

Now although this text is obviously Jewish, hear the words "Abraham," "daughter of Abraham," "Sabbath," "Synagogue," "Ruler of the Synagogue," "Law." This is obviously a Jewish setting, with a Jewish woman, but because she is referred to as the daughter of Abraham, they believe that this means that she was a Christian. This woman was not a Christian; she was simply a Jewish girl.

Number six is that they teach and believe that demonic warfare for saints is taught in the New Testament, and all that is based on a passage in Ephesians 6. The position of this church is that no such doctrine of fighting demons by Christians is found in the New Testament. I will be the first to say that Satan has power over demons, and it does seem to be logical. But I want to try to separate logic, experience, assumption, and presumption from Bible doctrine, and I want you to see the passage from which they get their idea. Turn to Ephesians, please, where we talk about spiritual warfare. The emphasis of the New Testament is that any fighting against evil is against the devil and not against all of these imagined, supposed demons.

Look in verse number 12, "We wrestle not against flesh and blood but against principalities, against powers, against the rulers of the darkness of this world, against spiritual wickedness in high places." Many people assume that these four names: rulers of darkness, spiritual wickedness in high places, principalities, and powers are names for orders of demons. They may be. They may just as easily not be. Principalities and powers may refer to the power of television, may refer to the power of Hollywood. Spiritual wickedness in high places may refer to things like Watergate, or things that go on in government that are wrong and immoral and ungodly. No clear-cut teaching says that this refers to demons. It is an assumption. It is a presumption. And, this Church's doctrine will not be built on assumption and presumption.

Verse 11 says, "Put on the whole armor of God that ye may be able to stand against the wiles of the devil." That means the way of the devil. It does not say the demons of the devil. It says the ways of the devil. Verse number 16 ends by saying, "Take the shield of faith by which you will be able to quench all of the fiery darts of the wicked." Now that is the word for the definite, the wicked, definite article, the one and only wicked one; the devil. It does not say we are fighting many demons. It says we are fighting the darts, the wiles, the attacks, the ways of THE ONE WHO IS EVIL. No doctrine exists in Scripture that specifically states that Christians fight demons.

Number seven is that they believe that the New Testament teaches exorcism of Gentiles and Gentile believers. FACT—it is the position of this church that exorcism is not only not for believers, but of any kind of Gentile; it is prohibited in the New Testament. Turn to Matthew chapter 10. I want to read to you a passage of Scripture, which is at the heart of their theology, and then explain something. In chapter 10 of Matthew, Jesus called together his twelve disciples and gave them power over unclean spirits to cast them out and heal all manner of diseases and all manner of sickness. And then they are named, and that is where they quit. That is not where we are going to quit, let us finish the command of Jesus.

Verse 5 says,

> Then Jesus said to the twelve as He sent them forth. He commanded them saying, "Go not, underscore not, into the way of the Gentiles and into the city of the Samaritans which were even half Gentile, enter ye not. You go rather to the lost sheep of the house of Israel. (This they conveniently forget.) And as you go, preach; saying the Kingdom of Heaven is at hand. Heal the sick, cleanse the leper, raise the dead, cast out devils freely. Freely ye receive, freely give."

Mark 16:16 makes it clear that those who would believe the Gospel in Jesus' day believed in an atmosphere of exorcism, of miracles, of signs and wonders, and of healings. And Jesus said, to be sure you do this to the Jews. Over in 1 Corinthians, as we will see when we start our February study of the wonderful book of 1 Corinthians, He says that God did miracles and wonders and signs in the face of Israel, yet they would not believe. Now you mark that down. Jesus is explicitly clear that this was hardly a ministry to believers and certainly not to Gentile believers, but to Jewish unbelievers.

Number eight is that they believe that virtually all human maladies are caused by demons. They believe that virtually all human maladies are caused by demons. One of their books that is so important in their ministry and school of thinking is called *Pigs in the Parlor*. The book lists about four, five, six hundred

CHAPTER 7: DOCTRINAL CRISIS—THE CHARISMATIC MOVEMENT 89

different supposed demons—demons who specialize in everything. Professorial demons inhabit professors who teach in the seminary. There are Pharisee demons. There are lust demons. There are cancer demons, depression demons, and any malady you can think of—physical, psychological or spiritual—has a particular demon. The position of this Church is that absolutely no such doctrine exists in the New Testament. They not only do not exist in the New Testament, but the Bible makes it clear that the demons that did exist, that were in unbelieving Jews, that were to be cast out as a sign for their conversion, and the consistent characteristics of demon possession where it did occur in lost people in the New Testament were blaspheming and cursing against Jesus. They had an extreme tendency to violence, to uncontrollability and to super human strength—hardly professorial demons and depression demons.

Number nine is that their position is that the conflict between these two ideas, whether a Christian can or cannot be demon-possessed, may be resolved with the following theology. Since the mind and heart have been redeemed, a demon cannot possess the mind and heart. Since the flesh has not been redeemed, a demon can possess the flesh. The position of First Baptist Church of Houston is, however, that while that is an interesting theory, absolutely no Biblical basis exists for it. It is strictly fanciful supposition. Incidentally, it is very interesting that the same mindset of a person that is into this, normally believes that healing for the body is in the atonement by the blood of Christ, which completely contradicts their own theology, by telling that the ornery degenerate nature of a body can be the home of a demon. But, Christ died for that body on the cross, and it is redeemed right along with the soul.

Number ten is that they believe and teach that God often sends demons to correct us. How incongruous this is with God sending something to punish us, to correct us, and then turning around and asking God to get rid of it because it is evil. The Bible is absolutely clear that such is not the case. It is, and shall remain the doctrinal position of this church, that Christ, according to 2 Corinthians 6:14-15, hath no accord with the devil whatsoever. And that God never uses Satan for good for any purpose, and that light hath no communion with darkness. Second Corinthians 6:14-15 says be assured, that God does His own correcting. He does not send it out to His neighbors when His children need correcting. You need not turn, I want to read to you Hebrews 12:5,

> My son, do not despise the chastening of the Lord, nor be discouraged when you are rebuked by Him; for whom the Lord loves He chastens, and scourges every son whom He receives. If you endure chastening, God deals with you as with sons; for what son is there whom a father does not chasten? But if you are without chastening, of which all have become partakers, then you are illegitimate and not sons (NKJV).

Well, they say, "but Job was corrected by God who used the devil to do so." That is their position. Let me tell you the doctrine of this church. One—Never attempt to determine New Testament Christian theology from the Old Testament. Two—God did not send demons, He allowed Satan. Three—He was not correcting Job. Job explicitly was stated to be a perfect man. He was obviously revealing the grace and sufficiency of God. Because of Satan's accusation, he only serves you for what he can get out of it. And God said, "let Me show you what a good man is." No correcting was present, no abuses were present, no collusion was present.

Number eleven is that they tend to believe that all experience is real. And so if it happens, it must be true. Generally speaking, the watchword and the cry of the charismatic movement, and many of the doctrines and movements that have spun off from it, have at their heart the cry, "But it happened." Experience is everything, they say. How can you argue with experience? But the position of this Church is that you must argue with experience. You must analyze experience, and that Biblical truth is to be arrived at not by bringing your experience to the light, but by bringing your experience to the light of the Scripture. And I care what you say happens, if it does not parallel New Testament theology. You have been deceived. That is why the Bible says, "Search the Scripture, rightly divide the Word, try the spirits." Satan, you see, is a counterfeiter and an angel of light can come and preach another Gospel.

Subjective truth is no truth at all. Suppose you are trying to arrive at truth by your experience, when precisely with that same experience, I arrive at a different conclusion. How do we know what truth is? A theological mishmash occurs. This caused the New Testament Church in the days of the Reformation to say "*Sola Scriptura*"—Scripture Only! We will not go by experience. We will determine truth by what the Bible says. Often, it is said that the first thing that happened in some of the counseling sessions is that one must determine if they are saved at all, because the obvious conclusion is quickly arrived at that a Christian struggling toward victory is probably not saved at all. And so they will get on their knees and say, "let's ask God to reveal to us whether you are really saved or not." HOLD IT!

We are not going to determine whether a man is saved by asking God. Suppose God revealed to me, "no," and God revealed to you "yes." What do we do then? Are we going to have a subjective faith that alters on the emotional whims of everyone's supposed revelation from God? We are going to determine salvation on the basis of, "Have I done what the Bible says to do to be saved?" PERIOD! Not by everybody's idea that comes along. Subjective truth is subject to everyone's emotional and spiritual and psychological states of mind and is no basis of truth at all.

Number twelve is that they believe that they have the right to believe and practice anything they will as a member of First Baptist Church. It is the position of this church, however, that in the name of the priesthood of the believer, you do have the right to believe anything you want. I'll be the first to say that, and I will be the first to defend your right to believe what you will. I'll go to the wall for my friend Austin Wilkerson or my friend Earl Banning or my friend Tim Smith, and other Assemblies of God preachers, to believe in tongues and instant healing on demand and falling from grace. I will fight for their right to believe that. And they are my friends, and I eat dinner with them. But let me tell you something. Earl Banning and Austin Wilkerson have not joined my church, nor begun teaching in my Sunday School. They do not hold meetings through the week with my congregation and attempt to seduce them theologically into doctrines not espoused by this church. And that folks, is a whole different ballgame.

Let me be as clear as I know how. I completely love and honor and respect any man who disagrees with this church's position at any point, but a man does not have the right, nor can this Church further tolerate the practice of using its facilities, its classes, the prestige and potential for ministry that it affords to any member of this congregation to evangelistically and perpetually spread doctrines with which the Church is in total and public acknowledged disagreement.

Let me say this in love with the responsibility God has given me as your pastor, to say, in conclusion. For 145 years, twenty-seven pastors have faithfully pastored the First Baptist Church of Houston. These pastors have given solid leadership to solid congregations and have built a solid Baptist church. I do not intend to go down in history as the pastor who stood idly by and watched in silence, advocating the responsibility entrusted to him by this church to preserve, preach, teach, defend, and perpetuate the doctrines and theological positions of this church and the tenets of the Baptist faith as we have understood them for over 2,000 years. Sixteen years ago, I became your pastor. In another fourteen years, probably, I will retire. And after these thirty years, I intend to leave exactly what I found—A SOLID BAPTIST CHURCH. Not something else, not a menagerie of theological mishmash; a Baptist church. The church and I are well-satisfied with the doctrinal position of our former pastors, my predecessors, such as Robert Smith, K. White, Boyd Hunt, Doug Hudgens, Eddie Head, Dr. Level, to name just a few. And those policies and doctrinal positions will not be changed.

They will not be voted on, nor is the jury still out, and the outcome uncertain; they are non-negotiable. They are issues that were settled hundreds of years ago when we took the name Baptist. We will continue to practice and believe as Baptists have in this Church for 145 years and for hundreds of years before us. We'll not change a thing. No, we're not going to start serving cocktails at the deacon's meetings. We're not going to tear down the education buildings and throw out Sunday School. We're not going to start raising money for missions by having BINGO parties and cakewalks. We're not going to begin teaching that salvation is by works, or that Christian victory is found through the exorcism of demons in the life of believers. These are teachings foreign to our faith that can no longer be tolerated.

In the office of the pastor of this church lies great blessing and responsibility. But with the territory comes the heavy burden of responsibility, and this day, I'm calling upon you with the authority that has been vested in me by this church and by the New Testament, which is clearly stated in Hebrews 13:17, "Obey the rule of them that God has set over you." Let me read it exactly in Hebrews 13:17, "Obey them that have the rule over you and submit yourselves for they watch for your souls." And in the name of the Bible, in the name of hundreds of years of Baptist heritage, of the pulpit committee, and deacons and congregation that called me to this church, and the Scripture that says obey the rule of them which are over you, I say to you, "stop the practice. Stop the spread of this doctrine in the congregation of the First Baptist Church of Houston."

I want to read to you a letter that came to me. It's not the first such letter.

CHAPTER 7: DOCTRINAL CRISIS—THE CHARISMATIC MOVEMENT

Dear Dr. Bisagno, I've been watching your TV program a couple of years now and recently started to support your ministry in a very small way, financially. It has recently come to my attention that a lovely girl, whom I have worked with and whose family I am acquainted with, was in your counseling program for mental problems. [Dr. Bisagno's insert: "This is not the church's counseling program. She is referring to the Deliverance Ministry, self-appointed counseling program that has been going on. It is this to which I have referred in this message."] While in this counseling program, somebody at your Church decided she was demon-possessed. To make a long story short, her family got to her just at the point of suicide, after the counseling. And there are other such stories. And I find it almost impossible to believe that you would countenance such a program in your church that could do so much harm to a young person. That's not what you preach, and I cannot believe that's the image you want for your congregation.

I don't believe we're going to change now, what we've stood for, for 145 years. Some time ago, I met with ten of our deacons—ten of the best men I've ever known. Good men. Godly men. Men who had been caught up in a doctrinal persuasion that was foreign to the position of this congregation. We met hours. We discussed, read, talked, and prayed many times. At the conclusion of those meetings, each one of those men looked me straight in the eye and said, "Pastor, we respect and acknowledge the concept of Biblical and spiritual authority of the church, and we give you our word, we will never publicly or privately teach or practice, from this point on, anything you do not articulate as the historical position of this Church."

I respect men like that, and I want you to know that this church requires that of its membership. May we pray?

Our Father, as well as I know how, I have attempted to discharge the responsibility, Biblically based, with explanation from Scripture, with a doctrinal defense and with love, the problem that has arisen in the church that most of us don't know anything about; never even heard of. And we commit it to Thee and leave it to Thy hands. And we know that good people, who are mature and love you, have heard the message from God, will respond to the Biblical admonition, because they believe the Bible, and we trust them that they will stop. And we pray that 1986 may be a year of cleansing and revival. I've never been as excited about a church year in my life. I've never looked forward to a sermon like next week to share with the church the direction, the plans, and the vision, and what I think God wants of us. We've come so far. We've weathered many a storm—financial, theological, racial. This old church has been through some battles, and we thank you, Lord that she still stands—one of the greatest churches that planet Earth has ever known. We commit ourselves again to maturity, to holiness, to the truth in love, to those positions and those things that we believe are right; by which we banded ourselves to the Unity of Faith in this congregation. In Jesus' name. Amen.[17]

Lessons

Houston's First Baptist Church faced a doctrinal crisis of never-before-seen proportions. All involved parties were charged emotionally for their side of the issue. The pastor of this fine church knew it was his responsibility to address the problem, and he knew he must do so without selfish emotion taking charge. If the reader will note, this pastor opened in a prayer that sought for all that he would say in the sermon to be, first and foremost, pleasing to the Lord. It is important that privately and publicly through prayer, the pastor asked that his heart and the heart of his people be focused only on God and His will. In this nerve-wracking moment, the church needed God's soothing, intervening Spirit to settle over the sanctuary that Sunday morning.

In this sermon on doctrine, Dr. Bisagno laid out the Scriptural support for the church's doctrine it espoused. With immense emotion, he dealt with each point of the opposing argument and countered it with Scripture. He demonstrated that many of the false beliefs were held by people who used only part of Scripture to defend their arguments without going into more depth of the text.

This was a necessary sermon for Dr. Bisagno's church. He knew the church's temperature and the devastating effect a non-biblical virus can bring. Recently, the executive director of the Northwest Baptist Commission of Southern Baptists said that 50 percent of the churches in the Northwest were being torn apart by the Charismatic Controversy which this church faced.[18]

---

17. John Bisagno, "The Unity of Faith," sermon archives of First Baptist Church, Houston, TX.

18. Bisagno, *Inside Information*, 7.

Bisagno defended the right of every believer to hold a different belief. He believes that every man has a right to believe as he chooses, even if that belief is incorrect. Further, he believes that the Christian has the right to reach out to those who have erred and guide them back to God's truth just as the Word of God says.

Though he defended the "Baptist" denomination and church historical beliefs, it is noteworthy that he has researched those beliefs to ensure that they were in tune with God's Word. To know Dr. Bisagno is to know that he is a Christian tied to the Bible first, and the church and the denomination only as they adhere to God's standard.

He was respectful to those who disagreed, but frank in calling out where they parted from Scripture. He told those ten who continued to voice the issue that he could be wrong, but he must preach what he believes is right until the Lord shows him otherwise. He sought unity in the body, and longed for the new year of working together.

At the conclusion of the sermon, the congregation sat deathly quiet. That afternoon at the four o'clock deacons' meeting, the chairman of the deacons commended him, and the deacons unanimously stood and applauded him. Six of those men, who held to the charismatic doctrine, left the church and started another church. He remained friends with all of them. The other four surrendered to the pastor's understanding of God's Word and continued to serve the Lord faithfully.

Chapter 8: **Doctrinal Issues—Calvinism**

Another doctrinal issue that has brought strife in churches is the subject of Calvinism. People in seminaries, denominations, and churches alike hotly debate the tenets of Calvinism. Again, great Christians, who are saved, are equally involved on both sides of the debate. Both sides can worship together in harmony, but when the theology of a church or a denomination harps on this topic as the only one that matters, trouble ensues. God's Word is too rich to spend on one mystery. Too many things need to be learned, so many Bible books to cover, and so many jewels to discover.

Without going further into the theological defense of either side, at times, a crusader brings tumult to the church, because he seeks to convert others to his stance, while undermining the pastor's authority and contradicting the beliefs of the church. When that occurs, the preacher has to bring calm through God's Word and the power of the Holy Spirit.

Situation

A Bible college in our town does a wonderful job of teaching God's Word. Unfortunately, the college seems to have taken upon itself the mission of sending out little five-point Calvinist evangelists to the area churches. I respect that college, and I admire their students. I have even recommended this school to two of my church members. With that said, right or wrong, I have strong disagreements in some areas. One of their students is a Sunday School teacher in our church. He has a heart of gold and a yearning to be all that God has called him to be. He is a great friend, and I am astounded at how God has changed him day-by-day. In his Bible lessons, I noticed that he tended to circle back to Calvinism with every lesson. He would bring out parts of the TULIP doctrine at every close. I finally had a visit with him and reemphasized my beliefs and the beliefs of the church. My only request was to stay away from that one emphasis. In all other doctrines, he and the church are in complete harmony.

He did great for a while, but then the TULIP began to bloom in his classes. I was teaching a youth class at the time and was not present to hear it, but after his class, several came to me with great fear and questions about something he had said. The teacher had taught that particular morning that "Some babies go to hell, that's just the way it is. No one deserves to go to Heaven so who are we to argue if God sends babies who die to hell?" The tragedy of the story, as well as my chief concern, was that a young mom was present who had just lost a little son. Additionally, another young mother in my church had a baby who died right after birth. Both women were extremely fragile, and both were new Christians. My only recourse was to take God's Word and explain to the best of my ability what I believe the Lord has to say on this subject.

Sermon

Johnny Teague

"Things a Son Would Do"

Genesis 37

Turn in your Bibles to Genesis, chapter 37.

So when Joseph came to his brothers, they stripped him of his robe—the richly ornamented robe he was wearing, and they took him and threw him into the cistern. Now the cistern was empty; there was no water in it. As they sat down to eat their meal, they looked up and saw a caravan of Ishmaelites coming from Gilead. Their camels were loaded with spices, balm and myrrh, and they were on their way to take them down to Egypt. Judah said to his brothers, "What will we gain if we kill our brother and cover up his blood? Come, let's sell him to the Ishmaelites and not lay our hands on him; after all, he is our brother, our own flesh and blood." His brothers agreed. So when the Midianite merchants came by, his brothers pulled Joseph up out of the cistern and sold him for twenty shekels of silver to the Ishmaelites, who took him to Egypt. When Reuben returned to the cistern and saw that Joseph was not there, he tore his clothes. He went back to his brothers and said, "The boy isn't there! Where can I turn now?" Then they got Joseph's robe, slaughtered a goat and dipped the robe in the blood. They took the ornamented robe back to their father and said, "We found this. Examine it to see whether it is your son's robe." He recognized it and said, "It is my son's robe! Some ferocious animal has devoured him. Joseph has surely been torn to pieces." Then Jacob tore his clothes, put on sackcloth and mourned for his son many days. All his sons and daughters came to comfort him, but he refused to be comforted. "No," he said, "in mourning will I go down to the grave to my son." So, his father wept for him. Meanwhile, the Midianites sold Joseph in Egypt to Potiphar, one of Pharaoh's officials, the captain of the guard.

Well, I'll tell you what. You read that passage, and you wonder—how did we get this far? I mean, last week we looked at the evil brothers, and now we are seeing the evil brothers doing even more evil, and we had to come back and remember, was not a promise made to Abraham somewhere and then to Isaac and Jacob? Was not a promise made about God giving them lots of land and a great multitude? Was not a promise made that God would bless those who blessed him, curse those who cursed him, and that he would be a blessing to all people? However, when I see these things, I realize that I am not seeing much of a blessing in this family. I have to ask, what is happening to that promise?

When we look at Genesis, chapter 1, how many words did God use to describe making the stars? Five words. "And God made the stars." That is it. The whole space, millions of stars—five words. When we look at Genesis, one-fourth of the whole book is committed to one guy named Joseph who is not even an heir to the Savior. It is amazing. Why would Joseph get one-fourth of a book? Well, we are going to find out today. The first thing we need to know is that they settled in Hebron. Hebron means fellowship—it is south of Bethlehem. Joseph was born to Rachel.

You may remember that Rachel was Jacob's favorite wife. He loved Rachel. He was tricked into marrying the other sister Leah, but he really loved Rachel. Rachel could not have children until finally, by God's miracle, Rachel became pregnant and had a little boy named Joseph, Jacob's eleventh son. The other boys did not like Joseph as you recall. Leah had six sons. I can imagine Leah up at night crying saying, "Oh, if only your dad loved me like he loves Rachel." The sons would see their mom cry every night and wish somehow that their dad could love their mom. I can imagine Leah saying, "You know what? He loves Joseph more than he loves you." And so, automatically the boys were jealous. And, as you recall, Jacob was given Bilhah by Rachel to have children,

CHAPTER 8: DOCTRINAL ISSUES—CALVINISM

and two sons were born. Jacob was given Zilpah by Leah to have some more children, and two sons were born.

I can imagine those boys hearing their moms say, "You know what? I'm sick of being treated like a servant. Your dad ought to love me. Your dad doesn't treat you well because he doesn't see us as equal." I can imagine that wore on the boys, and they did not like Joseph either. When Joseph was seventeen, his time had come to learn the family business of keeping sheep. He was learning how to take them to water, take them to pasture, and how to fight off animals. He had to learn how to fight off wild beasts and robbers. Did you hear about that in Oklahoma? Someone's been driving around Oklahoma in the pastures shooting thousands of cows. Did you see that? They have not caught them yet, but that is kind of what Joseph's job was to fight.

When you are a rancher or a cowboy, you cannot work cows by yourself. You need other people; to work sheep, you need more than one person. So, Joseph was sent to work with Bilhah's and Zilpah's sons. Bilhah's sons were Dan and Naphtali. Zilpah's sons were Gad and Asher. These were those from whom Joseph was to learn. Can you imagine? I can just picture them not wanting to work with *that* boy. He's daddy's pet. He's the favorite, and do you not know Joseph had something he had to prove to those brothers? Further, I think Joseph felt this pressure to conform.

When I worked at Level's Food Center in Glen Rose, Texas, I was a Christian. I had been a Christian about two or three years. I worked with some boys who were not Christians. These boys were always trying to get at me. They would feed me beef jerky for dogs, while telling me it was regular jerky. I ate it, and it made me sick. They put Ex-lax in my Dr. Pepper—that was not very funny as you can imagine. They always were trying to pick on me to see if I was as tough as they were. They wanted me to be like them. They tried to get me to eat food that was stolen.

One day Bob Montgomery comes in, "Hey, Johnny, you want some Pringles?" I said, "I love Pringles. Did you buy them?" Bob responded, "Oh, no, I took them off the shelf." I told him that I would not eat them, because they were stolen. To help pacify me, he crushed the can they were in, and said, "You can eat them now, they are not stolen. They were damaged in shipment!" (If food containers sustained damage in shipment, then the store allowed the employees to eat whatever it was.) I told Bob, "No, I am still not going to eat it. It is stolen."

Bob thought it was so funny that I felt so much pressure to do right, but what he did not know was that the pressure to conform was almost as strong. I know a lot of you feel this pressure in your jobs. You feel pressure to conform when you know it is not right. In school, friends want you to do what is wrong. Joseph felt that same pressure to do wrong—to conform, and then one day he caught his brothers doing something really bad. Maybe they were stealing from his dad. Maybe they were cutting their own deal with the flock. We are not sure what they were doing, but he caught them. Joseph had the opportunity to conform, to do what they were doing; that way they would accept him. You know that was a temptation. He also faced the temptation to conceal the act, not to tell Dad.

How many of you, as siblings, have been tempted to tell on each other? You know, that temptation is present to tell, and some commentators on this passage call Joseph a tattletale. They said he should not have told. Well, wait a minute, is it wrong to tell? You know, in our culture, not telling on people is a virtue. I have a relative whose daughter caught another student doing something wrong in school. The deed was really bad, and the principal knew that this daughter saw what happened. The principal brought her in and said, "Now, you need to tell us who did it." Though it was an awful thing, my relative's daughter would not tell. Then they called my relative in and said, "You need to tell your daughter to tell us." And my relative said, with his chest puffed out in great pride, "My daughter ain't no squeal. My daughter ain't no squeal." Of all the virtues one could have, "She ain't no squeal" was his banner? Let me tell you something. Sometimes it is alright to tell. The Bible says this about Joseph. Who were they robbing? His dad. He had an allegiance to his dad. He had a love for his dad. I think Joseph wanted his dad to be protected. So, he told. Joseph had a commitment to what was right. He had to tell, telling was the right thing to do.

If you make an enemy because you do what is right, so be it. I think that Joseph was pretty brave, because I know how brothers are. They probably said, "You tell on me, and I'm gonna rough you up," and yet he told. And the brothers detested him even more. Well, that wasn't enough. Rachel dies giving birth to little Benjamin, Jacob's twelfth son. Jacob finds himself clinging to Joseph all the more. Do you know what Jacob did for Joseph? He made him a real nice coat. It was multi-colored, lots of ornamentation. The coat was beautiful, and the amazing thing was he'd never done that for the other sons. He was playing favorites.

Well, the brothers were furious. They are probably thinking, "I would like to have that coat. How come dad never made me a coat?" And they could not stand it. They could not even talk to him because of it. That coat meant more than just a decoration. I think Jacob was saying, "Joseph's going to get my birthright. He's going to get the double portion of the inheritance. He's going to lead this family. He'll be the priest." And so, the brothers could not stand it.

To add insult to injury, Joseph had a wild dream. He told the boys about his dream. Joseph said, "I dreamed we were all carrying sheaves, brothers, and my sheaves went up to the sky, and your sheaves bowed down to my sheaves." One brother said, "So, you think you are going to rule over us, do you? Loser!" They were sick with jealousy, but you know what God was telling Joseph prophetically? "One day a drought is going to occur, and you are going to need someone to provide for you and I'm going to use Joseph to rescue you." But they did not see it that way. Then Joseph had another dream, and he said, "Guys, come here." You would have thought he had learned his lesson from the first dream. "Come here, guys. I had another dream. I dreamed the sun, moon, and eleven stars all bowed down to me." He even told his dad, and his dad said, "So, son, do you think your mother and I and your brothers are all going to bow to you?" Joseph said, "Yep." Jacob said, "No, no, son, don't say that. You are making people hate you." And yet, Jacob held all of this in his heart, because he knew God often spoke through dreams, but the brothers despised him.

Now we come to a scary thing. Was Joseph predestined to save the family? Well, yes he was. I am in seminary, finishing the work on my doctorate. In my seminary, a big thing is going on about this determinism. Some call it "Extreme Calvinism," while some call it other things. About 10 percent of our Baptist pastors follow this idea. You can be a great Christian, a model Christian, and hold this opinion. I am going to share some things from this passage that deal with this thought. The first thing we look at is the concept of "predestined." Was Joseph predestined to rescue his brothers? You bet he was. We read in Jeremiah, chapter 18, and Romans 9, that the potter can do with the clay whatever he wants. A lot of people have jumped off and said, "Well, that means that God molded some people for hell, and some people for Heaven and there's not much you can do about it." But, the reality is when you look at Jeremiah 18, what God says there is that God's intent for everything He makes is good. In fact, when we read predestination, we realize that it generally always refers to a function, a purpose. For instance, God predestined the Israelites to be the chosen people in their purpose. God predestined Jacob to be in the line of the Messiah. God predestined Joseph to rescue his family. God predestined Paul to rescue and be a witness to the Gentiles. I like what Romans 8, verse 29 says, "For those God foreknew, He also predestined to be conformed in the likeness of His Son." God foreknew.

Now, here is the question: Did God make Joseph good so He could use him, or was Joseph willfully obedient, so God used him? I tend toward the thought that he was obedient, and God foreknew it. Here is another issue about this passage. Should Joseph have told the brothers about his dream? A lot of commentators said he should have been quiet, that his telling the dream to his brothers was bragging or being egotistical. You know, I do not think that is the way he did it. I think what Joseph was doing was telling the truth. Now, a way exists to tell the truth, did you know that?

My friend Joe had an employee he had to fire. His employee would go around and tell his peers that they were terrible workers. When they were offended, he would say "You just need to know that. I'm a Christian, and I've got to tell you the truth." He might tell another peer, "You don't wear good clothes. I am just telling you the truth, I'm a Christian." One day this employee went up to Joe's boss and said, "You know what, Dave? Nobody likes you because you never let anybody else talk to you. I'm a Christian, and I've got to tell you the truth." When Joe's company let that guy go, he asked, "Why? I was just telling the truth." Well, there's a way to tell the truth, and it's always in love, and it should always be in a caring and courteous manner. See, I think Joseph was telling the truth. There was something they needed to know, but, perhaps it was the way he said it.

What's Craig Biggio doing these days? Do you know? He is coaching St. Joseph's High School baseball team. Isn't that cool? I like what Craig Biggio said in a *Houston Chronicle* article the other day. He said, "Kids want to learn to get better, and they want to hear the good things, BUT they've also got to hear the bad things." In fact, he said, "That way we learn how to work hard and do what we're supposed to do."

Jeremiah, chapter 23 says that preachers will come in the last days, and all they'll do is tell their listeners good stuff. They will say, "God wants to bless you. God wants to make you healthy. God wants to give you everything you want, your heart's desire." The thing they omit, Jeremiah says, is they do not tell their hearers that God will not bless their sin. They will not tell them that they have got to turn from that sin.

As I was praying this week, I was shocked to realize that I do not hear preachers these days say that Jesus Christ is coming again. Now, isn't that amazing? I mean, it is the greatest thing that could ever happen. Jesus is coming again, and nobody speaks about it. In fact, when He comes, He will take us to be with Him. I can't wait. And He will bring judgment, and that's why we are so active. We want people to avoid that judgment. We talked this morning in Sunday School about how to witness to one's family. How do you witness to your friends? If you really believe Jesus is coming again, you want them to know. I think Joseph was right in his message, but when he told them, they hated him for it.

Now, Joseph's brothers moved away from Hebron, away from fellowship. They went down to Shechem and to Dothan. Jacob, the dad, had gone so long without hearing from his boys that he thought, "There are dangers out there, and my kids can be lawless. They are often getting into trouble." Jacob needed to send someone to check on the boys. He needed to send someone who would not be tainted by his sons' sins. He needed someone to go who would come back with an honest report. Who do you think he should pick for that? The answer was clear—Joseph. He's already proven true. And so Jacob called Joseph. He said, "Son, I need you to go see your brothers." Without hesitation, Joseph said, "Dad, I'll go."

Joseph realized the dangers. He knew the distance. He knew the difficulties, and you know what else he knew? He knew his brothers hated his guts. Why did he go? Because, he loved his dad so much. When you and I look at doing God's will, it should be easy for us, because we love our Dad so much. So, Joseph goes on a three-day trip. He gets down to Shechem. You remember what happened in Shechem last week? Those boys did some bad stuff, didn't they? Remember, they killed all those people in Shechem. Returning to Shechem was dangerous for them. Someone was probably out looking for them.

Isn't it funny how we always go back to places where we got in trouble? I do not know about you guys. I do that all the time—go to the place where I should not be. The brothers went to Shechem, and then they moved on to Dothan. Joseph is looking for the boys. He's calling, "Hey, brothers—Reuben, Naphtali, Dan. Levi, Judah, hey, where are you?" And he's looking everywhere for his brothers. I think he probably has some lunch for them, and I think he is probably coming with good news, "Brothers, Dad loves you. He sent me to tell you that. Come home!"

As he was looking for his brothers, they were probably down the hill, chewing tobacco and telling dirty jokes. They look up. They see his gait, and he is wearing that ornamented coat. It is like a red cape in front of a charging bull. They were so angry, "Look at Dad's favorite! He's smiling at us. He thinks we're going to be happy to see him. Let's kill him." They begin to plan how to kill Joseph. Thankfully, Reuben steps up and says, "No, no, brothers. Let's not kill him. Let's throw him in an empty well, and leave him there to rot." Reuben's plan was to rescue him later. The brothers said, "Alright. That's a good idea. We'll leave him there to rot."

When Joseph reaches them, they rip his coat off of him. They rip it to shreds, throw him down in the well, and eat his food while he is down in the well screaming and crying, "Help, let me out. This isn't funny." And they are just eating and having a good time. Reuben goes to tend to the sheep. While he is gone, the Ishmaelites come by, headed to Egypt. Judah says, "Let me tell you something, guys. We can sell Joseph as a slave and make money on him, and we'll never see him again. Then we won't have to worry about his dreams anymore." They all agreed. I can imagine, they pull Joseph out of that well. Joseph is shivering and scared. He cannot believe his eyes. Judah says, "Hey, guys, what will you give me for my brother? How about fifty pieces of silver?" And the Ishmaelite says, "No, no, I'll give you five. He's kind of young and scrawny." Gad answers, "No, no, no, not five, forty! He's smart. He's got a big future." The Ishmaelite retorts, "No, I'll give you ten." Asher questions, "ten?" The potential buyer says, "That's fair, he doesn't have a lot of spirit." Naphtali jumps in, "Lot of spirit? You ought to see him at the house. Let's go thirty." The Ishmaelite gives his final offer, "twenty pieces of silver, that's it." And, as Joseph looked on with horror in his eyes, Judah says, "Sold." They sold their brother.

My brother Tracy is four years younger than I am. We were walking down a lane out in the country. We were heading home after getting off the school bus. Mr. Foss lived up on a hill—it was called Woodard Hill, up from our home. That day, I had a friend over. My friend and I started teasing my little brother and dared him to say, "Hey, Mr. Foss, you're a fat pig." That is what we tempted him to do. We said, "Do it, do it, you chicken, do it." And, Tracy did it. He yelled, "Hey, Mr. Foss, you are a fat pig." And you know what I said then? "I'm telling mama." I went, and I told on him. He got a spanking, and my parents took him up to Mr. Foss by the ear, and he had to apologize. I remember that look on his face.

It's the look of Joseph. He couldn't believe his brothers just sold him. As they tied his arms behind that wagon, he cried and he screamed in disbelief the whole way. The boys took the coat, tore it up some more. They killed a goat and put blood on the coat. The brothers took the garment to Jacob and said, "Dad, is this your son, Joseph's coat?" Jacob starts to weep. "That's my boy's coat. He's been killed by animals." He mourned, and he mourned, and he could not be consoled. We read in this chapter something interesting. It says, "And Joseph was sold to Potiphar in Egypt, the head of the command of Pharaoh." Now we are going to get into this in the weeks to come, but what we are going to find is this: God used Joseph.

God allowed him to move up into the kingdom of Egypt, to become second-in-command. When the drought comes, Joseph has a great, God-given plan. We will see that he rescues his family. He rescues all of Egypt, and everyone who will come to Joseph, he rescues. Joseph feeds them; he saves their lives. All they had to do was come to him.

We come to this thing called "God's sovereignty." Did God know what was going to happen to Joseph? God had a plan, did He not? Our God is sovereign. Those who are into the determinism or extreme Calvinism, they hold to the great truth that God is sovereign.

Hebrews 4:13 says this: "Nothing in all creation is hidden from God's sight; everything is uncovered and laid bare before the eyes of Him of Whom we must give an account." Isaiah 46:10 says this: "I made known the end from the beginning, from ancient times, what is still to come. I say my purpose will stand and I will do all that I please." We agree, God knows everything, but now let us look at "hard determinism." What is that? That is a phrase, which means that God pushes the matter. Hard determinism says that all things are caused by God. So, God caused sin. God caused Adam to sin. God caused us to sin. Then, God punishes us for sin, and God sends us to hell for sin. And we think, "Man! God's a monster. We're just play things." Well, that is not true, because Matthew 13:41 says this: "The Son of Man will send out His angels and they will weed out of His kingdom everything that causes sin and all who do evil." Well, if God caused sin, then is Jesus going to throw God out of Heaven? No. So, God must not cause sin.

First John 1:5 says, "This is the message we have heard from Him to declare to you: God is light. In Him there is no darkness at all." So, God does not cause us to sin in His sovereignty. Some other explanation has to exist then for why we fall short. It is called human choice. God gave me the faculty to see. God gave me the faculty to hear. God gave me faculty to speak. God gave me the faculty to choose. Genesis, chapter 2, verse 16: "And the Lord God commanded the man, you are free to eat from any tree in the garden but you must not eat from the tree of the knowledge of good and evil, for when you eat of it, you will surely die." They had a choice. Deuteronomy 30:19-20 says, "This day I call Heaven and earth as a witness against you, that I have set before you life and death, blessing and cursing," now catch this, "now choose life." You and I have a choice, and we can choose to sin against God, or we can choose to follow Him.

Now we go through certain points that follow the deterministic mindset. The first point is one's "total depravity." The extreme Calvinists and the extreme determinists say that you and I are all sinners. Some say "well, God created some good and some bad. Jeremiah 18 says, "All of us were created with good intent." So, we sin against God. We have this sinful nature, and we realize no one is good. Romans 3:12 says, "All have turned away. They have together become worthless. There is no one who does good, not even one." So, then they come across, and we hear this thing that "Yes, we're all dead in sin, but the reality is we are so dead that we cannot respond unless God calls us." And that is exactly right. The Scripture says this in John 6:44, "No one can come to Me unless the Father who sent Me draws him and I will raise him up in the last day." The reality is God calls—we could never be saved if God did not call. God loves you. We could not be saved if God did not love and call us. We would never even consider God without Him.

Okay, we know we cannot be saved unless God calls people. So, let us assume God calls some and does not call others. Calvinists and determinists say that is what Scripture says. No, God's Word does not say that. Acts 17:30 says "In the past God overlooks such ignorance, but now He commands all people everywhere to repent." Jeremiah 7:13 says, "While you were doing all these things declares the Lord, I spoke to you again and again, but you did not listen. I called you, but you did not answer." You see that the reality is, God is calling all men to be saved. We are depraved. We cannot be saved without Him. But He calls.

Then we come to the thing called "unconditional election." Now, when you press that to the extreme, what you find is the belief that some babies, when they die, go to Heaven and some go to hell. Well, that is not true. The reason I can say that is Jesus said this in Matthew 19:14, "Let the little children come to Me and do not hinder them. For the kingdom of Heaven belongs to such as these." When David's son died, David wept. He said, "Oh, oh, my son, my son. I can't bring him back but I can go to him."

CHAPTER 8: DOCTRINAL ISSUES—CALVINISM

We read about the age of accountability. At a certain age, a child has the knowledge to make a decision, and at that point, they are responsible for that decision, for what they do with Christ. Prior to that, they are covered by the mercy of God.

My wife Lori's little brother Danny died. Danny was about four months old when he died. Danny was buried near Galveston. Lori's dad graduated to be with our Lord in 2002. We buried her dad in Memorial Oaks Cemetery in Houston. We decided to move Danny and bury him next to his dad. Lori's mom said, "Johnny, I want you to do the dedication for the burial." As I thought about what to say to the Baklik family, it dawned on me, "Right here are the two ways to Heaven." You get to Heaven if you die before the age of accountability—a baby, for instance. Or, when you reach the age of accountability like Lori's dad, you can receive Christ and go to Heaven.

Think about this, God made us in His image; is that right? My friend Gabriel has six children. Do you think that Gabriel and his wife sat around one day during her first pregnancy and decided, "Let's keep this baby." Then she gets pregnant the second time and they decide, "You know what? Let's kill this one." She gets pregnant again, and they say, "You know what? Let's let this one stay at home with us." They have another and say, "You know what? Let's put this one out on the doorstep, out on the highway." Is this realistic? No. A balanced parent wants to keep all their kids. How much more does the Father long for all created in His image to come to Him?

We read about election, and election is true. Please know, I do not understand everything. I cannot even begin to understand this or so many other attributes of God. None of us do, but Ephesians 1: 4-5 says, "For he chose us in Him before the creation of the world to be holy and blameless." Now, is God's choice of each of us selective in that He chose Tate, yes; but Lori, no? No, He chooses those in Christ. Anyone who is in Christ is a new creation. All things are passed away. John 15:60 says, "You did not choose me, but I chose you and appointed you to bear fruit." Frequently, election deals with purpose. God chose us to be holy. God chose us to witness. An election element is present.

Next is this issue called "limited atonement." That is the belief that Christ did not die for everyone's sins, just some. I mean God only paid for certain ones and certain ones He did not. When Christ died, He only covered some people's sins. That is not what the Scripture says. John 1:29, "The next day John saw Jesus coming toward Him and said, 'Look, the Lamb of God who takes away the sin of the world.'" How about that?

First Timothy 4:10: "That we have put our hope in the living God who is the Savior of all men, especially those who believe." He died for everybody, but only those who receive Him get the benefit. John 2:2 says, "He is the atoning sacrifice for our sins but not only for ours but also for the sins of the world." This is important; Christ died for all of us.

Then we get into this thing called "irresistible grace." That means when God calls, we all have to answer—that none of us can resist God's call. That cannot be true. Look at Jeremiah 11:7-8, which says, "From the time I brought your forefathers up from Egypt until today, I warned them again and again saying, obey me, but they did not listen or pay attention." They were able to resist. Acts 7:51, "You stiff-necked people with uncircumcised hearts and ears, you are just like your fathers. You always resist the Holy Spirit." So, clearly, God's grace is resistible.

Now, why is one-fourth of Genesis written on one guy named Joseph? Well, I'll tell you why. Everywhere you touch Joseph's life, you see Christ. God loved His Son so much, and His Son never wanted to leave His side. His Son was obedient always, and because of the way Christ lived, men hated Him. You know why? Because it made them look bad. They also hated what Christ said, "You're a sinner, come to Me and be saved." And so men moved away from God out of His fellowship away from Hebron, and you know what? The Father said, "I need someone to go to them who will not be tainted by sin who comes back with an honest report." Who do you think He's going to send? Jesus. So, God sent His Son, and Jesus went without hesitation. He knew the dangers, the difficulties, the distances—He knew we would hate Him when He came, but He still came. And Christ saw us in our sins, and He said, "I've got good news, the Father loves you. The Father wants to save you, come home."

You know what we did? We plotted to kill Him. And they sold Him for thirty pieces of silver and crucified Him on the cross. Jesus "came into His own, but His own did not receive him." Sounds like Joseph, does it not? So, Joseph said this at the end of Genesis: "What men meant for evil, God meant for good." When Christ died, He died for our sins. Then God raised Christ to give us eternal life. And true, every knee will bow, and every tongue will confess that Jesus Christ is Lord.

Now, there is something very important for you and I to know. If not everybody can be saved, if the elect have already been chosen, if the nonelect cannot do anything about it, why share the Gospel? See, I believe there is a reason why we pray earnestly for those who are lost. I believe there is a reason why we preach fervently for those who are lost, because with emotion Jesus says in Matthew 23:37, "Oh, Jerusalem, Jerusalem, you kill the prophets. You stone those who are sent to you. How often I've longed to gather your children together but you were not willing."

I like the way God closes Revelation. Revelation 22:17, "The spirit and the bride say, 'Come', let him who hears say, 'Come'. Whoever is thirsty, let them come and whoever wishes, let them come. Take free the gift of the water of life." What a great thing to know. None of us are barred from the opportunity to be saved. God sends His Son, and His Spirit calls you today. If you do not know the Lord as your Savior, no better time than today exists to receive His eternal life.[1]

Lessons

God was faithful. The fears of the ladies and some of the other students were put to rest. The teacher even came and said that he was sorry for the trouble he had brought and would follow the pastor's lead. The pastor is to lead the best he knows how in accordance with how he understands God's Word. At times, the pastor's initial comprehension will be wrong and he must alter it to God's intent. This takes much study and searching. Thorny issues like this may never be settled this side of Heaven, but the pastor must pray and teach as God's Spirit gives him insight with fear and humility.

Spurgeon said that the preacher must always pay close attention to what is being taught in one's church. If there is a chance of a heresy being accepted by them, the preacher must quickly prepare a sermon, which, by God's grace, will slay the plague.[2] He said that preaching must "set the forests of error on fire."[3] This is what these last two sermons did. The leader of the church must attempt to deal with doctrinal disagreements on a personal basis, but when that does not work, or when such teaching spreads throughout the church, he must go to the pulpit for the health and well-being of the body. Scripture proves this out. Paul wrote in 1 Corinthians 5:6, "Do you not know that a little leaven leavens the whole lump of dough"?

I preach straight through Bible books in general. I lack the creativity to come up with novel and intriguing series. A comfort exists in preaching through a book. It means, corporately, my music minister knows what I am going to preach each Sunday, so he can plan our music. More in-depth, it

1. Johnny Teague, "Things a Son Would Do (Genesis 37)," January 20, 2008.
2. Spurgeon, *Lectures to My Students*, 88.
3. Ibid., 79.

means I will cover whatever God brings in His text no matter how hard or controversial. The amazing part of this situation is that I did not have to change our study to address the doctrinal crisis. I also did not have to bend the Scripture to fit some purpose. Never is that acceptable anyway. I was preaching through Genesis, and on that very Sunday, I got to the topic of Joseph and his brothers. God is wonderful. He brought a collision at the intersection of time. The Word of God collided with the crisis of the day.

The preacher's responsibility is to allow God's Word to shed light on a belief through him. That is not always easy. It may be drop-kicking a hornet's nest, but it is necessary. The preacher needs to anticipate questions that may arise from the doctrinal teaching and attempt to answer that question while there.[4] This will bring a more complete, comprehensive covering of the issue.

Legitimacy must be given to some beliefs, in that the preacher can explain how it is understandable why one could hold to a particular view. The goal of the message is not to win an argument so that we can show ourselves great. The purpose is to teach God's Word in a way that the listener can see the benefit of right belief. The preacher must love God's Word, because it is from the ultimate object of his love—God. Additionally, he must love the hearer, because he has been commanded to love, because he wants to love, and because he was first loved.[5]

---

4. Lotz, "Preaching on Controversial Issues," 41.
5. Pearson, "Sheep, Serpents and Doves," 16.

Chapter 9: The Sins of the Church

They pulled up in a twenty-year-old, dirty, rusted maroon station wagon, loaded down with no-telling-what on the inside, just barely room for the three of them to fit. Upon exiting from the car unkempt hair was revealed, along with skin suffering from tiny bites from the fleas that permeated the rotted floor of their dilapidated old trailer house. All three were overweight. She was a fifty-something-year-old single mom. The daughter was about fifteen, the son about twelve. When they spoke, it was apparent that all three had major learning disabilities. When the church served potluck meals, the mom always brought something, but everyone, knowing their struggle with cleanliness issues, was hesitant to eat their food. However, two things were certain—they were loving and they were faithful.

The young boy's name was Rheinart. He was a handful. Often during church, he would bark like a dog. Inevitably, his mom would get on him, chastising him in her whisper, which was a normal speaking voice to most everyone else. He would continue to bark. Then she would grab him to take him out of the sanctuary, and he would start to shout, "Mamma gonna hit me, Mamma gonna hit me!" Every Sunday, the same routine ensued. I was able to get them to sit near the back so that if she had to take her son out, the distraction would be lessened. A few in the church joined us in loving them and helping them with coping and social skills.

However, the majority of our members resented their presence. Many times, members called me for a meeting. I would be told that this family simply must act right or not come back. My answer to each was, "God loves them, and we must too. They do not know how to act and they are hard to teach, but God has brought them here." Many took it upon themselves to visit with them in an ugly way. Over and over, certain members meted out ultimatums, but this family always returned to me for reassurance that we loved them and that this church wanted them. Over time, the mom got a better handle on the boy. The daughter always was good, sweet, and quiet. Still, many members just absolutely resented this family.

Constantly, I had this family in mind when I preached to our members about loving one another. One year, I was so determined that our Lord needed to change this attitude in our church that I put in bold letters on the front of every church bulletin the Scripture, Ephesians 4:32: "Be kind to one another, tender-hearted, forgiving each other, just as God in Christ also has forgiven you". I even arrived at the point that before I preached, I had the church recite this verse with me aloud. I was probably preaching through Matthew at the time, and had many opportunities to show how Jesus dealt with people. The crowds that met Jesus near the Sea of Galilee were a lot like our people. Though some had not changed, many of our members began to develop a heart for this family.

Then came the day I received the phone call. Rheinart had died. He choked on a big piece of meat. His sweet mom saw him struggling, but had no idea what to do. Right at the dinner table in that dilapidated old flea-infested trailer, Rheinart died with his mom and sister watching. She called me that evening to let me know, and asked me to do the funeral. I told her that I would, of course. I visited with her several times before the funeral.

At the funeral, I expected very few people. You see, not only had some of our church members not been real friendly, this precious family of three was treated poorly by their neighbors and their own family because they were different and because they were easy to mock and humiliate. When I pulled up to the church, the parking lot was full. Every seat in the sanctuary was full with standing-room only. In that church were our precious members, many who had come a long way in loving this family. They were truly broken.

In our church were those who had resented this family, and now they sat in the audience broken for the way they had acted. In that church, were neighbors and family who had ridiculed these three. In the sanctuary were teachers of Rheinart's special education classes, therapists, and social workers who had worked with this boy. The message came from Matthew 18:1-6,

> At that time the disciples came to Jesus and said, " Who then is greatest in the kingdom of heaven?" And He called a child to Himself and set him before them, and said, "Truly I say to you, unless you are converted and become like children, you will not enter the kingdom of heaven. "Whoever then humbles himself as this child, he is the greatest in the kingdom of heaven. "And whoever receives one such child in My name receives Me; but whoever causes one of these little ones who believe in Me to stumble, it would be better for him to have a heavy millstone hung around his neck, and to be drowned in the depth of the sea.

And Matthew 18:10, "See that you do not despise one of these little ones, for I say to you that their angels in heaven continually see the face of My Father who is in heaven". At the end of the service and the following week, our church changed. Some rejoiced that God had given them the opportunity to minister to this family. Others were those who had been difficult with this family, but were now resolved never to be that way again. All rejoiced that our church had never given up on this family.

What is this story all about? The story is about sin in the congregation. It is about the need for the church to be refined. It is about the journey that a pastor leads his church through as God sanctifies them through His Word and through the events His sovereignty brings. A church is composed of sinners. Some are lost sinners, and the rest are saved sinners, but all are sinners. The sermon moment each Sunday is where the flint of human hurt caused by sin strikes a spark on the steel of divine revelation found in God's Word.[1] To avoid the sins of the church for fear some will believe the preacher is "picking" on them is easy. One way to avoid that temptation is to preach through a book systematically. In this way, one addresses sin, but no one can accuse the preacher of a deliberate attack from the pulpit. Rather, they can know what the sermon text was the previous week, and they can know where the sermon text will go the next week.

Thus, the people are not given any other explanation than that which was addressed is God's view of the subject. Dietrich Bonhoeffer said that a leader who "allows himself to succumb to the wishes of those he leads, who will seek to turn him into their idol. . . . This is the leader who makes an idol of himself and his office and who thus mocks God."[2] Many pulpits are guilty of this today. The one who stands behind the pulpit desires to be held in high esteem among the people. He will cater to their wants instead of standing behind the Word of God and allowing God to deal with whom He will deal and comfort whom He will comfort.

Many contemporary parents desire to be their kids' "friends" instead of embracing their rightful role as parents. The result is a double-negative. The parents end up lacking respect, and their children end up being uncontrollable. Thus, it is with the church. The preacher must love the members enough to bring the full counsel of the Word without hesitation or watering it down.

The church is laden with sin. Mac Brunson and Ergun Caner did a masterful job of identifying the sins that characterize different believers who attend church each week. Some are gossips, and some are grumblers. Some are nearsighted or farsighted when it comes to church vision. Some,

---

1. Tucker, *Primer for Parents*, 73.
2. Gordon MacDonald, "Speaking into the Crisis," in *Great Preaching—Practical Advice from Powerful Preachers*, ed. Paul Woods (Loveland, CO: Group Publishing, 2003), 44.

because of their neglect, are dried-up springs who live off their past righteousness. Some attend the business meetings just to be difficult. Some are the hardhearted who never allow God's Spirit to move them on Sunday. Still others have problems with bitterness and jealousy, while some in the church grapple with forgiveness. They are like Sigmund Freud who said, "One must forgive one's enemies but not before they have been hanged."[3]

Some attending think they are the most righteous people in the world, and definitely the most righteous in the church. Some are never happy with what occurs; no mountain is ever high enough. Some are just plain needy. They have to speak about some issue with the pastor every day, or they just do not feel they can cope. Some are great workers, but they get disheartened quickly because, in their opinion, no one else is working. Some are perfectionists. They desire people to help, but the people who do help never seem to meet their standards. Some are timid and wear their feelings on their sleeves, while others do not know God's Word, do not want to know God's Word, and they reject what He says. With that said, they still like being in church. Others are those who seem to have the gift of discouragement, while still others sit waiting to be offended.[4]

Pastor beware! Sins are rampant in the church. Worldliness, covetousness, prayerlessness, wrath, pride, slander, lust, lying, and the like do not take long to sweep into the heart of a church.[5] The church should be a light to the world around it; instead, it often reflects the world. In the church, a businessman is accustomed to employees obeying his commands and expects the same at church. In the church, a woman feels worthless and loathsome, so she projects this negative view onto her church. A laborer in the church is faithful, but has big issues with authoritative figures which results in his unwillingness to follow direction.[6]

Each of these must be addressed through preaching. Never forget that each problem is a spiritual one.[7] The preacher must deal with the spiritual problem by speaking to the sins of the businessman, of the single mom, and of the laborer. He is to deal with the temptations of the times and the needs of the age.[8] The preacher must take the needs of the church in one hand, and the Bible in the other and bring the two together by means of

---

3. Powell, *Basic Bible Sermons*, 18.

4. Brunson and Caner, *Why Churches Die*, these "types" come throughout the book, specifically 17-201.

5. Spurgeon, *Lectures to My Students*, 87.

6. Gunnink, *Preaching for Recovery*, 48-50.

7. Brunson and Caner, *Why Churches Die?*, 205.

8. Spurgeon, *Lectures to My Students*, 79.

the spoken word.⁹ He serves the position of the priest to stand between God and man, bringing man's pain to God and God's message to man. God's messenger, who is sent to speak to the sins of the church, should try to walk with these people and observe their needs, rather than guess at them from a distance. At times, this discovery requires no real research. The people are shouting their needs.[10]

At times, even with the best gift of discernment, the messenger cannot decipher the complexities that are presented. That is the beauty of God's Word. The preacher does not have to find the text. The text will find him.[11] As a result, with each text that a pastor is led to preach, he should look deep into the text and consider, "What was the purpose that the Holy Spirit had in mind when He led me to this passage?" Truly, the Bible assures its reader that every passage has its purpose.[12] The preacher may see the text as completely irrelevant to his congregation. The preacher should preach it anyway. He would be surprised to learn what lies out among those pews. All he has to do is let the text root out the sin, confront it, and offer deliverance. The Bible brings solutions; this is why people come to church—they want solutions to their life's drama. Preaching simply has to allow God to speak through His Word. Allow God to carry the weight of correction. Only He can change the heart.

To be used of God in dealing with the sins of the people places the preacher in a fine group of servants. Amos addressed oppression, materialism, injustice, and prostitution. Malachi dealt with divorce and tithing.[13] Paul dealt with sexual immorality, legalism, and pre-Gnostic thought. Moses dealt with idolatry and faithlessness. Jesus dealt with hypocrisy, the heart of sin, the need of deliverance, and salvation. These used different approaches. Sometimes they addressed the sin head-on, no candy-coating. Other times, they laid before the listeners an innocent story about somebody else, which packed a punch at the realization that the innocent story encapsulated their own sin (i.e. Nathan with David's sin of adultery).[14] God leads the method, often determined by adhering to the text.

---

9. Gunnink, *Preaching for Recovery*, 69.
10. Ibid., 75.
11. Tucker, *Primer for Preachers*, 54.
12. Chapell, "Fallen-Condition," 29.
13. Gunnink, *Preaching for Recovery*, 55.
14. Ibid., 60.

Situation

Mike Robertson pastored a church that struggled with its finances. They had trouble meeting their bills, payroll, annuity contributions, and so forth. Additionally, they had difficulty planning, because they never seemed to know where they were financially. Their business administrator controlled the money, and he kept a tight rein on it, almost with the strength of a dictator selectively giving out information. He literally controlled the church through the avenue of money. You see it coming, do you not?

This business administrator was more than a paid staff member. He had worked his way up through the church from a member to a deacon to a staff position. The church had given him that position, because he had earned the trust of the people through the years. In addition, he was a lightning rod for the people with the previous pastor. He helped lead the charge to remove this pastor due to "ethical" issues. He said he just felt this church deserved better leadership than it was receiving. To no surprise, he had gained honor in the sight of the people through this.

The church called Mike to be their pastor. As he began to wrap his hands around the financial crisis, the church reached a point where many realized this business administrator might be the root of some of their challenges. When enough people began to be enlightened, the church was able to move him to a strict pastoral care position, but even in this position, he continued to meddle in the finances, especially through the treasurer. The church moved to a new location. Mike began a series of sermons in the book of Joshua. The previous Sunday, he preached about the victory of Jericho. The next pericope up was the defeat of the Israelites at Ai.

Sermon

Mike Robertson

"Valley of Trouble"

Joshua 7

Only in the Cross do we understand that on some days only great defeat seems to be present; and yet, that day brings great victory. The Cross teaches us in the midst of unbearable pain, Christ won a battle for us that we could not win on our own. The lesson is that no enemy will be able to withstand defeat by our Lord God Almighty. Indeed, my friend, we are taught that times come in life when we will experience great victory. As disciples of the Lord Jesus Christ, we must understand how to attain that victory and to live in the glory of it, as we did last week when we talked about the Israelites conquering Jericho. My friends, we learned that it is not about methodology; rather, it is all about theology, and God wants to show us incredible greatness in the midst of troubled times and in glorious times as well. Today, we are going to look at a different passage of Scripture and connect the dots. Right in these verses in chapter 7 of Joshua, the people of Israel faced their first massive defeat. After having attained this incredible victory in their life and walk with Jesus Christ, they were learning that; indeed, in the moments of great victory, defeat can occur.

I want to present this picture to you today, because you are going to need to know how to have victory in times of your troubles. You are going to need to know how to have victory over your times of trouble as you walk with Jesus Christ. You must have that engrained solidly in your minds today. Thus, as you look at the passage of Scripture today, I want you to connect the story here. Joshua and the Israelites had just finished forty years of wandering in the wilderness. They just spent all this time learning what putting one foot in front of the other meant, simply trusting every day for God to provide, or else they would perish. Scripture says that the whole time they wandered, their shoes never wore out; they were never without food in the mornings, they were never without quail at night, and they always found water.

God cared for them, and shadowed over them at all times. They learned obedience through a test of adversity for forty years. They stepped into the Promised Land, and their first victory experienced in Jericho threw them another test—a test of prosperity. For the very first time in their lives, they had won a victory! This was the first time they had seen anything like this before, and right in front of them stood the collapsed wall of Jericho. Every one of them just walked right in and conquered the city, but in the midst of that great conquering, a great defeat happened as well. Joshua, chapter 7 records that story for us, so if you are in Joshua, would you stand with me as we read these verses together.

> But the Israelites acted unfaithfully in regard to the devoted things; Achan son of Carmi, the son of Zimri, the son of Zerah, of the tribe of Judah, took some of them. So the Lord's anger burned against Israel. Now Joshua sent men from Jericho to Ai, which is near Beth

Aven to the east of Bethel, and told them, "Go up and spy out the region." So the men went up and spied out Ai. When they returned to Joshua, they said, "Not all the people will have to go up against Ai. Send two or three thousand men to take it and do not weary all the people, for only a few men are there." So about three thousand men went up; but they were routed by the men of Ai, who killed about thirty-six of them. They chased the Israelites from the city gate as far as the stone quarries and struck them down on the slopes. At this, the hearts of the people melted and became like water. Then Joshua tore his clothes and fell face down to the ground before the ark of the Lord, remaining there till evening. The elders of Israel did the same, and sprinkled dust on their heads. And Joshua said, "Ah, Sovereign Lord, why did you ever bring this people across the Jordan to deliver us into the hands of the Amorites to destroy us? If only we had been content to stay on the other side of the Jordan! O Lord, what can I say, now that Israel has been routed by its enemies? The Canaanites and the other people of the country will hear about this and they will surround us and wipe out our name from the earth. What then will you do for your own great name?" The Lord said to Joshua, "Stand up! What are you doing down on your face? Israel has sinned; they have violated my covenant, which I commanded them to keep. They have taken some of the devoted things; they have stolen, they have lied, they have put them with their own possessions. That is why the Israelites cannot stand against their enemies; they turn their backs and run because, they have been made liable to destruction. I will not be with you anymore unless you destroy whatever among you is devoted to destruction. "Go, consecrate the people. Tell them, 'Consecrate yourselves in preparation for tomorrow; for this is what the Lord, the God of Israel, says: That which is devoted is among you, O Israel. You cannot stand against your enemies until you remove it.'" In the morning, present yourselves tribe by tribe. The tribe that the Lord takes shall come forward clan by clan; the clan that the Lord takes shall come forward family by family; and the family that the Lord takes shall come forward man by man. He who is caught with the devoted things shall be destroyed by fire, along with all that belongs to him. He has violated the covenant of the Lord and has done a disgraceful thing in Israel'!" Early the next morning Joshua had Israel come forward by tribes, and Judah was taken. The clans of Judah came forward, and he took the Zerahites. He had the clan of the Zerahites come forward by families, and Zimri was taken. Joshua had his family come forward man by man, and Achan son of Carmi, the son of Zimri, the son of Zerah, of the tribe of Judah, was taken. Then Joshua said to Achan, "My son, give glory to the Lord, the God of Israel, and give him the praise. Tell me what you have done; do not hide it from me." Then Joshua said to Achan, "My son, give glory to the Lord, the God of Israel, and give him the praise. Tell me what you have done; do not hide it from me." Achan replied, "It is true! I have sinned against the Lord, the God of Israel. This is what I have done: When I saw in the plunder a beautiful robe from Babylonia, two hundred shekels of silver and a wedge of gold weighing fifty shekels, I coveted them and took them. They are hidden in the ground inside my tent, with the silver underneath." So Joshua sent messengers, and they ran to the tent, and there it was, hidden in his tent, with the silver underneath. They took the things from the tent, brought them to Joshua and all the Israelites and spread them out before the Lord. Then Joshua, together with all Israel, took Achan son of Zerah, the silver, the robe, the gold wedge, his sons and daughters, his cattle, donkeys and sheep, his tent and all that he had, to the Valley of Achor. Joshua said, "Why have you brought this trouble on us? The Lord will bring trouble on you today." Then all Israel stoned him, and after they had stoned the rest, they burned them. Over Achan they heaped up a large pile of rocks, which remains to this day. Then the Lord turned from his fierce anger. Therefore that place has been called the Valley of Achor ever since."

Father God, today there are times when your children are in trouble, and Father Lord, today, teach us carefully how to have victory in a time of trouble. It is in Christ's name we pray. Amen.

Thank you for standing during that rather long reading. I want you to understand today that there are ways you can tell that you are in trouble. Turn your attention to the screen, for those of you that drive, this might be an indication to you that you are in trouble. We do not know who the driver is of this vehicle. We assume they might be in the water this very minute. The next one, for those of you who do not drive, this is a good indication to you that you might be in trouble. I do not know how you solve that problem, but it looks like gravity is going to have its toll on that little mule before much longer.

Perhaps you wonder, "Brother Mike, I don't relate to cars very well, but what about Sunday School?" I want to read to you a top ten list of things that if you hear while teaching Sunday School class, you might be in trouble. These are actual recordings of actual children in Sunday School classes. The first one said, "Noah's wife was called Joan of Arc; Lot's wife was a pillar of salt by day, but a ball of fire by night; the Egyptians were all drowned in the dessert; Moses went up on Mount Cyanide and got the ten amendments; the first command was when Eve told Adam to eat the apple; the seventh commandment is 'Thou shall not ADMIT adultery'; Moses died before he ever reached Canada; then Joshua led the Hebrews in the battle of Geritol; Solomon, one of David's sons had three hundred wives and seven hundred porcupines; Jesus annunciated the Golden Rule which says 'to do one to others before they do one to you'. If you are teaching a Sunday School class today, and teachers, the children in your class come back with those answers, you might be in trouble.

Church, I want you to know today that there are times when we, as we walk with Jesus, will have great moments of victory. However, it is often in the victory that we fail the test of prosperity. For the first time in their entire remembered existence, the Israelites here in this chapter face prosperity. They had been slaves, and then they had been wanderers, and now they were in the land, and before them was a valley, a valley of trouble. While they were conquering this great and mighty city, one of their men named Achan (his name means "troubler") took something that he should not have from the Canaanites in the city of Jericho (or Geritol—however you want to say it). In chapter 6, verse 18, he stole what is known as the accursed thing. What that simply means is that things were being used in the city of Jericho for pagan worship. God told the people, "When you go into the city, guys, you can't take anything with you. You can take the silver and the gold if you want, but you cannot take anything with you that is accursed or has been

CHAPTER 9: THE SINS OF THE CHURCH

used in the worship of other gods. You are to destroy that completely, one hundred percent."

However, Achan, the troubler of Israel, in Israel's victory saw among their things beautiful ornaments, beautiful silver and gold. He wanted and coveted these for his very own. So in verse 18 of chapter 6, after he had been warned by God, "and you by all means abstain" (abstain that means leave it alone), "abstain from the accursed things unless you become accursed when you take of those accursed things and make the camp of Israel accursed and trouble it." God's ability to see things in front of us is amazing, is it not? He saw that the Israelites needed a good solid warning not to get involved in the idol worship that faced them in the land of Jericho. Thus, He warned them, "Guys there are some things in that city that you are not to mess with, period, end of story. If you do so, you yourself may become a curse and trouble the whole nation." Chapter 7, verse 1 of this passage tells us that after this mighty victory, the people did not know how to handle it.

Prosperity tripped them up, and made them fall on their faces. Prosperity made them stop being serious about obedience, and it caught up with them in verse 1 of chapter 7. Prosperity lists Achan and his family line, and the records says that he troubled Israel when he himself took of what was forbidden, the gold and the silver and the things that were accursed and used to worship foreign gods. They could take the gold and silver, but not the things that were used in foreign worship to foreign gods. Thus, through one man's sin, the whole nation fell. And so I want you to see very first in your outline today, that you and I, we never sin alone. When you sin, it affects other people's lives. Most often, and by clear implication of this story, it affects those people that you love the most and are closest to first. It hurts them above all else. Other people may not even know what some other individual's sin in this room might be, but that individual's wife knows, his kids know, his close family knows what is going on in their lives, and they are the ones that take the brunt of this.

Do you understand that, as we go through times of trouble, we must comprehend the serious nature of sin in our lives? We must understand that God does not treat it lightly when we have stumbled and missed the mark. In fact, I want you to understand from the passage that you guys just read, two definitions of sin are present in this passage. One you see listed, means to miss the mark. They were supposed to adhere to a standard, and they were aiming at it, but they missed it. They did not hit true center; they missed the mark. The other in verse 1 tells us that a trespass had been committed, an unfaithful act that had taken place deliberately, crossing over God's line.

I want you to know something very clearly. This one man's sin cost the entire nation their victory that day. What a sad thing it is in our day, and in our time, for people to think that for just one itty-bitty instant that they could do wrong against God and not affect anyone else around them. Somehow, they get the idea that they can do whatever they want to do, and it does not affect the church where they come to worship on a Sunday morning. I want you to understand something; we are affected, because if you are not right with God, corporately WE cannot be right with God. I have to tell you something, that is the way it has always been in Scripture, and it is the way it will always be in God's church.

How do I know that? Well, another man, thousands and thousands of years ago, made a mistake, a mistake that you and I are still living with to this very day, and his name was Adam. Adam made a mistake; he deliberately trespassed and walked over a clear line that God had set out for him, and in doing so, you and I inherited the curse that was placed upon him. The seriousness of sin was put inside of our nature. Even to this day, we do not need to teach anybody to miss the mark; you do not need to teach your children how to cross a line that you have set clearly for them. They will learn that all on their own. Amen? Because it is already inside of them, you are going to have to teach them dear church, and dear mothers and fathers and grandparents, you are going to have to teach them to walk right. You are going to have to teach them to live righteously. You are going to have to teach them the importance of living in obedience to Almighty God. You are going to have to teach them that, but you do not have to teach them to be wrong, because inside of them, there is a nature towards it, and then we get pretty good at practicing it, do we not?

We are even able to do it and put on a mask as if we are not doing it, you all nod your head. We somehow get to show in our everyday walk a small smidgen of hypocrisy, don't we? We all carry a mask around with us and, indeed, it is not an unclear thing in this passage of Scripture. Achan, for his one hidden sin, almost destroyed an entire nation. The sin entered his eye and sunk deep into his heart. The sin was carried out by his hand, and he hid the whole event from the rest of the people of Israel. Sin's specific conviction always comes to those who walk away from God. Follow the story for a minute with me as we look at this chapter in particular.

The way I understand it, the first thing that happened was that a defeat occurred. The men of Israel saw that Ai was a small town, and they said let's not all go, let's just send a small group of people there, and we'll take the town that way. So go, let's do it! So, they sent three thousand. Thirty-six men were returned home dead, and they said that's not high casualties, but in Joshua's eyes any casualty is a casualty, an indication if you will that God was no longer with them. They suffered this massive defeat. Joshua is broken. Joshua is mourning. Joshua in his heart is just completely unsure of what has happened. He does not know what is going on or how to process what he just lived through. In these verses, God tells him, "Hey Joshua, what are you doing with your face on the ground? Get up, there is a problem, and I'll tell you what it is Joshua. Someone inside the nation of Israel has sinned. They have taken of the accursed things." By the way, that phrase is said seven times in this passage, "accursed things."

"Someone's taken it, and I'm going to show you who. Tomorrow I want all the people to come before Me, the whole nation, tribe-by-tribe, and I'll pick a tribe. Then all of the families of the tribe will come before Me, and I'll pick a family. Then all of the individual leaders of the families will come before Me, and I'll pick a leader for you." And when it was all said and done, one man named Achan was left, and he knew exactly what he had done wrong because God through Joshua says, "Tell us what you did." And he describes in accurate detail exactly what he did; he knew exactly what it was. I want to tell you something—that is a real good test whether or not you are walking with God or you are in the valley of trouble guilty. A good test for knowing if you are guilty or not is when God narrowly, specifically convicts you.

People tell me, "Why Brother Mike you stepped on my toes today." Well, I understand that phrase, and let me tell you something—I was aiming for your heart. Amen? I pray the Lord God Almighty, even in this room; He'll aim for your heart. I believe God always is accurate when He gets to convicting His children. Amen? A whole lot of people sit in churches like this under the conviction of false guilt. My friend, that is something I do not want you to think about today. If God is unpleased with you, He is going to be very specific about what you have done wrong, very specific. He is telling you right now. He may have said it three or four months ago, and you did not do anything about it. He will just keep bringing it back to you until your heart is so calloused that you are not listening to Him anymore.

"Brother Mike, is there a difference between what happens to a believer when he sins and what happens to an unbeliever when he sins?" Well the answer is: "yes, there is a difference." When a person who does not believe in Jesus Christ sins, there is punishment that comes upon their life. What I mean is their sin is recorded in a book in Heaven, and it stays there. But, when you become a believer, my friends, God takes your name, and He takes your name from the books and all of the account of it, and He blots out all the stuff you did wrong. He just takes a big ink blotter, if you will; you cannot see it anymore, it is gone. God blots it out through the blood of the Lord Jesus Christ. And in that blotting-out process, He takes your name, and He transposes it to another book—the Lamb's Book of Life, where it stays forever. And you as a Christian in the Lamb's Book of Life WILL sin, you are going to make mistakes, you are going to get into the valley of trouble. It is going to happen to you, but those things that you have done, past and present and future, have already been blotted out by God when you trusted Him as Savior and Lord, and they are gone. Is that not good guys? That is what the cross did for us, that is shouting ground for the Christian today. I do not have to face the punishment of my sin anymore, but those without Christ have to face the punishment of their sin. What a dreadful thing it is, indeed, for that to happen.

We never sin alone. No matter what, we hurt people, and it is almost always the people who are closest to us first. The second thing you need to see here in these verses today is that when we sin, when we are in the valley of trouble, we lose God's power and presence. Thirty-six casualties were inflicted by just a few people from Ai. For the Promised People in the Promised Land not to have victory was wrong. It was not right. It should have been a victorious day, but because of one man's sin, the power of the children of Israel was completely evaporated, and thirty-six men died in that one day in that one battle. That they should lose the power of God was the tragedy of all tragedies in Joshua's eyes.

They just saw the city of Jericho fall down flat before them, and now they cannot stand before a weak few. Sin will do that; it will zap you of your spiritual strength, and you will wonder what happened to it. You wonder what is wrong, you wonder why you cannot hear God anymore, and you wonder why you cannot see Him moving anymore. It is because sin has zapped your power! "Brother Mike, I'm not a charismatic person, and

I do not believe in charismatic theology. Are you teaching us that today?" No. I am teaching you that the Spirit of God wants to fill you today, and when you are filled as a believer, the Holy Spirit's power in your life is strong for tearing down strongholds. In that condition, you can put the weapons of warfare upon you and stand against the schemes of the devil in victory, but when we sin, we lose God's power.

It is like one of these fans that is blowing behind me, somebody reaches up here and pulls the plug. The fan is still here, you are still here, it still looks like a fan, it still smells like a fan, it still sits in the place the fan always sits; but, I have to tell you something my friends, it is no longer doing any good! A whole lot of Christians are like that, unplugged to the power, because sin in their life has pulled them free from the presence of Almighty God.

I want you to see what verse twelve says. God tells Joshua one of the scariest things that I have ever seen about this passage of Scripture. "Therefore," verse twelve, "the children of Israel could not stand." They could not stand anymore. Their power was gone. They had incredible power. The Red Sea stopped up in front of them and divided; the Jordan River, for twenty-five miles, dried up; the city of Jericho fell down flat! I am going to tell you something, if we had that kind of victory in Baptist churches, we would have program after program exalting the power to pull the Red Sea apart. That's power. But this verse says that they could not stand; they lost their power. It happens to you. It happens to me. They turned their backs before their enemies, and it said that they had become doomed to destruction. God tells him, second part of verse twelve, "Neither will I be with you anymore."

Yep, that is the story of the Bible. You see a man and a woman named Adam and Eve walked in the cool of the day with God Almighty, their Creator, and there they had intimate and perfect fellowship in the presence of Almighty God. Not fellowship like potluck dinner fellowship, but about fellowship of the soul, fellowship of the heart and the mind, fellowship that was pure and innocent and sweet and powerful and joyful beyond all measure, but then they sinned. And God took Adam and Eve away from His presence, and He blocked the gate into the garden so they could no longer come into God's presence again. You see, that is exactly what death is, separation from God's power. The Bible tells us that the wages of our sin, what we earn justly from sinning, is death. And really, a great definition of death in that verse is simply to be separated from God. When those without

Christ die, they are separated from Jesus for eternity. They live on physically and spiritually, but they do not live in the presence of God anymore. Heaven is the presence of God. That is what we need today, my friends, as do churches all over the world today, the powerful presence of God.

"Brother Mike, I need my friends here in this place, I need their presence." Good, I need you, I need the staff, I need the choir, and I need the sound guy. I want you to know something, more than anything else, my friends; we need the presence of God here. Because it really does not matter if you come to this place to meet me or anybody else in this room; it matters if you come to this place to meet God. A whole lot of people in the valley of trouble have caused trouble to the whole body of Christ, until the presence of God is removed in a very tragic way; and so we just continue. Sometimes we just go on, and we do not even know it. All the while God is telling us, "Get up! There is a problem amongst you, and I am going to put my finger on it right now." You know, in these verses, it is very, very clear that God quickly tells them what is wrong. "There is something wrong amongst you." The tragic thing that I see here is that they lose God's power and presence. I do not want to lose it, Church! We cannot lose it! I will not lead a church away from Him. I will not allow us to turn our eyes blindly from little small sins, because it affects us all. That cannot happen. We must have God's power and presence.

Last, in your outline I want you to understand, we never sin alone, we lose God's power and presence, and this is important guys; we lose life itself. Thirty-six dead in this story, Achan himself dead, his wife, his sons, his daughters dead; all his possessions, donkey, sheep everything dead; this story is about someone losing their life. Does Achan repent in these verses? This is one of the questions I ask myself, in verse twenty. Is he really repentant? If so, why did God take his life? The answer is no, I do not think he repented, and I will show you why. He does say, "I have sinned," but he does not admit that the things he had taken are accursed; he does not do that. He says, "God, I sinned," but nowhere in here does he admit that the thing itself taken was idol worship.

He coveted these things and did not admit to coveting these things. He himself did not, in this verse at all, give any idea that he was disgraced or shamed about what he had done. He admitted that he sinned, but he was not ashamed. I want you to understand what the word confession means in Scripture—that you say exactly what God says about your sin, that you agree with His estimation of what you are dealing with and the trouble you have entered, that you say to God "I know what I have done not only is a sin but it is a disgraceful thing that I have done," that you confess and say and agree with God of the deplorable nature of your actions, that you tell him you are completely wrong and that He is completely right, that you submit yourself to His righteousness, and you say to Him, "God I know that not only have I walked across a line, that when I walked across that line, it brought disgrace to Your Name. Nowhere in here does Achan say, "Guys, I am sorry for seeing thirty-six of my friends die." He does not repent of that so, therefore, his repentance, in my opinion, is shallow and false.

A lesson to us today, I want you to understand something, that when God gets on you, He expects you to agree completely with His estimation of your sin. Completely submit to His definition of right and wrong, and say, "God, I am wrong, and it has hurt and destroyed my life and people's lives all around me!" Achan did not do that, so he did not, in my opinion, confess it to God like he should have; and, as a result, he faced punishment. He had been warned. He had been warned more than once not to touch the accursed things, not to be an idol worshiper. That was the issue with that beautiful Babylonian garment that he just could not take his eyes off of, and the silver and the gold he stole that he wanted for his very own. It is recorded that he put it amongst his own stuff, and he hid it.

Do you ever notice that? When people are wrong, they often try to hide their sin. Have you ever had a child that you knew wrote a nice little letter to you with crayons on the wall of your house, and while they came with the crayon tucked in their back pocket, they came to you and said to you "I do not know who did that"? They try to hide that particular transgression; they might even take that crayon and throw it in the trash just to make sure. "We do not even have that color crayon Mom, it does not even exist Dad. I know it is red there; we do not have red. I do not know who did it, maybe the mystery bandit did it and wrote it on the wall."

When I grew up, I had two brothers. The best thing that I ever learned was to blame them for the stuff that I did, because when we are wrong, we try to hide it, don't we? Most of the times, we do not know we have done wrong, and we do not try to hide it. When we know we are wrong, it is different. As Achan did, he knew he was wrong, so he covered it over. He dug a hole, literally, in the midst of his tent, and he covered it over. They went, and they dug it up, and they brought it out for all of Israel to see. And there it was, his guilt lying before him, and they took his life.

Well is it fair? We are going to take the life of his whole family. I asked myself that question. I have struggled pretty hard with it, and here is the answer I believe. They lost their lives, because some way somehow, God is tying the fact that they knew what was going on, and they themselves were guilty likewise. They knew what was happening. They saw what he did; you cannot hide gold in a tent with fifteen people, can you? They knew about it you all. They knew about it, so they tried to hide it also. So they all were punished, that is harsh, isn't it?

Does a Christian lose his or her life if they disobey and walk in disobedience to God? I do not believe so, not all the time, but you can lose abundant life and lose it quickly. If you are a Christian today, and I want you to know something, you can sin. When you sin, you are going to lose a glorious part of the life God has for you. It is not going to be as good as it should be, as it could be, as God wants it to be. You are going to lose some glorious things in your life like the power and the presence of God, and it is going to destroy those that are around you first, because you never sin alone. God will punish you and bring you back; I do not think he takes your life. In the Old Testament system, God took this curse very seriously. I want you to know something, He warned him, if you do this, you are going to die, and he did it anyway. That is just like us, isn't it; because we are prone to wander? All we like sheep have gone astray. Each one of us has turned to our own separate ways, and the Lord has laid upon Him, Jesus, the iniquity of us all.

Here is the great news and the conclusion to this message today. You can have victory over the valley of trouble. This picture on the screen today is actually a picture of a road going off into Death Valley, in California, one of the hottest places on earth apparently. I want you to know something, that even in the midst of the Valley of Death, we can have the shadow of the cross to save us. Even in the midst of a valley of trouble—that's what the name Achan means "trouble," even in the midst of that trouble, you can have victory. How can you have victory? First of all, you have to confess. First John 1:9, we must confess our sins. That means we must agree with God that He is right, confess them. Now I want you to know something brother and sister in Christ, I do not want to hear all that. I am talking about confessing them to Almighty God. He already knows it. He needs you to admit it, confess. You also need to repent. To have a radical change in your thinking, that means you have to say, "You know what? This has killed my life. This has hurt other people. And the power and the presence of God is no longer with me."

You have to say, "I hate that life," and turn away from it completely. Do not go back to it right after lunch. Hate it! And ask God to help you develop a serious hate for that sin again, repent. Confess, repent, and believe. It is not simple. God wants us to believe Him to be the cure for our troubles. You see, that is the way it should be, that is what the Gospel teaches. That the wages of sin is death, but the second part of that verse tells us that the gift of God is eternal life through Jesus Christ our Lord. Only one way exists to that gift, that gift of forgiveness and mercy and grace and help in our time of trouble, and that gift is through believing in the Lord Jesus Christ. That is victory my friends! God has, indeed, brought us out of the Valley of Death, and so when we pass from this earth, only the shadow of the Valley of Death passes over us. We have life my friends, and victory through Jesus Christ. He does not want to make it hard for you. He wants to make it simple for you to come out of the valley of trouble and into the victory of the cross.

I want you to have victory today. Today, in this room, in a moment, I am going to ask you to stand, and you are going to come forward, and you are going to say one simple thing—"I want victory!" Some of you guys in this room today, some of you need victory over sin and hell itself. If you have not trusted Christ as your Savior and Lord, a time is going to come when you admitted you confessed it all to God that you were wrong, and you knew you were wrong, and you did it anyway. There was a time when you said that, there was a time when you said, "I will repent of that lifestyle and I am going to trust in Jesus to be my Savior, the One who brings me out of the valley of trouble." But, you never did that, and you need that kind of victory today. Some of you in this church family, you have been in the valley a long time. Maybe God has awakened you to an accursed thing, an idol that you are coveting, something that you keep close to your heart that you desire more than you do God.

Maybe a problem exists in your life that you do not even recognize that it has cost you the power of God and the presence of God, and it has hurt other people around you. You were not even seeing that they are hurt, but God has awakened your heart today to the pain that you are inflicting because of your own sin. He has shown you that you are the reason why. You are in the Valley of Trouble, and it is no one else's fault. You are going to come down in a minute and say, "I'm a believer, and I know Jesus has saved me, but I've been in a valley way too long, and I want victory today." Staff is going to be here to receive you, and I want to encourage you. You have a great high priest named Jesus who gave his life for you that you might have life today if you will believe in Him. The door is wide open; His arms clearly are laid out open before you today. Church, He wants to receive you if you will only come.

Father God, we love you. We thank You Lord that we can have victory from the valley of trouble. Lord, we thank You that we have gotten into that valley and have and will do it again, God, we thank You that there is a way out through Jesus to the forgiveness that is offered to us through Your Word. And today, Father I pray, today in this room, someone here in this place realizes their need and realizes You are the One who meets that need, and they are going to come and trust You as Savior and Lord to free them from the Valley of Trouble. We pray for Your Spirit's power to move amongst us and change lives. In Christ's name we pray it.[15]

Lessons

Brace yourself for a blessing! From a preaching standpoint, Robertson "just happened" to be preaching from Joshua. As stated earlier, he had preached about the victory of Jericho the week before, and then, the following week, he preached about the defeat at Ai. The very next day, Monday, a bag of money was found in the church vault, containing three hundred dollars in cash, some old checks including tithe checks, and some miscellaneous things. The old administrator had never told anyone that this bag existed or what was in it. The sin of this man was discovered in the "camp" the day after the preacher brought this message.

That did it for the personnel committee. They were inspired by the passage just preached the day before. The committee got involved, and the man was asked to leave the church due to his lack of repentance. Robertson said, "I was blown away to be living out the story of one man and how his sin had literally destroyed the victory for an entire congregation. At the time and still today, I take it as God's providential hand that led me to that passage. I moved with greater confidence and conviction after that message than I would have if I had preached the message after the bag was found. God gave me the greatest alibi."

15. Mike Robertson, senior pastor, Wichita Falls, TX, "Valley of Trouble (Joshua 7)," September 23, 2007.

CHAPTER 9: THE SINS OF THE CHURCH

Sin is prevalent in every congregation, but the man of God does not face this on his own. He is merely God's instrument that the Loving and Just God uses to tend to His sheep and His Church. At the intersection of time, a collision occurred where the Word of God met the need of man. Every pulpit occupier should stand with a confidence as this preacher did, knowing that the text will find him at just the right time to deal with the ugliest, most complex crises.

Chapter 10: The Power Struggle

A church in Houston that had a long history of pastors with short tenures interviewed me. Every potential pastor thinks he is the one to break the tradition of short, troubled pastorates. He thinks in his mind, "Yes, but I'm different than those other guys." He thinks that the reasons the other ministers left were that they were not bright enough, cordial enough, organized enough, or strong enough. As I visited with the head of the pulpit committee, I found him gracious, kind, and humble. He poured out his heart at how the previous pastor had been so abusive and had become mentally irrational and fiscally irresponsible. He was honest in saying that to take this church would be a hard task, uncomfortable, but how his church needed someone to help right a sinking ship.

I agreed to meet with the pulpit committee and found them as cordial and hopeful to turn things around. Never in any of the discussions did a hint of financial catastrophe exist. Each time the head of the pulpit committee met with me, he was humble and kind. In addition, he happened to have been a member of the church for thirty years. He was chairman of the deacons and even sang on the worship team. The last day before I was to make my decision after several visits, he rolled out what seemed to be the full financial information on the church. By the way, he was over the finances of the church. You see this coming don't you? He explained that they were losing money each month, but had cut back and were making up the difference rather quickly. He explained that once the church began to grow again, the money would take care of itself. He even showed me an aggressive building strategy that he calculated the church could meet with strategic financing.

After prayerful consideration, I accepted the position. A celebration took place at the church, and the journey began. Before my arrival, the church had been in a traditional church building in an upscale part of Houston. It turned out, the former pastor and this chairman of the pulpit committee had strong-armed the members to sell the traditional site and buy on credit an eight-story building on a major highway in Houston. Their goal was to keep up with a megachurch down the road. The church went from the business of the Kingdom to the business of managing an office building, with Sunday services on the first floor of this building. The location was poor, and circumstances were difficult.

In my egotism, I just knew I could help the church grow at that location. The service attendance almost tripled in the first three months, but offerings did not follow as quickly. I noticed the chairman of the pulpit committee began to act very erratic. He would explode in a rage of temper and would work to run people off at will. All of his tirades had what I thought were reasonable causes, though I disagreed with the verbal explosions. They all seemed justified, that is, until he turned them on me.

In a moment of anger, he showed me the finances, the true finances of the church. The church was giving $25,000 per month in offerings, but expenses were running over $75,000 per month, including the burden of the building. I was shocked to view this stark truth. When I found out the amount of money left in the bank, I realized our church only had four months to go before it would be out of money. Another secret revealed was the church, under this man's direction, had already borrowed almost $1,500,000 to keep the church afloat up to this point. His answer to the shortfall was to borrow another million. I told him that I did not believe that was the path to take. He told me it was, and that the deacons would approve this decision.

The deacons' meeting was that Saturday. When I arrived, they asked me to step outside for a while so they could talk. I did. They talked for almost an hour. Then they brought me into the room. This man explained the financial situation of the church, and told me the deacons agreed to borrow another million. And, another thing, "We have decided you are the problem in this church." Only eight months at the church, after all the years of struggles in this church, I was the problem. I could not believe my ears. I polled the deacons one-by-one with the question, "Do you think I am the problem?" One-by-one, they all replied with "yes." Some stated that trouble existed, and it was my responsibility. Some just said emphatically "yes."

Only one deacon spoke on my behalf. He said, "We are in a lot of trouble, but I do not believe you are the problem." The most stinging words were from the guy who sat directly across the table from me. He said, "We made a mistake calling a rural pastor to lead an urban church." I was crushed. They asked me to step down. I said I would not, and I was going to tell the church Sunday where we stood financially. The man who had been so humble, the man who was the chairman of the pulpit committee and who ran everything else, looked at me and said, "You will not, and if you do, you will be gone for sure." What a nightmare!

It happens all over the country—power struggles, that is. Gunnink's survey,[1] the Titus Task Force survey,[2] and most others place power struggles near the top of their lists as a chief cause in church crises today. Dr. Jerry Vines was asked, "What are the biggest struggles pastors will face in the coming days?" He responded that the number one trial that lies ahead is the "challenge to the role of the pastor and the challenge to the authority that the New Testament gives the pastoral role."[3]

Because of the nomadic movement of many pastors, churches have come to rely on existing leaders like deacons, elders, or financial backers to be the overriding authority in their church. As a result, the church ceases to function as God designed. It is said that a man visited a town and asked a business owner where the Church of God was located (this was the visitor's denominational background). The businessman replied, "Let's see. The church on Main Street is Mr. Story's church. And the one across from the school is Mr. Johnson's church. The church east of here is Mr. Allen's." The businessman then looked at the visitor and said, "You know, come to think of it, I don't think God has a church in this town."[4] A church that is alive and well is run by the Lord and His Holy Spirit. A church moving to the inconsequential state is run by people.[5]

Few pastors would come to a church if that church was honest with the candidate and told him who actually ran it. Every pastor would think twice if he asked the pulpit committee, "Do you have a deacon rotation plan here?" and the answer was, "Son, around here we rotate pastors."[6] This is not what the committees tell their prospects. Sadly though, Dr. Jekyll the recruiter will resurface as Mr. Hyde the critic at some point.[7] That point of transition usually occurs when things in the church get out-of-control. What that means, to the powerbroker, is that things are getting out of *his* control.[8] Mr. Hyde will often work to make the pastor look incapable. He will make demands on the pastor, which he does not follow personally.

Truman Dollar tells of such a situation in one of his pastorates. He was pastoring in Kansas City. A bright man, who was an executive for a large

---

1. Gunnink, interview.
2. Fraser, interview.
3. Vines, interview.
4. Charles Clark, "The Suicide of a Church," *Preaching* 15, no. 4 (January/February 2000): 30.
5. Ibid.
6. Powell, *Basic Bible Sermons*, 98.
7. Jim Berkley, "Have I Come to the WRONG Church?" *Leadership* 7, no. 2 (Spring 1986): 51.
8. Jackson, interview.

corporation, served on the church's finance committee. For two years, he came to the pastor and complained that the church was 1 percent to 2 percent over budget in some areas. Dollar listened, checked the finances, tried to keep a tighter reign, but every quarter, the same complaint was brought by this man. This executive continued to heckle and harp on the pastor for his poor performance—1 percent to 2 percent over budget.

Finally, Dollar called the comptroller of the corporation this executive worked for and asked what budgeting margins the company maintained. The comptroller told him that they seldom ever hit their budgeting margins and were already $88 million dollars in the red for the first half of the year. The next time the executive complained about the church budget, the pastor told him that it was not right to expect out of the church more than his own corporation could maintain. Dollar was not being ugly with the man, but wanted to send the message that complaining and throwing weight around with a double standard was not acceptable behavior.[9]

Yet, this goes on every month in many churches. There are meetings where a key leader will demand a weekly call to go over the sermon, its focus, and things on which the preacher should work. There is the big giver doctor who demands to give a "devotion" to the pastor every morning during the week for the pastor's growth (true story). There is the monthly meeting where the pastor is required to answer for the state of the church. The meeting's real intent is to criticize and condemn the pastor "in Christian love for his development".[10] These all say they want good leadership, but in reality, they hate it. They are afraid the preacher will overstep the bounds they have for him, and take some of their authority.[11] To prevent that, they keep close tabs on him.

Such aggression is terrifying, knowing that God's people are perpetrating it. They will seek to take constitutional steps to limit the pastor's authority. They will make wild accusations; they even throw child-like fits. They seek to withhold their tithes in an effort to starve-out the pastor. They condemn, make calls, write letters, and exhibit abrasiveness to the pastor's family. They attempt to master *Robert's Rules of Order* to circumvent the pastor's speech or actions.[12] They call moderators to deal with the pastor, and often, they call a vote to remove the pastor. They change the locks on the doors of the church so the pastor cannot enter.

---

9. Shelley and Miller, "Fundamentally One," 16.
10. Qualben, *Peace in the Parish*, 21.
11. Powell, *Basic Bible Sermons*, 40.
12. Hicks, *Preaching Through a Storm*, 52.

In those days, the bulk of the congregation sit on their hands silently, either too wrapped up in their own struggles or too afraid of the powers-that-be in the church. Some retreat to the position that getting rid of a pastor is easier than getting rid of a deacon.[13] At this point, the pastor knows, like never before, that he has entered a spiritual war. He wants to ascertain if he is on the right side. If he feels he is, the hymn "Onward Christian Soldiers" goes from being a grand old Church song to being his personal anthem for the battle just entered.

Situation

Many preachers have reached this point. Moses faced it from Aaron, Miriam, and several others. Even guys like Johnny Hunt, former president of the Southern Baptist Convention, have had to stare at the frontal assault for power from deacons, patriarchs, and layleaders.[14] Hunt chose to preach, and so did I. I noted the circumstances in the introduction to this chapter. Keep in mind, the deacons had asked me to leave. They had told me that if I let the church know where we were financially, then I would be fired immediately.

In preaching that Sunday's sermon, God's Word had to be the central concern. My emotions were running wild, my heart was broken, and my legs truly trembled. I made a decision that I would not use God's Word to berate the strong opposition I faced. I would not name names, nor would I cancel the preaching moment to deal with the financial crisis. I decided I would preach God's Word from His text, taking the pericope that I had worked on that entire week. My intention was to preach the message from the text God had given me. This message totally was unrelated to what we were facing as a church, but it was the message God had laid on my heart and compelled me to preach even in the face of this crisis. I decided that I would preach this message and then call for a response as the Spirit led. After the invitation, I decided that I would then let the church know where we stood financially. I fully expected the chairman to interrupt me. What follows is the sermon that I preached that Sunday (which, incidentally was Father's Day).

---

13. Tucker, *Primer for Pastors*, 101.
14. Hunt, interview.

Sermon

Johnny Teague

"What a Dad!"

Job 1:1-6

Turn your Bibles to *Job*, Chapter 1, beginning with Verse 1.

> In the land of Uz there lived a man whose name was Job. This man was blameless and upright; he feared God and shunned evil. He had seven sons and three daughters, and he owned seven thousand sheep, three thousand camels, five hundred yoke of oxen and five hundred donkeys, and had a large number of servants. He was the greatest man among all the people of the East. His sons used to take turns holding feasts in their homes, and they would invite their sisters to eat and drink with them. When a period of feasting had run its course, Job would send and have them purified. Early in the morning, he would sacrifice a burnt offering for each of them, thinking, "Perhaps my children have sinned and cursed God in their hearts." This was Job's regular custom.

My dad used to lay rock for houses, rock walls, amphitheaters, gateways, and so forth. My brother and I helped. I mixed the mud or cement. Tracy was younger, so he was the errand-boy. Dad laid the rock, and he was very good at it; in fact, my dad was an exceptional rock mason. In this work, my dad had an interesting habit. When we got near the end of a job, he took a bottle and wrote a note about his life. He then wrote the date, wrote about his family, wrote about our hometown of Glen Rose, and he wrote a little biography on his sons Tracy Teague and Johnny Teague (my brother and I). He would slide the note in the bottle, put the cap back on, and put it in the wall and then finish the wall, sealing the bottle inside.

Why did he do that? I think part of it was that my dad had this yearning to be remembered. In his mind, he may have reasoned, "If someone finds that bottle maybe they'll remember that Jim Teague lived." Amazingly, our rock-laying days are twenty years behind us; yet, in the past month, we have gotten two phone calls from people who had found those bottles as they remodeled or as they had some additional work done to their homes. Dad wrote his home number in the bottle, and that number has not changed in over thirty years. These callers have asked my stepmom if my dad built their wall. She affirmed that he had built it. They ask questions like, "We learned so much about your family. How's Jim?" My stepmom tells them, "He has been sick for quite a while, but he gets out some." They ask, "How's his boys?" My stepmom answers, "Well, Johnny is living in Houston. He's a preacher now. Tracy is working for the county and doing fine."

Dad's time capsule idea is working to this day. You see, my dad wanted them to know something about who built that wall. Figuratively, I have a bottle in my heart. My dad wrote some notes, which he slid into the bottle, and they are still present. As I open that bottle from time-to-time, I realize who built this wall—who helped make me what I am. Maybe you know what having a bottle in your heart is like, because of your dad or your mom.

Today, I want us to look at one fact and four principles about fatherhood. The one fact is this—dads are human. Did you know that? Dads are human. We expect dads to be these great pillars of stability. We expect them to be error-free. We expect them never to lose their temper. We expect them to be the model of perfection. On the contrary, what we have found in our lives is that father-figures are not quite that way. They are human. I played high school, college, and semi-pro football as a quarterback. I was slow—real slow as a runner, but I could pass the football. My dad's biggest claim-to-fame was his speed.

Even when I was playing at Tarleton State University, my dad would come and say, "Hey, kid, let's race." My dad weighed 270 pounds at the time. He had short, pudgy, fat little legs. He would say, "Let's race." I'm like, "Okay." So, we would all get in our stance—my brother, me, and Dad. My stepmom would station herself down at the end of about forty yards on the road. Dad would yell to my stepmom, "Alright, Carrol, start us off." She would yell, "Go!" And those fat little legs of Dad's outran me *every* time. Unbelievable, that at 270 pounds, he could outrun me. He loved that. He loved to say, "Let's race." We would debate some issue, and he would ask, "You want to race for it?" I would answer, "Well, no, I don't." My dad was human. My dad is still living, but he has always been human.

My dad could be mischievously mean. I grew up in the country. My dad would always say, "You know when you're the daddy, you pretty much get to sit in the chair and make other people do stuff. When you're the daddy, that's what you do." He practiced what he said. When we would pull up to a gate, he would say,

"Kid, get out, get the gate." We would return home, and he would see the newspaper at the end of our lane, and he would say, "Kid get out, get the paper." You realize early on, when you are a child, you are a virtual slave! You know that, don't you?

Parents hate it when the kids grow up, because then they have to do all those things. In the country, we had cows on our place, and so we had livestock gates. I remember when I was about eight years old, we came to a livestock gate, and Dad says, "Get out, open the gate." Now, this was the most unusual gate that I had ever seen. Only one long wire ran across it. I came back and asked Dad, "How do you open that gate? It's just a wire." He said, "Oh, just grab it anywhere." And so, I went back and grabbed that thing. It was electric! I was shocked literally and figuratively and was crying from the sting. My dad laughed until he could hardly sit up. I told mom on him. That got him in trouble, but to this day, he still cries laughing about the day my feet flew up in the air as I was being electrocuted—hair extending straight out. He loves that. Let me tell you something, that was mean. We have an electric fence at our place now, and I will not let my daughter touch it, that is, unless she deserves it!

My dad could lose his temper. He had a wench truck. He was in the tree business for a while and you know, these wench trucks have a huge boom on the back. And Dad told me one day, "Look I've got to take both my trucks to the job. You drive the wench truck, and we'll go to the gas station, get some gas, and then we'll run out to the job." I said, "Okay." So, I get in the wench truck, which I had never driven before. I get in, and I know I've got to get gas, so I drive into the ARCO station. I drove under that covered area and Man! That truck popped a wheelie inside the covered area, because the top of the metal cover caught the boom on the wench truck. That threw the tires up, and I'm like, "Oh, no! What is happening?" Finally, I put it in neutral, and it rolled back. My dad comes running, screaming, yelling expletives I won't share—and he drew back to hit me in the face. But then, he dropped his arms. He said, "Son, I'm sorry. You've never driven this wench truck before." I cost my dad $15,000 in damages. I probably deserved a good hit, but he would not do it. See, my dad was human.

My dad was an alcoholic. When Mom and Dad divorced, he started drinking. He drank straight gin every morning for twenty years. My dad is dying at this moment with cirrhosis of the liver. He is on hospice—does not have long to go. My dad is human. When we look at a guy like Job, we like to picture him as an angel or some fictitious character, but you and I need to understand that Job was a human. Job's underarms smelled; Job got hungry; Job sweat; Job lost his temper; Job knew what it was like to go through hard times. You know what that is all about! His name means "persecuted."

Job lived in the patriarchal period of time, sometime between Noah and Abraham, probably 2000 to 1400 B.C. He lived in the land of Uz. Now if you know anything about archeology, some question exists about exactly where Uz was, but most believe Uz was—that's a great rhyme—that Uz was located in the area of Damascus, Syria. Now, that is interesting, isn't it? The Bible has Job, one of God's most choice saints, and he is not Jewish. Did you know that? He is Syrian. He is of Arab descent. You understand that even in the darkest, most vile, most adulterous place on the earth, God still calls people to be saved, because He did not come to save just the Jewish people. He came to save any and all who would come.

Now, I want to talk to you for a moment about Uz. Uz was a desert region, where Job lived. Do you know when Paul became a Christian, he immediately went to Arabia? Most likely, he spent eleven years in Arabia—that is the land of Uz. Why was Paul in a desert area called Uz? Because that was the place where God prepared him for what He had for him to do. God sent Moses to the desert. God sent Abraham to the desert. God sent John the Baptist to the desert. Do you know why I think dads know so much? Because I think at some point in the life of a dad, he has been to a place called Uz. He has been in a desert place in his life. My desert place is different than your desert place. Unfortunately, I keep frequenting those desert places, but they are a place of training. Maybe today you find yourself in a desert. God loves you, and no matter what desert you are in, He is going to bring you through it. He will use you in a mighty way. He has a plan. So, dads are human.

Now here comes the first principle. Dads are to be providers, are they not? You know I heard of a guy sitting in the courtyard of a mall one day. He gave money to his daughter. He sat on a bench for a while. Then here comes another daughter. He gets up, pulls out his wallet, gives her some money, and sits back down. Here comes another daughter, he pulls out the wallet, gives her money, sits back down. When he stood up and he turned around, you know what his t-shirt said? "Human ATM." Isn't that cool?

Dads are to be providers. We know that. We expect that. That is God's call, but additionally, they are to model how to be a provider. Many people today do not want to work. We want what our parents had, but we do not want to work for it. No one wants to start at ground zero anymore. We want to start where our parents are and build from there, but our dads teach us about provision. My dad trimmed trees part-time. My dad laid rock part-time. My dad was a welder part-time, but my dad worked primarily for General Dynamics. He made the F1-11 airplane; I think that's a bomber if I'm not mistaken. Further, my dad worked for the Santa Fe Railroad as a boilermaker. My dad works. He now owns a trash business that he built himself. My dad has never in the past tolerated laziness. Job was like that. He was a worker.

You know what? In this Scripture, we find his number one work—you see what that is? He had seven sons and three daughters. Dads, father figures, your number one occupation is your children. Job had seven sons, three daughters. Now, in that day when you were working the land, you needed many kids—that is cheap labor, right? Thus, he had seven sons, three daughters. God's Word says, "As arrows in the hand of a warrior, so are the children a blessing from God. Blessed is the man whose quivers full of them." Job also had seven thousand sheep—can you believe that—seven thousand sheep. That is a lot of sheep. What does that tell you about his work? He was in the clothing industry or wool industry, and probably in the meat industry. He had sheep, seven thousand of them.

I hate sheep, but he had sheep. Additionally, he had, and this is really cool—three thousand camels. Why camels? What does that tell us about Job? What other business was he in? Perhaps, the shipping industry. In a desert, the only animal that can carry things and make it is a camel. I have researched camels this week, and I am amazed by what I have learned. A camel can carry one thousand pounds on his back, did you know that? Some camels have one hump; some have two. Do you know what the camel carries in that hump? Everybody says water. That is not what it carries. It carries meat, food, the sustenance it needs. When camels eat, their humps get bigger and bigger. Camels fill up with sustenance, and then when they go a long time without food, those humps start getting smaller. Did you know that? You know a camel is really hungry when you see its hump is concave!

Camels can eat and live off thorns. They have such tough tongues they can live on thorns. I think about Robert's dad who, when he tried to get his cow to kiss him, his cow licked and literally ripped his lip off his face. I mean, they have tough tongues—tougher than cow tongues. That is amazing. The other thing about camels, from what I have read, they can go thirty days without water. Isn't that amazing? Thirty days without water, and you know what? When they do drink, they can drink thirty gallons in ten minutes. Now that is sucking it down. That is a fire hose, backwards, right? And when they walk, they can start off carrying three hundred to five hundred pounds of water. Another thing about camels is, they do not sweat.

We can learn something from the camels, can we not? When you are in the desert of life, do not sweat it. God loves you. And when you are dry and thirsty, if you are a Christian, a reservoir of living water is inside of you, and you can make it through whatever you are facing.

Job had five hundred yoke of oxen—generally, two oxen are on a yoke. That means he had about a thousand oxen. What does that tell us about Job's business? It showed that he was into cultivation. He was into vegetables. He was growing fruits and vegetables with those oxen. He used them to till the ground. He had five hundred she-donkeys. Now that is interesting. Why would you want five hundred female donkeys? That is kind of interesting, is it not? Well, one is he did not have horses; he had donkeys, because they are easy to care for; they go longer without water and require less food. When you ride a donkey, you are riding on a delicacy. Did you know that? They say their milk is a great delicacy. Now that is a delicacy of which I would rather not partake! Job had many servants. He had plowmen, overseers, and shepherds. You know what? I think he probably had camel jockeys—that is where that phrase comes in—camel jockey. He had servants.

Job was a worker, and he lived the example. Kids, if you are going to make it in this world, you must be willing to work. Fathers, you are the model for that. Dads are the model to instill the values of family, to instill harmony in families. My dad never missed a family reunion. He went to every family reunion we had, and when a relative was sick or old, my dad always went to see them. He calls them all the time, even in his poor health now, he calls older relatives who are struggling. My dad was always present in a crisis. There were days in my life when I went through trouble, and I would go to my dad. I remember one specific crisis where I had to admit to something I had done, and I was scared about it. I went and told my dad what I had done, and my dad said, "So, are you going to go and do the right thing?" "Oh, yes sir," I answered. "Do you want me to go with you?," he asked. I answered with a plea, "Please, go with me." And Dad went. There were other crises I have faced in my life when I did not live near home, and my dad would call me and say, "Johnny, I'm gonna come stay with you for a week." You see moms do that. You do not see dads do that a lot. I said, "No, Dad, I'm okay but I'll call you if I need you." Dads, father figures, you are to instill the value of family. There are people out there who need you to instill the value of family.

Job had kids, and those kids grew to be adults who had homes, jobs, and families. Those kids still loved each other. They loved to reminisce. In fact, it says when their birthdays came along, everybody would go to the birthday boy's or the birthday girl's house, and they would celebrate together. There is something beautiful about seeing families that get along. You know why that is so beautiful? We do not see it much, right? Do you know what God says about Job's kids? Nothing. He has no reproach for them at all.

However, when Eli's kids acted up, God spoke sternly about them. When Samuel's kids acted up, God spoke sternly about them. Even though their parents were righteous, God spoke sternly about their kids, but we do not hear any reproach regarding Job's kids. What does that tell you? It tells you they learned something. It tells you they tried to be like their dad. It tells you they had a good time together, and their parties were wholesome and not wild whooping parties. It teaches a lesson. Christians, we can have a good time. Did you know smiling is okay? Laughing is okay. Telling a joke is okay. Making fun of each other is even okay as long as it is done with taste and care, and they know you love them. It is okay.

You know we do not have to get together and gossip and lie to one another. We do not have to drink to have a good time. We do not have to do drugs to have a good time. We can have a good time without sexually explicit stuff occurring. One of my favorite memories as a kid involves a church outing. Our church had a fish fry out in the country. The reason I remember this outing more than anything is that we had just gotten our first new family car—a 1972 Plymouth Fury, four-door, brown, headlight things dropped down. Oh, it was a great car! It smelled new. I thought I was the richest kid in Glen Rose. Dad took it down the highway at 120 miles per hour to show us what it could do—that was not a good thing. We went to the church fish fry, and Dad had a great time with the men. I hung out with the kids. We used to have watermelon parties at our house with homemade ice cream, and the whole church would come. We would play volleyball. We had a good time. Christians, we can have a good time and do it right, and then when we are done, no issue of conscience ensues.

Another principle about fatherhood: Dads, you are to model righteousness—a living relationship with the living God in front of all who watch you. My brother and I went to a funeral together on Monday. One of my good friends was killed in a motorcycle wreck last Friday. Tracy, who is four years younger, rode with me. We know Dad is dying, and Tracy said, "You know, I'm gonna miss Dad when he dies." "You know what," I said, "I am too." What Tracy said next really struck me. He said, "I want to be like him in every way."

He said that for a reason, because my whole life I have told my dad, and I have told my siblings that I want to be like Dad in every righteous way that he lived. See, my dad had an alcohol problem. He struggled with womanizing. He cheated on some things, and he did some illegal things. These were things he had done when he had strayed from the Lord. He has rededicated his life, and he is living for Him again. But you see, I told my brothers, "You know, there are a lot of good attributes that I want to copy of Dad's, but the bad ones I want to leave behind." You see, father figures, you have to understand, as irrational as that sounds, people are watching you, who want to be like you in every way, including your bad habits, including your weaknesses. They want to be like you, and when they are like you, they will say, "I am just like my dad. I can't help it." Oh, dads, look at the impact you are making. Kids, look at your dads and realize they are human. Do not be like them in every way. I have not met a perfect man yet short of Jesus.

What does God say about Job? God says that Job was blameless. It was not what others said about Job. It was not what Job said about Job, because he was humble. What God said about Job is that which matters. What God says about you is that which matters. You and I may think that we are all good people, and I really respect this person or that person. You know what? It does not matter what we think. What matters is what God thinks, because He is with us all the time.

The word "blameless" is the same word used for Abraham and Noah. Blameless does not mean sinless, did you know that? Job was a sinner. What it means is Job was right with God. None of us are without sin, but we can all be right with God. How do you get right with God? You seek His forgiveness. When you mess up, you say, "Lord, please forgive me." Job did that all the time. And then, it seems, he would sacrifice every time he sinned, every time at the end of the day or the morning.

He would sacrifice because of his sins, and when he sacrificed, perhaps he knew a day would come when God would pay the ultimate sacrifice for man's sin, abolishing the need for animal sacrifice. Job said things like, "Search me, oh, God and see if there be anything in my heart that is not pleasing to You. Search my attitude, my thoughts, my sight." Job is the one who said, "I have trained my eye not to look upon another woman." We all need to learn that lesson, do we not? Job wanted to be righteous. So, he was blameless.

I remember when my dad was serving the Lord. He would have people over after church, and we would gather around the piano and sing together. I remember him being the Training Union director. How many people even know what a Training Union director is? That is like Sunday night Sunday School. He would come up and tell a few jokes, do the headcount, then pray. My dad did not model some righteous things, but Job was always blameless, always—even when he sinned, he made himself right with God. Blameless has to do with character. God says he was blameless, but he also was upright, and this has to do with conduct. Upright means he did not deviate. He was straight, and we read in Job, chapter 29, beginning with verse 11,

> Whoever heard me spoke well of me and those who saw me commended me because I rescued the poor and cried for help, and the fatherless who had none to assist him. The man who was dying blessed me and I made the widow's heart sing. I put on righteousness as my clothing; justice was my robe and my turban. I was eyes to the blind, feet to the lame. I was father to the needy. I took up the case of a stranger. I broke the fangs of the wicked and I snatched the victims from their teeth.

Dads, we must be active. If someone is hungry, let us feed them. If we know a woman in our church or outside the church who is widowed and struggling, we help them. If we know someone is in the hospital, we go see them. If we know someone cannot afford groceries, we go buy them. Dads, if we know someone is lonely, we give them our time. That is a father figure, and God will bless you for that.

Job was upright. What kills me is that we will see people who have a relative who is doing horrible things, and then you will go talk to the mom of that relative or that friend and the mom will say, "Well, I know they're doing those things. I know they are not living right, but deep down, they are a good person."

Let me tell you something. That is a lie. If you are upright inside, you will not be crooked outside. If you are crooked outside, something is wrong inside. Job was upright. Furthermore, he feared God. That is good enough reason to be upright; to fear God is the beginning of wisdom. He feared God. It was not a slavish fear. It was not a terror fear. It was a respect, a reverence, knowing God is holy, God is Almighty. It is the attitude, "God has given His Son for me, and I'll give Him the utmost reverence." And if you fear God, dads, you're going to shun evil. Not only are you going to stay away from it, you are going to hate evil. And you do not want to be near it.

You know the trick of a Godly man is this. Do not see how close you can get to sin; rather, see how far you can stay away from sin. That is shunning evil. The number one priority of a dad is to model a right relationship with God. The only way for him to perform number two is to be number one. Now, here is the number two most important thing for a dad: You have to be a priest for your family or for those who look up to you. How many of us consider ourselves priests? How many of us walk up to David Jones and say, "Well, hello, Pope Jones. How are you doing?" See, we do not do that, but dads we are to be priests. My dad was not much of a priest later on in life, but let me give you a little insight. When I was seven years old, the preacher called me in his office, and he said, "Don't you want to go to Heaven?" I said, "Yeah. I never really thought about it much, but yeah." He said, "Well, pray this prayer with me, okay?" I prayed the prayer with him. He then said, "Let us baptize you tonight." I said, "Okay, let's do it." I got baptized. My family said they were so proud of me. I wondered, "What did I do?" They kept saying, "You're a Christian!" My attitude was, "Oh, that's cool, okay, good."

Did I really become a Christian? No. I just prayed a prayer, and someone dunked me. When I got to be about twelve or thirteen years old, I started to worry that if Christ came, I would be left behind. If I died, I would not go to Heaven. I would go to hell, and I knew why—because I was a sinner. At Latham Springs Baptist Camp, I sprinted down that aisle at the first invitation. I knelt before Holy God, and I asked Him to be my Savior, and I meant it. Then I was baptized again. I made my profession public at our home church that Sunday.

At that time, my dad was divorced from my mom, and he would pick me up after church each Sunday. I did not know what he would think, because he thought I was already a Christian. I feared that he would think I was a nut, but several people told

CHAPTER 10: THE POWER STRUGGLE

Dad before I got out of church. They said, "Hey, we are proud of your son. He just became a Christian." When I got to the car, Dad asked, "What'd you do today?" I said, "Well, Dad, I gave my heart to Jesus." I thought he would be disappointed. He said, "Son, I did the same thing when I was a boy. I did not know what I was praying at that time. Later, I came to realize that I was not saved, and I gave my heart to Christ, and I was baptized again. I know how you feel. I have been there, and I'm proud of you."

As it turns out, I am in a long line of double-dunkers, because my daughter prayed the same prayer at age seven. She just did not understand. She went to camp last year, went forward, and gave her heart to Christ sincerely. She came home and thought I would be upset. I was not upset. I had the great joy to preach that Sunday, with my full suit on and her full clothes on, we stepped on that balcony, into that baptismal, and I baptized my daughter. You see, we are in a long line of double-dunkers. My dad *had the potential* to be a great priest. Job *was* a great priest.

Father-figures, you are to be priests. We live in an age where parents say, "I do not want to push my religion on my kids, because I want them to make that decision for themselves. I want them to decide what is best for them." We get them braces; we take them to dermatologists; we teach them social skills; we pick their schools; we make sure they make good grades, and yet when it comes to eternity, we say, "It is kind of up to you—whatever you think." We have it backwards. I would rather go through life with rotted teeth and enter Heaven than to go through life with shiny teeth and spend eternity in a place called Hell. Parents, what are we thinking? Dads, what are we thinking when we say, "I do not want to force my religion. I want them to choose for themselves." You guide them in everything else—guide them in what is most important.

Other parents say, "You know, it is okay to have some sin. I want my kids to explore. I want my kids to see what it is like. I want my kids to not regret later that they did not do something." I have a friend in my home town. He has that attitude. His son and daughter are free to bring friends over every night. They raid his refrigerator; they go through his freezer, primarily because this dad wants to be best friends with his kids and not a father. He lets those kids—the friends of his children—drink in his house, smoke in his house, and have sex in his bedroom, and says, "I feel better about it, because I know they are going do it anyway. I would rather them do it at my home." Do you know what his children's friends call their house? "Casa de Fun-Fun." Do we not understand? It just takes one sin to ruin a life.

Do we not understand? One sin separates us from God for all eternity. My friend, Jim, came to my house in Beaumont, He was driving a Ford Taurus, and I saw when he was backing out of our driveway that a lot of fluid was dripping underneath his car. I yelled out, "Wait a minute, wait a minute, stop!" He was heading back to Dallas. And I said, "Jim, you have a horrible leak, let me look at it." Doing my best impression of Mr. Mechanic, I popped the hood and looked for leaks in the hoses just like my dad had taught me. If you see a hose with a leak, men what do you do? You cut up above it, and then you re-clamp it, right? Well, I told Jim, "You've got a leak. Here's what I'd do. Give me that pocket knife." And so I cut it, clamped it and sealed it. I sent him off so proud, "Well, have a good trip. Be safe, God bless you." Two and a-half hours later his car was in flames. I did not get all the leaks, another one was up above it. It was just a little leak, but it ruined a $16,000 car.

Guys, one little sin in your kid will ruin their lives. Do not tolerate it. Job would not. Did you read what Job does? After the kids have their party, Job sends for them to come to him, and he asks, "What'd you do last night?" And he watches them for every motion, every attitude, and every gesture. He is reading them. "What'd you do?" And he knows even if they didn't do anything, they might have had bad thoughts. When we are not thinking of things of God, we forget God, and we sin.

Did you read about that girl from Michigan that got on Facebook? She was e-mailing back and forth with a kid in Jericho—a 25-year-old; she was not quite sixteen. She e-mailed him, and he asked her to marry him. Sixteen and he is twenty-five, a terrorist, for all we know. They go back and forth, finally she agrees, and asks her mom, "Mom, I need a passport." The mom asks, "Why?" The daughter says, "Well, my friends are going to Canada for the summer, and I need a passport so I can go with them." The mom agrees, drives the daughter to get her a passport. Two or three weeks later, the girl tells her, "Mom, will you take me to the train station? The Simpson family is going to Canada. I'm going with them." The mom says, "Okay, but I am not going to let you out until I see you are with the family." Well, you know the girl is already sweating it. Finally, the mom calls Mrs. Simpson and says, "Mrs. Simpson, when are you guys leaving for Canada?" Mrs. Simpson surprised exclaims, "Canada? We are not going to Canada." She looks at her daughter and says,

"What are you doing?" And what did her daughter do? She blew up at her. "That is none of your business."

Her mom was so silly, she drove her back home and left her at the house by herself. The girl immediately catches a cab, goes straight to the bus station, goes to the airport, and gets on an airplane with the ticket that this twenty-five-year old guy had purchased for her. Eventually, they catch up to this daughter in Amman, Jordan, about to be a stranger's wife. Do you think maybe that could have been stopped? How could the mom have stopped the daughter's actions? Well, you ask your kids questions. You know, in my home—and my home's not perfect, but in my home, we have no secrets. We do not have secret drawers. We do not have secret diaries. We sleep with our doors open. Our kids are not forbidden to go through our dresser. We are not forbidden to go through theirs. You see, Job looked for the first sign of defect in his child, because he wanted to stop it right there.

Kids, I know you are probably thinking, nobody better go through my stuff. Well, let me tell you something. It is to protect you. Your parents should be free to read what you write. And kids, I know you think it is like the Gestapo. I know you are going to think I am an idiot. When you go home, you will tell your family, "That guy's a nut. I'm glad he's not my daddy." Parents, you need to be active in your kids' lives and look through their stuff. You will be surprised sometimes at the good stuff that is there.

Job consecrated his kids before the Lord. What does that mean? He took each child, and he brought them and said, "God, this is my son, Darrel. Darrel is a man that I have raised, and I love. God, I do not know what sins are in Darrel's life, but I dedicate Darrel to You for the rest of his life. Lord, keep him righteous. Sally, come here. God, this is Sally. And I don't know what sins are in her life." Probably, each time the kids had a party, the next morning Job would bring his kids before God and pray, "God, this is Sally. You know how she has a temper. You know how good looking she is. Men want her. God keep her, please. She's Yours. I set her apart for You." And then he would sacrifice an animal for each child. Is your first thought—I might drive my children away from the Lord? I bet it is, right? Let me tell you something. If you drive them from the Lord by obeying Holy God, they were going anyway. If you do not obey the Lord and watch over your kids, you are going to lose so many more. Be radical with kids. Make them accountable.

Brittany went to camp this week, and they had a great camp. The preacher questioned the campers, "How many of you are tired?" It is Thursday night after three services a day, Monday through Thursday. The preacher, at the last service that Thursday night asked, "How many of you are tired today?" All the kids said, "I'm tired." He said, "How many of you are worried when you go back home, you're not going to keep the commitment that you promised here at camp today?" And he said, "If you are worried about it, will you stand up?" And several kids across the room stood up. Many said, "You know what, I'm afraid as much as I love God I might stray." And what did the camp director do, the preacher? He had people go around and stand around them and pray that God would keep them holy. Let me tell you something, I will always stand behind Brittany, and I will make sure she does not stray from Holy God. With every ounce of my being, I will fight for her righteousness, and she will never stand alone. I will be picky, and I will be nosy, and I will dictate, and I will pray, and I will love, and I will provide, and I will care, and I will be a model. Will you?[15]

Lessons

When one is in a crisis of power, it is important for the preacher to remember that if he has to tell the church continually that he is in charge, then he is not in charge. Power is earned and granted, not assumed automatically. It often takes a major crisis for the church to see their pastor as their true leader.[16]

I preached the previous sermon on Father's Day, 2006. My plans were to mold the sermon around my dad and his life and the impact he had made on me. I referred to Job, a man of Uz, and talked about men who have been to Uz in their lives. I spoke about the fact that when a Christian faces a trial, God is faithful to give His child all that he needs. It is amazing to me that I had been led to preach this passage from Job, of all books, and I had worked on the message with no idea what lie ahead for me at the deacon's meeting that Saturday. At the intersection of time, God brings a collision between God's Word and man's need.

I preached this sermon. God's Spirit was all over it. After the message, three people were saved, and two more joined the church. All were amazed at the Lord's Presence. Many who knew what I was facing were especially in

---

15. Johnny Teague, senior pastor, Church at the Cross, Houston, TX, "What a Dad! (Job 1:1-6)," June 11, 2006.

16. Bisagno, lecture.

awe at God's goodness. The power of God's Word breaks through any crisis. The goal was to focus on God, not on the church and not on me. We had scheduled the Lord's Supper that day, but I suspended it because, Biblically, we were not in the right spirit to partake. I definitely was too conflicted to serve it as the Lord commands.

I then told the church that I had something I had to share. I told them we were in a financial mess, and that we would need to meet next Sunday to make a decision on what we must do to right the ship. The church agreed. The chairman of trouble sat tense, angry, and silent. The church, out of the blue, gave me a standing ovation for my stand on the matter. The support was much needed. The chairman then called the deacons to the back corner of the sanctuary to dismiss me as pastor, but many members who knew or caught wind, or heard them speaking, approached the chairman and told him, "You will not get rid of my pastor!" That was all it took. The deacons were greatly outnumbered, more so than they knew. I, like Elisha, sensed there were more with us than against us. That was the last service for the chairman. He left, and God has continued to hold me and His church in His hands.

Losing that chairman was hard; he contributed over 25 percent of the offerings. An old preacher told me long before, "If you preach God's Word and lose good givers because of it, God will make up the difference." The next Sunday, the offering was a record! God is so good.

Sometimes, the power groper will stay. They may stay simply to haunt the preacher, or they may stay hoping they can regain the power the minute the pastor slips. Rest assured that, in most cases, if the pastor continues to feed people God's Word by the power of the Holy Spirit, the star of the groper will fade, and the love and following of the pastor will rise.[17] Even in the toughest crisis, the spokesman for God has the chief responsibility to bring God's Word. In most cases, let God take care of the defense. If self-defense is necessary, one should carry it out in love and honesty, using God's Word as the sword, knowing it is double-edged.

One other positive note is that the other deacons all stayed through this crisis. The two who were against me the most adamantly next to the chairman (one of them was the one who said they made a mistake calling a rural pastor to take an urban church), stayed. They have become my closest friends in the church and have grown in the Lord, and have been transformed before my very eyes (as have I).

A preacher going through a power struggle and coming out of one, must be a Christian leader who has the ultimate capacity to forgive. Joseph, after

---

17. Berkley, "WRONG Church," 52.

being mistreated and sold by his brothers and reaching the capacity of power, forgave those brothers and loved and provided for them their whole lives.[18] The man of God can know he is pleasing God when he has preached something difficult in the face of fear without succumbing to that fear or adjusting the message in light of the consequences that may come.[19] A "steeled" resolve lay in the prophets, the disciples, and Jesus, who carried the Gospel to where it is today. Today's preachers must carry that same resolve. As my Dad always said, "Never mistake kindness for weakness." Stand!

The greatest ally in all this is the Lord Jesus Christ Himself. Many a minister, including this one, has felt the Lord's gentle hand on his shoulder. He has brought His Word to comfort the mind of the pastor. The words, "Be still and know that I Am God," resound with clarity. The one under fire will cling to the passage, "If God is for us, who can be against us." Or, as the Psalmist wrote, "The Lord in Heaven laughs" at those who try to come against His will.

For the preacher who finds himself in a power struggle, he can take a tip from the movie "The Alamo." Though surrounded by the Santa Anna's troops, Davy Crocket stuck to his guns, fighting for what mattered. Jim Bowie, wounded and bedridden, held on to his guns and the Bowie knife, and died fighting from his bed. They both died for the cause of freedom. The pastor must be willing to stand for the freedom of Christ, and he must do this in the position where God has placed him. Many a prophet died sharing God's message. Who knows, maybe for "such a time as this," God has asked you to be His martyr or His victor, knowing in the end, we are more than conquerors. Preach the Word!

---

18. Michael Milton, "Hit by Friendly Fire: What to Do When Christians Hurt You," *Preaching* 21, no. 1 (July/August 2005): 38.

19. Wagner, "Preaching from Down Under," 144.

Chapter 11: **The Unexpected**

Surprises—everybody loves surprises. On the contrary, in the ministry, often they do not. I was preaching a wedding for a couple in our church. I tell every young couple that what they are about to do is a glorious thing. To do so in the church with God's Word as the sourcebook of their union is honorable even more. Good counsel for every couple contemplating a wedding ceremony is to tell them, "Something will go wrong; count on it." The flower girl will stumble, the ringbearer will be shy and run, or someone will suffer hurt feelings. The photographer will be late. The preacher may stumble on a name. The couple may be so nervous that they forget their vows or where to go. The catering truck will wreck. Wedding-day calamities are only natural. However, with all this, I remind the couple that the mistakes or the surprises on their wedding day will, for years to come, be things they will laugh about and remember most. In fact, those mistakes on the wedding day will add to their fondest memories. This couple chuckled, but understood the point I was making when I warned them. We prayed together, and I told them I would see them that Saturday afternoon for the wedding.

Contrary to my prediction, everything was going just great. The wedding party entered, and the ushers had seated parents of both sides. The pianist hit the notes for "Here Comes the Bride." Everyone stood. And just like that, the lights went out in the church. Not just in the church, the lights went out in the whole city. Darkness prevailed. No stage lights worked. Thankfully, the couple used candles. I also discovered that night that, without electricity, the soundboard does not work either. A church member checked during the music and informed me that the whole city was without electricity and would be so for at least two more hours. The groom, already somewhat superstitious, asked me, "Is this a bad omen?" I could not believe that question in church. I told him, "Remember what I told you about things happening." We continued with the wedding, no microphones, no favorite songs piped over the speakers, and no lights for good photography. I tied the knot really tight for their marriage, and they were off to wedded bliss.

Surprises. This is the life of the preacher. Sundays have occurred when the musicians and the music leader all fell ill on the same Sunday morning with no time for replacements. Days have occurred when traffic jams even made me late for church. Most of these are funny, but some are surprises that are more serious. The music minister gets caught buying beer at the local convenience store. You receive word of a church member's arrest (not as much of a surprise as it used to be). A beloved member of the church graduates to be with the Lord. A youth minister resigns in the middle of a youth event, and remarks, "I was just here for a season." (Pardon my bitterness, but I think this is by far the most used phrase for quitting and the least Biblical. This excuse can often be a copout for leaving when the going gets tough. I know God says a season exists for everything, but as I recall in that passage, God determines that season, but I digress.)

Jim Jackson found a great surprise in a building program. Jackson believes that if you cannot raise the money, you do not build. Leveraging the church puts the church and the pastor in an unfavorable position. In his first building program at Chapelwood Methodist Church, the church was involved in a 12 million dollar program. The church pledged the full amount, and all were happy. Some money was for reconstruction, which Jackson said is a harder project to estimate, because no one really knows how bad things are until they start to pull boards apart. They found horrible things in the process of which they were not aware, and further, the furniture and equipment was underestimated. They went from being over-pledged to needing 4 million dollars extra.

The church had pledged an extra 3.5 million for a community activity center in its area. Chapelwood's desire is that any time they build something for the church, they also build something for the community or for a mission. When they ran short, the consultant advised three options: take the money out of what they were planning for the activity center, cut the project back, or borrow the money.

Dr. Jackson called his leaders together, and they prayed. He felt strongly that he should ask the congregation for more money. The consultant "freaked out," saying, "you will make your people who feel good now, feel like failures and they will turn on each other." He felt if he had failed, he might be run out on a rail. Jackson's opinion is that one can be fired one of two ways—moral failure or failing to raise money. He said that you can outlast nearly anything else.

Dr. Jackson brought a message relevant to their need, and then at the end of the sermon asked for the shortfall. God's people were not offended; they got the first 2 million quickly, but then it ceased. He felt that if God did not do something, his ministry would come to an end. In his mind, his credibility was at stake. He could not back off, nor could he reason how to work it out or manipulate it. He just prayed. Then came a visit from a man who loved Dr. Jackson, the church, and Christ. He said if something does not happen, this will all turn on you, and then we will turn on each other, and we will never get over it. The guy gave a challenge grant of $500,000, with the understanding that the money would be used to get the congregation to come up with the rest. Dr. Jackson stood up before the people with renewed confidence. He announced the challenge to the church, and they opened their purse strings, raising an excess of $500,000 over what they needed.

Jackson says that in the midst of a surprise or an unexpected event, credibility and faith are important—"People want to know you are going to give them the truth." They are seeking to do things in the name of Jesus. The question is, "Will you waffle on your principles when you get down to it and no way out exists, or will you make a stand in faith and honesty? This separates the men from the boys, becoming all or nothing; and the preacher knows, if it works, it has to be God.[1]

Paul faced his own surprise, and he provided a perfect Biblical analogy of what a preacher is to do in the midst of a storm, as recorded in Acts 27. Paul is on a ship as a prisoner heading for Italy. They were sailing in the stormy season and the winds on that voyage were abnormally violent, perhaps even of hurricane-force. The ship continued to deteriorate beneath them. Paul then spoke. He spoke the words God had given him. He brought comfort to the sailors. His message steadied the people and provided reliable direction. In a church that is facing surprises and a future unknown, the role of the man of God is to look to Him for direction and convey that direction to God's people.[2]

Situation

Churches in transition face many unknowns—who will stay, where will we meet, how will we make our bills, and so forth. Surprises to a steady, mature church are uncomfortable, but they often have the resources to respond. Many churches today are living on a whim and a prayer. When our little church sold that eight-story office building, we began to meet at a movie theater in an area that we felt should be our new mission field. The theater was a nice, multi-screened movie complex. The manager was a Christian man and provided much of what we needed at little or no cost. We purchased the things we needed to do the "church-in-a-box" thing. The sound

---

1. Jackson, interview.
2. Gordon MacDonald, "Speaking into the Crisis," in *Great Preaching—Practical Advice from Powerful Preachers*, ed. Paul Woods (Loveland, CO: Group Publishing, 2003), 43.

system plugged in nicely. They moved their movie times around to accommodate us. All was going swimmingly.

I thought it odd that the manager, who said he would retire at that theater, suddenly took a new theater that was being constructed. He told us that he had changed his mind, and that he loved a challenge. He left us in good hands with a new manager. One day, we went to our church mail and received a letter from the movie theater's corporate office which said they were sorry for the inconvenience, but we needed to be out in two weeks. The movie theater had sold and they were tearing it down for an office building. Two weeks! We had searched hard to find anyone to house our little church.

With this egregious and unconstitutional separation-of-church-and-state mentality, no one was open to having a church in their park or business. Our church had already been through so much. Our church members seemed to think they had a black cloud over their heads. Some thought we were paying for past sins of the church. The ironic thing was, the vast majority of members had joined since all the ruckus. It was too late to change my sermon. Even if I could have changed my sermon, I could not think of an appropriate passage with which to deal with the news. Thus, I preached the sequential next pericope in Genesis.

Sermon

Johnny Teague

"When We Go Where God Leads"

Genesis 26

Genesis 26:1-33 Now there was a famine in the land—besides the earlier famine of Abraham's time—and Isaac went to Abimelech, king of the Philistines in Gerar. The Lord appeared to Isaac and said, "Do not go down to Egypt; live in the land where I tell you to live. Stay in this land for a while, and I will be with you and will bless you. For to you and your descendants I will give all these lands and will confirm the oath I swore to your father Abraham. I will make your descendants as numerous as the stars in the sky and will give them all these lands, and through your offspring all nations on earth will be blessed, because Abraham obeyed me and kept my requirements, my commands, my decrees and my laws." So Isaac stayed in Gerar. When the men of that place asked him about his wife, he said, "She is my sister," because he was afraid to say, "She is my wife." He thought, "The men of this place might kill me on account of Rebekah, because she is beautiful." When Isaac had been there a long time, Abimelech king of the Philistines looked down from a window and saw Isaac caressing his wife Rebekah. So Abimelech summoned Isaac and said, "She is really your wife! Why did you say, 'She is my sister'?" Isaac answered him, "Because I thought I might lose my life on account of her." Then Abimelech said, "What is this you have done to us? One of the men might well have slept with your wife, and you would have brought guilt upon us." So Abimelech gave orders to all the people: "Anyone who molests this man or his wife shall surely be put to death." Isaac planted crops in that land and the same year reaped a hundredfold, because the Lord blessed him. The man became rich, and his wealth continued to grow until he became very wealthy. He had so many flocks and herds and servants that the Philistines envied him. So all the wells that his father's servants had dug in the time of his father Abraham, the Philistines stopped up, filling them with earth. Then Abimelech said to Isaac, "Move away from us; you have become too powerful for us." So Isaac moved away from there and encamped in the Valley of Gerar and settled there. Isaac reopened the wells that had been dug in the time of his father Abraham, which the Philistines had stopped up after Abraham died, and he gave them the same names his father had given them. Isaac's servants dug in the valley and discovered a well of fresh water there. But the herdsmen of Gerar quarreled with Isaac's herdsmen and said, "The water is ours!" So he named the well Esek, because they disputed with him. Then they dug another well, but they quarreled over that one also; so he named it Sitnah. He moved on from there and dug another well, and no one quarreled over it. He named it Rehoboth, saying, "Now the Lord has given us room and we will flourish in the land." From there he went up to Beersheba. That night the Lord appeared to him and said, "I am the God of your father Abraham. Do not be afraid, for I am with you; I will bless you and will increase the number of your descendants for the sake of my servant Abraham." Isaac built an altar there and called on the name of the Lord. There he pitched his tent, and there his servants dug a well. Meanwhile, Abimelech had come to him from Gerar, with Ahuzzath his personal adviser and Phicol the commander of his forces. Isaac asked them, "Why have you come to me, since you were hostile to me and sent me away?" They answered, "We saw clearly that the Lord was with you; so we said, 'There ought to be a sworn agreement between us'—between us and you. Let us make a treaty with you that you will do us no harm, just as we did not molest you but always treated you well and sent you away in peace. And now you are blessed by the Lord." Isaac then made a feast for them, and they ate and drank. Early the next morning the men swore an oath to each other. Then Isaac sent them on their way, and they left him in peace. That day Isaac's servants came and told him about the well they had dug. They said, "We've found water!" He called it Shibah, and to this day the name of the town has been Beersheba. Let's bow before this great God of ours. Father, I'm so thrilled when I look out, Lord, to see so many faces and so many families. Many people, Lord, could find a reason to stay home today or do other things, but Father God, they remembered Your fourth commandment that says, "Remember the Sabbath day and keep it holy."

And so, Father, we have come and we know that when we honor You, You bless us, but we know the greatest blessing You can give us right now is Your Word and Your Spirit and Your Presence and that You might do spiritual surgery in each of our lives. Oh, Lord God, we pray that You might make us in Your image. Please, Father God, let me get out of Your way so that You might be able to speak to these, Your people, and that Lord God, we might all be changed, for Jesus it's in Your holy name we pray, Amen.

Let me look real quick at Joshua, chapter 18. I am just going to read one verse for you. Joshua 18, verse 3 says this, "So, Joshua said to the Israelites, How long will you wait before you begin to take possession of the land that the Lord, the God of your fathers, has given you?" I read a little bit of a book by Tony Dungy called *Quiet Strength*. Tony is the head football coach of the Indianapolis Colts. In that book, Dungy talked about graduating from the University of Minnesota as a quarterback. When the NFL draft came, no one drafted him to play, and so he began to debate what to do. The Canadian Football League called and said, "Hey, we'd like for you to play for us. You can play quarterback. We'll give you a $50,000 signing bonus. We'll give you a good salary." But, Tony Dungy wanted to play in the NFL. He said, "I want to play with the best." When the Pittsburgh Steelers called him, his old football coach, Tom Moore said, "Tony, I'd like for you to come play for us. You can't play quarterback. We've got a pretty good one named Bradshaw. And you really can't play receiver. We've got a couple of good guys named Swann and Stallworth, but we can make it work. We'll find some other position for you. And by the way, we'll give you a thousand dollar signing bonus, and we'll pay you about, oh, $1,500 a month."

Though the offer was not great, Dungy really wanted to play in the NFL. He began to pray, "God, I want Your will. What do You want me to do?" Dungy said in his book, "I would have loved for God to have spoken in an audible voice and say, 'Tony, go to the Cowboys, but He didn't do that." And he continued, "Yeah, I wish God would have written on a scoreboard at some football field. I wish God would have put it on a billboard. But God didn't do any of that." Dungy began to read about Elijah and how he sought God to speak to him and God sent a storm, but He was not there. Then, God sent an earthquake, and He was not there. Then God came with a soft still voice.

Today, we are going to make a decision on what we will pursue as a building, as a place to minister. And I know this, as I visit with each of you, we do not really know what God wants. He has not spoken in a strong voice. He has not put it on a billboard. He has not put it on a scoreboard. We really want the Lord's will, and so I think we have to come here and say, "Lord, I'll listen to Your still soft, quiet voice." In the Old Testament, they used a thing called the Urim and Thummim, which are, in essence, like dice. They cast it, and they trusted that God would help them make their decision, but in the New Testament, the body of Christ began to vote as a people. I have no idea if those votes were unanimous, but when they voted, they must have assumed the outcome was God's small voice.

So, today, we are going to decide where we are going to go, where God is leading us, and we are going to pursue that. God may close the door that we choose, or He may open it wide. I think it is pretty cool that Genesis, chapter 26 has a lot to say about what we are about to do. We are going to go over five points.

When we go where God leads, famine will occur. You need to understand that. You can be perfectly where God wants you to be, and hard times will be present. And the question is, what do you do in a famine? What do you do in a hard time? Well, you know, I have a ranch and cows. With all this rain God has blessed us with, our ranch is covered with tall grass. If I have a calf missing, I do not walk in the tall grass, because I am a little scared of snakes. Where do I walk? I walk in the path. You know, cows tend to walk single-file. And just like those cows, I will walk in a path they have trod. I have no idea where the cows were going, but I walk in that path.

I wonder about what Isaac was thinking, when the famine came in the land. He probably asked, "What do I do?" He saw a path his dad had taken down toward Egypt, and he thought, "Hey, I think I'll go to Egypt." Now, Egypt in the Scripture represents things of the world. The reality is that when you and I go through famine in our lives, we tend to fall back on old ways, and on what the world would do. When we hit a famine in our lives, we work a little harder. Maybe, we party a little more. We try substances that we think will help alleviate those issues. Maybe we try a new relationship or an illicit relationship.

All of these are the paths of the world. Isaac was thinking about going to Egypt. God said, "Isaac, do not go to Egypt where trouble is present. Live where I tell you. Stay where I am." And God says to Isaac, "If you will do that, I will bless you. I will bless you with descendants, I'll bless you with land, and I'll make you a blessing." What is God saying? God is saying that when a famine exists, you and I need to stay where God is, and He will bless every aspect of our lives.

How do we know that? God pointed it out in Genesis, chapter 26. Look at Abraham. God could easily have said, "Isaac, look at your daddy. He made mistakes, but he came to Me, he sought Me, and he listened to My voice. Did I not bless Abraham? Isaac, I will bless you, too." God says the same to us. When we go where God leads, yes, famine will occur, but you and I need to be very careful to listen for His voice.

The second thing we need to know is when we go where God leads, failure will occur. We are going to make mistakes. I am so thankful again that, in Scripture, an acknowledgment is made that everyone who stands on this earth struggles with sin. I do not like being a sinner. I hate being a sinner. I wish you could have voted for a perfect pastor. The reality is, when we go where God leads, failure will occur. Isaac decided to go to Gerar as God led him, and he started noticing some things. He started seeing men combing their hair. He started seeing men kind of shine their shoes. They asked Isaac, "Hey, who's that babe with you?" And Isaac remembers the old cow path of his daddy, and he says, "She's my sister. Yeah, she's my sister. That's it. She's my sister." What a bonehead!

When you and I step out of faith, you know what we step into? Fear. Every time we step out of faith, we step into fear. I think it is interesting that in 1997, the Associated Press published a story about a convenience store in Massachusetts. A lady went into the bathroom at this convenience store and found a $20 bill on the stall floor. Now, I like finding money, but with my fear of germs, if it is in the stall, I may not touch it. But, there it was on the floor of the bathroom—a $20 bill. The lady picks it up and unfolds it. She finds a note in it. The note says, "Help. I have been kidnapped. Call the highway patrol."

On the back side of the note, it gave the phone numbers of the supposed kidnapped person's office. A description was also given of her blue-and-cream van with Oklahoma plates. Sure enough, the lady who found the note called the highway patrol. They sent out an all-points bulletin trying to find this couple. The couple's name was George and Rita Rupp. The police began a 24-hour search; they put the couple's pictures on the television. They searched the highways. They searched every blue-and-cream Ford van. About two days later a phone call came into Mr. Rupp's office. The manager of his office answered the phone, and he immediately recognized the voice.

The voice says, "Hey, I'm down at the beach enjoying the weather. How are things going there?" The manager says, "George?" Rupp answers, "Yeah, what's going on?" The surprised manager says, "You have no idea what's going on, do you?" Rupp concerned says, "No. What's going on?" The manager informed him, "We have a note that you were kidnapped. They've been searching for you on national television." George got real quiet and said, "I'm so embarrassed. My wife has a big fear that we are going to get kidnapped one day. So, she has kept a $20 bill in her purse with a note just in case we get kidnapped. I guess it fell out of her purse."

Fear. We all do things because of fear. As we look at where God wants us to go, we have some fears. We are afraid that we are not going to have enough money. We are afraid that we are not going to have enough land. We are afraid that we are not going to be able to do renovations, or we are afraid we will not be safe. Psalm 23 says, "The Lord is my shepherd I shall not want." God's Word says, "Though I walk through the valley of the shadow of death . . ." What? "I will fear no evil." You see, when we step out of faith, we step into fear, and when we step out of faith, we step into sin.

What did Isaac do? He lied. He said, "She's my sister." You know what? Some days in your life and mine, lying looks pretty strong, does it not? I mean, our nature is like, "Hey, I've got to protect myself. This lie's a pretty good one. The truth's pretty weak." And the reality is, no matter how strong a lie looks, it is always weak, and no matter how weak the truth looks, it is always strong. A lie will never be a port in the storm. Do you agree with me that God is truth? Are you debating that? I mean, do we agree God is true? If you do not believe it, do not nod your head. Do you believe Jesus is the truth? Jesus says, "I'm the way, the truth, and the life." Do you believe the Holy Spirit is called the Spirit of truth? This Book that I preach from every Sunday, is this Book true?

The last thing the world expects from you is a pack of lies spewing forth from your mouth. We are people of truth. Isaac was just like you and me. When you and I resort to a lie, when we say, "In God we nearly trust," when we trust a lie and not God, we will be embarrassed. Isaac is out with Rebekah. He says she's his sister, but you know men, some days you just want to hold your wife. Some days you just want to give her a big smooch, right? And there's Abimelech, the leader of the Philistines, the Gerarites. He looks out the window and sees Isaac and Rebekah really smooching. I am talking heavy stuff. Abimelech runs down and says, "What are you doing? She is not your sister! You lied to me!" Abimelech says something that is very convicting. If one of my men would have slept with your wife, you would have brought judgment on my country.

Now, I think it is interesting. I will give you a parenthetical comment. If Abimelech was afraid that if one man committed adultery, it would bring judgment to his whole nation, what are we looking at as a nation when we tolerate adultery on the big screen, and we promote it in our books, and we allow it in our neighborhoods? If one man will bring judgment on a nation, what are our sins doing? For you and I to be people of truth is so important. As it turned out, Isaac had nothing about which to fear or worry. So, you and I need to know that when we go where God leads, failures will follow. Isaac failed. But, we need to return to God's Word.

When we go where God leads us—here is another scoop for you—people are not going to want us present. As good looking and as kind as you guys are, people will not want our church to be present. They will not want me to be present. Isaac—he gets caught in his lie. He admits it. He goes on. He plants crops. And when he plants his crops, he gets a hundred times what everybody else gets. Now, you and I have to ask the question, "Why would God give a liar great blessings?" You know why? Because 1 John 1:9 says, "If we confess our sins, He's faithful and just and will forgive us of all our sins and cleanse us from all unrighteousness."

God is faithful when you are not faithful. And the reality is, if you, while in your sin, come and confess and begin to walk with God again, God will continue to bless you. God did that for

Isaac. Isaac had more herds, flocks, servants, and crops. And do you know what that did to those Philistines? They were mighty jealous. They could not stand that everything they did, and Isaac did—ended in victory. Isaac used the same dirt, the same sun, the same rain, the same methods, which reminds me of football coaches. They say this about good football coaches. On any day, a good football coach can take his team and beat the sap out of your team, but here is the real definition of a coach. On any given day, he could take your team and beat the sap out of his team, too. That is a good coach.

Now, Isaac is winning, but it is not because Isaac is a good man, but because Isaac serves a good God. That is why he was being blessed. And so the Philistines began to try to fill up his wells with dirt. And that does not make a bit of sense to me. Here, the land is in a famine. Water is so vital. And they are trying to cover the water up with dirt. You know what? We see that happening today. The Philistines needed the water, but they did not want the water, and they did not want anybody else to have the water either. That is pretty sorry.

I am reminded of this guy who had been a drunkard his whole life. This man comes out to the city square, and he gets up on a little box, and he begins to tell people what Jesus had done in his life. Everybody was listening, and the crowd began to grow, and he talked about how he had wasted his life. He had not been good to his family, had treated them poorly, and one cynic in the crowd yelled, "Hey! Shut up! You're dreaming." And that is when a little girl tapped the cynic on the sleeve. She said, "Mister, that is my daddy you are talking about. Let me tell you something. My daddy, when he was a drunk, he would come home, and he would beat my momma, and she would cry all night. Let me tell you something about my daddy. He would spend our money on whiskey, and I wouldn't have shoes to wear to school." She said, "Mister, let me tell you something. You see these new shoes? You see my pretty new dress? My daddy's got a good job now. Do you see that woman over there smiling at him? That's my momma. She doesn't cry anymore. She sings at night. Mister, Jesus has changed my daddy, and Jesus has changed my family. If my daddy's dreaming, please don't wake him up."

People do not want to hear about Living Water, even though it changes lives, and it makes things well. Because of that, people will not want us where we go. The Philistines asked Isaac to leave, and he did. They asked Isaac to leave their land, and my question to you is, whose land was it? Did God not say, Isaac, this is your land, not theirs? And we read later on, as we preach through the Bible, about David running those Philistines out, and they will never return. When we go where God leads us, people will not want us present, but take heart. Our God has given us the land, and our God will drive out everybody who tries to silence His Word or run out His people. When we go where God leads us, there will be people who will want us to be silent about what God does. It is always going to happen that way. We read about Isaac. He leaves that part of Gerar, and he is working in the valley. He finds more of his daddy's wells that had been covered up. So, he begins to re-dig those wells and dig back down to the good water.

You and I live in a world today where a lot of Christians are saying, "We need something new. We want the new wine. We want the new water. We want something new in our churches." Let me tell you something. Revivals never came by some new wine. Revivals came when Christians began to dig back down past tradition and apathy and false teaching, and they got back down to the Truth, the Living Water of God's Word. That is when revival comes, and God's Spirit begins to move. Isaac's men did dig some more wells, and they found living water there.

Do you not love it when God shows you truth in His Word that you have never seen before? Is that not the coolest thing? You know, when I prepare for a sermon, my prayer is, "Lord, show me something that the commentators did not see. Show me something a preacher did not preach. Show me something I have never read before. God, show me something. Empower me to preach Your Word from talking to me." Let me tell you what. When you as a believer begin to read this Word, you are going to find God speaking to you and you are going to celebrate it, and Satan is going to hate it, because a Christian who reads God's Word is stronger than a Christian who does not—every time.

Sure enough, Isaac's men, they dig a well, and they find water. And what did the Philistines do? They said, "That is our water! Get away! That is our water." And Isaac names that first well Esek. "Esek" means contention. When you and I speak God's truth, they are going to say, "Oh, no, no, that is our truth. That is Islam's truth. That is Buddha's truth. That is Mormon's truth. That is the Catholic truth. That is the Baptist truth." People are going to contend for the truth, but there is just one Truth. Isaac goes on and digs another well with his men, and they find water, and as sure as they find water, the Philistines contest, "No, no, no, that is ours, too. That is ours, too!" It is like being in the nursery with some kids. "That is my toy! And that is my toy, too!" He named the well Sitnah. "Sitnah" means hatred. The Hebrew word

"Sitnah" shares the same root as the word Satan. Hatred—the world hates God's Truth, and they hate God's Name.

How many of you have seen the Ten Commandments movie that has come out? I have not seen it, but I plan to view it. Have you heard about the advertising for the movie? The powers that be do not want them to advertise anything saying God's Name. Did you hear about that? Or, how about in Pearland, Texas this week—I have the article right here—maybe you read it. At the school board meeting in Pearland, the trustees voted not to begin their meetings with opening prayer anymore because they feel like that makes people uncomfortable, because Hindu temples and mosques are in their area. Thankfully, about two hundred Christians showed up to one of their school board meetings and said, "We want prayer back in this school board." So, the school board, fearing for their jobs, came to a mutual consent. Every meeting will begin with a word of devotion or a word of kindness or maybe a prayer, as long as it does not mention Jesus' name, or preferably they just have a moment of silence. People do not want God to be mentioned, or Christ to be lifted up.

I thought these San Diego fires were interesting. Fox News interviewed an official on Monday night. The interviewer asked this big official over fighting these huge fires in San Diego if we, as a nation, could do anything to help? And it is amazing what the official said. He said, "You know, the best thing ya'll can do for us here is sometime this week give us a moment of silence." Let us say something here. Silence never did much for anybody. I know that sometimes you wish I would be silent and you'd find a little peace, but the reality is, silence has never helped anyone. Prayer is what makes a difference—not just prayer—prayer to the Living God. When you look at Ezekiel, chapter 37, what was it that made the dead bones come to life? The Word of God did.

So, Isaac leaves that place. He goes to another place. He digs another well. He looks around, waiting on the Philistines to come. No one comes. No one argues. He is finally far enough away, and he names that well Rehoboth. "Rehoboth" means room. And Isaac says, "Now, we can flourish, because God has given us room." I am ready for Rehoboth for our church. I am ready for room. I am ready to flourish. I interviewed several preachers Monday. These preachers talked about being in their temporary settings. One preacher said that they were twelve years in a temporary place meeting in a strip center, and they grew to thirty-five people. He said, "The minute we finally got situated in a place of our own, we have grown to more than 350 people in four years." The reality is, God can bless us here. No doubt exists about that. But, my heart's desire is the yearning for room to flourish. Now, God may stake our church in another temporary setting, and that is okay. We will serve Him there, and we will be faithful.

When God leads us to where He wants us to go, people will want to silence God's Word. And you know what you and I have to do? We have to keep digging and we have to keep making God's Word available to others. That is what we do here. When we go where God leads, at some point in the future and maybe various times in the future, people will come and say, "You truly have the Word of life." And they will be right. Isaac goes to Beersheba, and Beersheba's a special place. That is where Abraham and the Philistines made a peace agreement. And while Isaac is in Beersheba—the name means well of the oath—God appeared, and God said, "I am the God of your dad, Abraham. Do not be afraid. I will bless you." How cool is that? If you read God's Word, if you follow His truth, if you are fervent about loving Him, many days in your life, God will come and say, "I'm the God of your fathers. Do not be afraid. I will bless you." How do we respond when God does that? We do what Isaac did. He followed one path that was right. He built an altar, and he called upon the name of the Lord just like his daddy. He pitched a tent. Do you know what he found? He found strength. He found power.

When God comes to us, we should be at our altars, and we should call on His name, (that should be a daily practice anyway). That he prayed is a good thing. It is a good thing he found strength, because no sooner did he get up from his prayer time, than here the Philistines come again. Whew, whew! He is so glad to see them. And he possesses so much courage, that he asked, "Why are you here?" What courage, Isaac! All of a sudden, he has got courage. "Why did you come? You have been hostile to me. You have made me leave every place I have gone." And what did the Philistines say? They said, "We see clearly God's hand is on you. We want a peace treaty." Everything they tried to do to Isaac, he always came out ahead. If you serve the Lord, no matter what Satan tries to do in your life, you will always come out ahead, always.

So, they make a peace treaty. He fixes a meal. This makes me think about Psalm 23, "Thou preparest a table for me in the presence of my enemies." That is exactly what He did for Isaac. Do you know what you read in this passage? As soon as the Philistines left, one of Isaac's men says, "Isaac, we found water!" Again.

You know what, I think Isaac smiled and said, "God, when I follow you, I just can't lose." And that is the truth.

Isaac never won a major war. Isaac never built a mighty city. All Isaac did was dig wells and make them available to others. I want you and me to be like Isaac. I want us to dig wells and bring Living Water. God's Word is compared to living water. People have come, and they have tried to dispute this Bible. They have tried to discredit this Bible. They have tried to destroy this Bible. This Bible has been under more attacks over four thousand years than any other book, the very book in your lap or hand right now.

I think about the Roman Caesar Diocletian. Diocletian hated Christ, hated Christianity. In 303 A.D., he began to kill all the Christians he could find. His main goal was to destroy every Bible in existence. He nearly did. About twenty years later, these Bibles began to pop up everywhere, and Constantine became a Christian—amazing. Roman Caesar Julian came along and said, "Hey, when I killed the Christians, that did no good. They just multiply. And when we tried to kill the Bible and destroy it, it just keeps coming back up. What I am going to need to do is to discredit the Bible." So, he looks in the Bible and tries to find a prophesy that he can make come untrue. He turns to Luke, chapter 21, verse 25 where Jesus spoke about the fact that the Temple will be destroyed and remain so throughout the age of the Gentiles. You read on in the Scripture and you see the inference that the Temple will one day be restored when the Jewish nation becomes a nation again. Julian said, "Hey, I've got it. I am over Rome. I am over Jerusalem. I will build their temple and that will make the Bible untrue."

So, he began to try to build the Temple. He got all of Rome, all the money, all the Jewish people he could recruit, and they started to try to build a temple on the Temple Mount. As soon as they cleared the land, a huge explosion occurred right on the Temple Mount, and they could not extinguish the fire. The fire burned several workers. Finally, they said, "You know what, let's just shelf this project for awhile." They were never able to discredit the Bible.

In the 1700s, Voltaire said, "Within a hundred years, the Bible will be useless, just an antique, and Christianity will be wiped from the face of the earth." Fifty years after Voltaire died, the Geneva Bible group decided to buy his home. Some say they are printing Bibles there right now. God's Word is an anvil. People come with hammers trying to destroy this Word and they cannot—all they do is break their hammers, because

God's Word stands. Jesus said, "Heaven and earth may pass away, but My words will last forever." I think of the Bible like a four-thousand-year-old man. Everybody kept trying to kill him. They threw him to the beast, and they tore at him a little bit, but they could not swallow him. The Bible is like a four-thousand-year-old man. They tried to chain him up, and he kept getting out. The Bible is like a four-thousand-year-old man. They chopped him into little pieces, and the meat came back together, the wounds healed, and he continued to walk. The Bible is like a four-thousand-year-old man; they hung him until he was dead, and when they lowered him down, he jumped back up and began to walk again. The Bible is like a man who was thrown into a fire, and when they thought this man had turned to ashes, they opened the furnace and out he walks, not even smelling like smoke. God's Word is like a four-thousand-year-old man. When they gave him poison, he was not even harmed. When they put him in water, he would not drown. That is the Word of God.

You and I come on good footing. Our responsibility, Church at the Cross, is to dig wells and not back down from God's Word. John said, "In the beginning was the Word, and the Word was God, and the Word was with God." Jesus Christ is the Word. He said to the woman at the well, "Let him who is thirsty come to Me and drink Living Water and you will never thirst again." Today, perhaps you do not know our Savior. Maybe you have been in church forever. Maybe people think you are a Christian, but you know better. Do not leave this place lost. Give your heart to Christ.

One thing is certain; you will not be embarrassed, you will be embraced. In church, we are to be united. No matter where God leads, I want to be where God is, and that is what we will do.[3]

Lessons

Vance Havner said, "A preacher should have the mind of a scholar, the heart of a child, and the hide of a rhinoceros."[4] I never knew that guy, but he sure knows what he is talking about. To handle the arrows that come to the pastor purposely and inadvertently takes a lot of nerve. More than anything, it takes a great reliance on the Lord. In a world of instability, the church has

---

3. Johnny Teague, senior pastor, Church at the Cross, Houston, TX, "When We Go Where God Leads (Genesis 26)," October 28, 2007.

4. Powell, *Basic Bible Sermons*, 44.

to know that Jesus is the Rock. No matter what the surprise, people come to church to see what God has to say to them in what they face. The more they see that God has an answer, the more they will rely on Him for that answer. And, so will the preacher.

This passage showed how Isaac continued to face surprises from the environment, his nature, and the people with whom he lived. With every surprise, a lesson was present. With nearly every surprise, a trust in God was present to carry them through. This is the word for the preacher facing surprises. Each one is a lesson to guide in the sanctification journey of the preacher and the church members.

With each move, Isaac dug new wells. What this meant was that each place they left, they left a well. What a teaching point for our church! I told our church that no matter how many times we move, may we leave a well of Living Water that will lead those who have seen us to the Lord Jesus Christ. The text found our church where our need was. At the intersection of time, another collision occurred for God's Word meeting man's need.

Chapter 12: The Dying Church

When our church was looking for a place to relocate, we found numerous church buildings with a capacity of four hundred to seven hundred seats, with only twenty people meeting every Sunday. To witness so many fine edifices virtually empty was amazing. They are on every corner, in nearly every city in the United States, and in other countries also. They consist of huge sanctuaries, nice facilities, and equipped gymnasiums, which are serving only a handful of people. One pastor referred to these as "museums of revivals long ago."[1] These are precious churches with precious people in locations where God has done great things in the past. Most, I am sure, long for God to do the same again. Others just want others to nurse them through their older age at that location, because it is their home church. They have even taken legal measures to leave the building to some other ministry or purpose when the church loses the ability to continue. For still others, the church in decline is their last vestige of power, so they will hold on until the church pries itself loose from their cold, stiff fingers. Churches still exist, which live in the past and cling to tradition. Regardless of how times have changed, they simply will not change or adjust in an effort to reach the lost person of the day. Where churches sometimes choose bumper stickers to describe their church's mission for the year, some churches in grave decline could easily post bumper stickers, which read, "Last one out, turn off the lights."[2]

The Pew Forum on Religion and Public Life revealed in their Religious Landscape Survey that "the percentage of those affiliated with Protestant churches is shrinking."[3] America is reported to be in a great deal of flux, in which almost half of the adults have not kept the faith of their childhood. Stephen Klineberg, a Rice University sociologist, could not have summed the consequences better when he said, "This is where the American future

---

1. Brunson and Caner, *Why Churches Die*, 33.
2. David F. Nixon, *Leading the Comeback Church* (Kansas City, MO: Beacon Hill Press, 2004), 59.
3. Jeannie Keever, "As Americans Change, So Does Their Religion," *Houston Chronicle*, 26 February 2008, 1 (A).

is going to be worked out."[4] For the Christian with any Biblical knowledge at all knows the future is dim for the nation that ceases to follow the God of Heaven, the God of the Bible, and His Son Jesus Christ. In the Pew Forum study, practically every religious group was in decline. The one group that made the largest jump in growth was the one comprised of atheists, agnostics, or no religion in particular.[5] Clearly, churches are dying, people are content being lost, and a nation is at stake.

Truly, God can grow a church. Man can grow an organization that may or may not be called a church, but only God can grow a true church. God's watchcare over His church is so mighty that no one could ever kill a church, but a church does have the ability to commit suicide.[6] Dr. Jim Jackson says that man cannot make things happen; only God can. All that man is able to do is to keep things from happening. Man does not have the power to fire things up, but he has the power to shut things down.[7] That dying churches knowingly choose to close their doors or dismantle their buildings is not likely, but the decisions they make will accomplish that task just the same.[8]

When things start to grow is interesting, because often churches will stop the growth, because the harvest seems threatening to them. They become afraid of the very work of God for which they prayed. In times of heavenly activity, members can become more fearful for their facility than for souls. One pastor found that to be true in a former church that he pastored in a downtown area. This church was an architectural marvel beaming with incredible stained glass. The church building was the pride of the members and a beautiful landmark in the city, but the church itself was dying.

The young pastor began a street ministry to feed suffering people. One day each week, the impoverished of the area would come to the basement of this grand old church building to receive a meal. Members began to squabble against this ministry for fear someone might accidentally leave a stove on and burn down their beautiful building. The pastor told them if that was a concern, "Build me a building or buy me one. We are going to reach out to these people." They came to a compromise, and he was able to get local restaurants to give his church their surplus cooked food at the end of the day, which was served in the basement, already cooked. This soothed the sanctuary worriers and grew the ministry of the Kingdom. Not long after, the whole church became excited at the way God

---

4. Ibid.
5. Ibid, A4.
6. Clark, "Suicide of a Church," 29.
7. Jackson, interview.
8. Clark, "Suicide of a Church," 30.

was using them. However, the measures needed to move the dying church to a thriving church were immense.[9]

Success is never guaranteed. Because of this, seldom will one take a dying church willingly. Very few Calebs are present out there, who in their eighties are not content with a rocking chair in a retirement home near a stained glass window. Very few Calebs see an impossible situation as a mission field from God promised for conquest.[10] They want a church that is on the move. They want to step-in-and-ride-the-wave of the planting, watering, and weeding of others. They are unlike

Bro. Bruce Wells who has spent over twenty years with a church that had once been in decline, which is now content to "plod along," hardly noticed, ever upward. Even today, his church has reached a good size, but not to the point of being recognized even in its state. Wells is content in the mission God has given him, and overjoyed at the way God is changing people through him slowly, but surely.[11]

Often, success is defined in terms of fannies in the seats and acreage in the church compound. The megachurch holds a dream and a draw for some preachers and a competitive trump for the consumer-minded churchgoer. Big churches offer vast opportunities for service, a "smorgasbord" of ministries.[12] Huge, thriving churches can be a great blessing in carrying the Gospel of Jesus Christ to multitudes. In a consumer-mentality culture, these churches are in a position to reach lost people who might never darken the door of a church for any other reason.

Has the small "plodding" church lost its usefulness? Does such a church have no call from the Lord? What about those areas that are downtrodden and in decline where megachurches cannot or will not reach? Do the people in these areas not need the Lord? They have churches in them, but they are churches that are too weak to make an impact. These are the churches that preachers often overlook or run from in escape. Have preachers forgotten the lesson of nature? Although a slow-growing tree may require several years of growth before it can ever shade a house, generally, that tree will live longer than a fast-growing tree. Because of its slow growth, it will often have deeper roots and stronger branches enabling it to withstand droughts and windstorms much better than the faster-growing tree.[13] These are exactly

---

9. Jackson, interview.

10. Brunson and Caner, *Why Churches Die*, 41.

11. Bruce Wells, senior pastor, Liberty City, Texas, personal phone interview with project leader, May 27, 2008.

12. Nixon, *Leading the Comeback Church*, 113.

13. U.S. Department of Energy, "A Consumer's Guide to Energy Efficiency and Renewable Energy: Landscape Shading" (September 12, 2005) [on-line]; accessed 28

the areas that are untended and populated by near-empty church buildings, which need the shade of the Savior.

When one looks at Houston's First Baptist Church, they see the fruitful, active product as it is today. When people visit the Brooklyn Tabernacle Church, they see the global ecclesiastical giant that is now. For some reason, people never realize these were dying, near-dead, last-breath kind of churches. These were churches in areas that needed the Gospel, but lacked the resources to make an impact. Dr. John Bisagno came to the second oldest Baptist church in Texas—Houston's First Baptist Church. He did not come to a megachurch. In fact, he left a much bigger church to take this one. He came to a church with old deteriorating facilities, which could seat two thousand people, but had barely three hundred attending. He first preached to a near empty sanctuary.

When Jim Cymbala arrived at the Brooklyn Tabernacle, it was not the apple of the church's eye; rather, it was more of a blight. A young pastor had left, and the sparsely attended church in a crumbling structure had to face the probability of closing with less than ten dollars in the bank. Cymbala's father-in-law was an unofficial overseer of a few small, independent churches. He was not willing to let the church close. He said, "I'm not sure God is finished with that place quite yet."[14] He was right. Through prayer, preaching, and perseverance, God used one of His servants to do a mighty work with that small dying church.

When Charles Haddon Spurgeon was called to Park Street Church in London, he began preaching in a fifteen-hundred-seat sanctuary with fewer than two hundred people attending. Nine years later, this church built and relocated to the Metropolitan Tabernacle, built to accommodate thousands who flocked to hear him preach. During his thirty-year pastorate, six thousand people regularly attended worship in a church that reached a membership of fourteen thousand.[15] Did you catch the optimal phrase, "he began preaching"? There it is. God said if Christ be lifted up, He will draw all men to Him. This does not say, "If Christ be lifted up, I will make you a Megachurch." Jesus said, "Come with Me and I will make you fishers of men." Jesus takes responsibility for the church's success.[16] He has a plan for each one. The preacher's prayer should be "Lord I want to be exactly what You made me to be, nothing more and nothing less." With that said, it is the

---

July 2008; available from http://www.eere.energy.gov/consumer/ yourhome/landscaping/index.cfm/mytopic=11940; Internet.

14. Jim Cymbala, *Fresh Wind, Fresh Fire* (Grand Rapids: Zondervan Publishers, 1997), 15.

15. Nixon, *Comeback Church*, 47.

16. Ibid., 51.

preaching of the Word of the Lord that God has called His servant to do in any and every church and church-type.

What does one preach in a church that is dying? He does not come condemning and berating the congregation from the pulpit saying, "You people are too old-fashioned!"[17] He can come before the congregation honestly if need be. One pastor came to his church and told them that because of the neighborhood shift, "Within two years the church will be dead if we do not do something." Instead of killing the church, it began to work with a new mission. The church mobilized, it visited, it started new classes for all age groups, and soon it began to grow.[18] More than anything, the preacher preaches God's Word faithfully, backing it up with a prayer life and a love for God and the people.

Situation

The New York Avenue Presbyterian Church was founded in 1859 in Washington D.C. It had a host of great preachers lead it through defining moments in the history of the United States. This church has often been called the "Presidents' church." It was the church of Abraham Lincoln. The New York Avenue Presbyterian Church's pastor at that time was Dr. Phineas D. Gurley. He had a strong relationship with President Lincoln during the years of the Civil War. He helped President Lincoln through many difficult times, including the death of Lincoln's son, Willie in 1862. Additionally, he presided over President Lincoln's funeral and accompanied Lincoln's body from Washington D.C. to Springfield, Illinois for burial.

Needless to say, a young Scottish preacher was thrilled when asked to take the pulpit of this historic church, which was in rapid decline in the years leading up to World War II. He began his ministry there in 1937. A movie based on his life entitled "A Man Called Peter" was produced in 1955, based on the biographical account written by his wife Catherine. That movie covered the initial sermon he preached in that beautiful, but dying church stoked in tradition.

---

17. Willimon, *Preaching About Conflict*, 83.
18. Ibid., 13.

CHAPTER 12: THE DYING CHURCH

Sermon

Dr. Peter Marshall

New York Avenue Presbyterian Church

WASHINGTON, D.C., 1937

It has been said that a new minister's first sermon, while he is still strange to his congregation and his congregation is strange to him, frequently has far-reaching repercussions. You have your ideas of what your pastor should be, and your pastor has his ideas of what your church should be. I have come practically as a stranger to this imposing old church, a church whose history is almost as old as this country. A church whose traditions and legends I respect and find thrilling and exciting. Now, history and tradition and legends are fine. We could not live without the past, but past glory has never been enough for a nation or a church or even an individual. The all-important now and the more important future are present always. I look out this morning on a church not even half filled. Now, this in no way injures my personal pride, my vanity. I am not here to recruit fans for a fellow named Peter Marshall. Nor, am I here to sell anything.

That which we call salvation, and a most comprehensive term it is, is a free gift. You cannot buy it; neither can you earn it. It is not a reward dangling before the Christian like a carrot before a mule. It is not something that the church has to peddle. In addition, probably no idea hurts me more than suggesting that I am a salesman endeavoring to sell people on the idea of religion. I resent it bitterly. Religion is not for sale; it is given away. So today, as I start my ministry in this hallowed old church, I think it only fair to explain that it is not the church or religion I am trying to present, but Christ.

Not the pale, anemic namby-pamby Jesus, the gentle Jesus meek and mild, but the Christ of the Gospels—striding up and down the dusty miles of Palestine, suntanned, bronzed, fearless, the knuckles big in His carpenter's hands; the Christ who upset the money lenders, the Christ who had a good time at weddings and who would not allow His host to be embarrassed by running out of wine; the Christ who loved people, all kinds of people, but particularly red-blooded folk. For He Himself was red-blooded. The Christ who called a spade a spade and who let the chips fall where they might; not the Jesus of the perfumed cloisters of pious sentiment, but the man who walked the streets of the city; stopping here and there to pass the time of day in places where you and I could not afford to be seen and getting a huge kick out of it.

Let us be honest. Let us recognize that the kind of people that Christ liked best were not the kind that the average church appeals to at all. Think of the people that He personally invited to be His friends—Peter and Andrew, James and John—fish merchants; Zacchaeus and Matthew—unpopular tax collectors; Saul of Tarsus, an aristocrat and a persecutor of the church; Mary Magdalene—once a prostitute; and Jo Anna—wife of Herod's chancellor, a so-called society woman.

I am sure in Washington, countless people fall into just this category. We cannot afford to be indifferent to them. We must invite the sophisticates, the irreligious, the lost, and the lonely. We must extend to them our fellowship and introduce them to Christ. That is our business, nothing else. For Christ likes people, all kinds of strange people, people whom we might have to think twice about before cultivating them. He wants them. He enjoys their life and vigor. He wants to hear laughter, a joke, if it is a good one. A man of sorrows and acquainted with grief, that He was, but it was in order that our joy might be full. That is the Christ that I know; that is the Christ I would have to dwell in this historic old church. His big carpenter's hand stretched out in welcome. Let us pray.[19]

Lessons

In this dying old church, Marshall faced a great variety of obstacles. He faced opposition at times because of his nontraditional clerical wardrobe. Further, his common language in a refined city drew questions. His target of all kinds of people for salvation troubled many in the congregation who lived upscale, powerful lives. With all that, Marshall preached God's Word.

When a preacher preaches to a dying church, he must lift the vision of the church beyond the four walls that house the sanctuary. He must have them look beyond people "like themselves." He has to point out to them the mission of the church, Christ's mission for the Church. He does this by preaching God's Word, purely, soundly, and faithfully. He does this by hungering for lost people in the highways and byways of life. He does this by finding the needs and launching the ministry to meet those needs from the pulpit and in leadership.

19. "A Man Called Peter," 20th Century Fox, 1955; see also Catherine Marshall, *A Man Called Peter* (Grand Rapids: Chosen Books Publishers, 1951).

Further, he must prepare his people to be accepting of the variety of people who walk through the church doors. Marshall did an excellent job in this sermon by describing the type people who were meeting Jesus on the shores of Galilee and in the streets of the bordering cities.

When I took over my first church, in my first sermon, I broached the kind of people that our church should welcome. I described the hypocrite, the lost, the rich, the poor, the promiscuous, the virtuous, the young, and the old. Further, I said that one Sunday, a homosexual couple might even show up in our church. I said, if such come, they are sinners like the rest of us. I said that we will preach against the sin, and strive to lead them to repentance, a saving knowledge of Jesus Christ, to experience a break from that lifestyle, and then fruitful, active membership. I never in my life expected to see such a couple, but then two years later, two young girls came that fit that exact description. No one knew the girls were gay; I certainly did not. They were young, college girls; we just assumed they were roommates.

Then one evening, they had my family over for dinner. After the meal, they shared with us where they were in their lives. I shared with them what God says concerning that lifestyle, prayed with them, and encouraged them to follow the Savior. Not too long after that, they both left that lifestyle, separated, and over time began to serve the Lord themselves. God can do that in a church that preaches God's Word and is open to touch the sinner with the Gospel and love of Jesus Christ.

Special note: This sermon was transcribed directly from the biographical movie of Dr. Peter Marshall's life. In my research, I sought to find assurance that this was actually the sermon preached by Peter Marshall at New York Avenue Presbyterian Church. I wanted to make sure this compelling sermon was actually his and not some Hollywood movie guess. I visited with dignitaries at the church, but they had no sermon transcripts dating that far back. I visited with his son Peter John Marshall, but he was not born at the time this sermon was preached. Confidence exists that it is Marshall's though, in that it is noted that his sermons were transcribed by his secretary Mary Wood.[20] The movie in which this sermon was preached was based on the biography of his life by Catherine Marshall and was filmed shortly after his death with Catherine's oversight.

---

20. New York Avenue Presbyterian Church, Washington D.C. [on-line]; accessed 18 August 2008; available from www.nyapc.org; Internet.

Chapter 13: **Church In Strife**

Behind every statistic recorded in this book, broken pieces exist. Innocent people in broken churches have no idea what has happened, nor what will happen. They look for someone to come and pick-up those broken pieces, to put their church back together, so they can go back to the work of bringing their lives to a state of glorifying their Creator. Many churches never recover. If they continue to exist, they exist as a shadow on the church map. They exist as a church that had that "big fight back in 1973." They exist as a church that really made a difference—once upon a time. They exist calloused, skeptical, holding their church close to the vest. They placate themselves by saying that "we are small, but at least we are a 'family.'" What they do not realize is that a lot of cults and religions call themselves the same thing.[1] The good news is that many more churches long to recover. They want to move forward. They want to thrive again. In fact, like people in their individual lives, they prefer not to deal with the past anymore.

Pastors called to take such churches receive very familiar comments. Men at a local barber shop will get into a conversation while waiting for a haircut. They exchange pleasantries, find out what each other does for a living, and then continue to speak based on that information. Assuming one is a pastor, a guy at the barber shop may ask him, "Where do you pastor?" The pastor will reply, "I preach down at Fourth Methodist Church, in Middletown." The questioner will say, "I'm so sorry to hear that. That church sure had a whale of a fight a few years back. Are they still as poisonous as they used to be?"

Or, perhaps the pastor is visiting with a member of the Fourth Methodist Church. At some point, the member will feel comfortable enough to comment, "I wonder what you did wrong to get pulled into all this mess." Pastors who take strife-torn churches seldom have the full disclosure on all the happenings of the past. Pulpit committees major on getting the complete history of a candidate—prior church experience, education, married life, and so forth. Rarely, do they reciprocate. The minister may spend the rest of his pastorate chastising himself for not being more thorough in the

---

1. Qualben, *Peace in the Parish*, 155.

CHAPTER 13: CHURCH IN STRIFE

interview process. Really to discover pertinent information takes due diligence on the part of the pastoral candidate.

Most of this is hindsight. The greatest blessing for the Israelites in the wilderness came when they looked forward to what God had in store for them. The pastor is served best by looking at the now and the not yet. His job is to build the house of God for His glory. This job involves using damaged bricks, knowing that no matter how long it takes, the goal is to save the lost, grow the Christians, and make the church fruitful.

One particular preacher followed a pastor who had fallen to immorality. His goal was to lead the church beyond the crisis to restoration. He found great success in the process, so much so, that a seminary student asked him, "How did you do it?" The pastor informed the student, that it was not due to pastoral work, or teaching, or administration, or psychotherapy. He said, "All I did was preach."[2] Now that is simplistic. Surely, he did other things, but his focus was on preaching the Word of God to the strife-torn church.

Bruce Wells took a little church in a rural community called Rainbow, near the town of Glen Rose, Texas. This church had suffered through much strife. The pastor before the previous one had split the church and began a new one a few miles away. The ensuing dispute was very bitter, and those who stayed were bitter and hurt. The pastor they hired following that one was a sight to behold. He was kind and pastoral, but he had a bad habit. He loved baseball—not that baseball is a bad habit, but he loved it so much that when the Texas Rangers were playing during worship times, he would carry up to the pulpit a transistor radio with an earphone in his right ear. Throughout his sermons, he would listen to the ballgame and give the congregation score updates. He was asked to leave before long.

Then came Bro. Bruce Wells. He had a mess on his hands, a church that was the textbook illustration of strife-torn. He took the pulpit knowing more than anything that this church needed to be fed the Word of God. He did not come to correct them, but to shepherd them through. When bitterness and control issues arose, he simply encouraged them with the instruction of Jesus. That church became the fastest-growing church in the county. People were converted, baptisms always took place, and people on their knees before God covered the front of the church during the invitation.[3]

Mac Brunson took a church that had made some mistakes in its past. The longer he was at the church, the more the past presented itself. Brunson realized that corporately, this church needed to go back and repent of some things. From the pulpit, he began a series on the topic of

---

2. Gunnink, *Preaching for Recovery*, 18.
3. Wells, interview.

repentance. Through this sermon series, he addressed issues which the church had not handled correctly. He led them through this series to a heart of repentance. The church members were in one accord in their repentance. The biggest obstacle he found was that, though the church repented, they found it much more difficult to forgive. As a result, Brunson continued for a lengthy time on the issue of forgiveness, displaying for all to see the Biblical mandate and example.[4]

Situation

John Meador's church faced an issue of strife, and Pastor Meador, for the life of the church, had to address the reluctance of some members to forgive. He set a visual backdrop for the sermon by decorating the stage with a cornucopia of luggage types, shapes, and colors. This was his sermon prop as he began to walk among the luggage, picking up different types, and explaining how luggage lends itself to describe areas in which people will not forgive.

Sermon

John Meador

"Life Won't Wait on the Unforgiving"

MATTHEW 18:21-35

I am so very glad that you are with us this morning. I am going to ask you to take your Bibles today and turn to Matthew—the Gospel of Matthew, chapter 18, for just a few moments. As you are turning, you may notice that we have a few pieces of equipment up here on the stage. Most of you would call it luggage; others of us would call it baggage. The last couple of weeks we have been talking about different aspects of bags or baggage in our lives. We have been looking at the fact that life will not wait on the wounded. This week, "Life Won't Wait on the Unforgiving." Now, as I look at these pieces of baggage up here today, I am thinking about how diverse they are. I want them to be in front of you during our entire worship service so that you might think about them for just a few moments. These represent the bags that are not only in the room, but in our lives that we do not often speak

---

4. Mac Brunson, senior pastor, First Baptist Church, Jacksonville, FL, telephone interview with writer, April 22, 2008.

about. It is like that eight-hundred pound gorilla that is sitting in the room that no one ever talks about. You know it is present, but you do not quite know what to say about it. This baggage represents the same kind of thing in our lives.

All kinds of bags are in here for us—there is a big bag right here—really big—it has something in it, too, so it is pretty heavy. It may represent something in your life that is pretty dramatic, pretty huge, something that you still carry around with you. Something that you have had in your life for many, many years, and you do not quite know what to do with that bag, but you know it is heavy—you know it is hard to bear.

Here is an old one. I do not know how old this is, but you will not find this on the carousel at the DFW Airport, will you? You just will not see anything like this. It is old and ancient looking—almost looks like an antique. That might represent something that happened to you fifty years ago—*fifty years ago*—that you still carry around in your life.

This bag looks like kind of an old work bag—an old briefcase. Maybe something happened to you at work years ago, and you have yet to forgive the person that did that to you. Here is something kind of small. Women typically carry their make-up in this bag. Maybe something has been said about the way you look, and you still deal with that—you still struggle with unforgiveness toward the person that said that to you.

Over here is a bag that might represent something your mother or father did to you when you were a small child. This looks like a child's suitcase. Maybe you are carrying with you the issue of unforgiveness; you have never yet dealt with that. You have never yet been able to look at them in the face and say, "I forgive you for what you did to me." Maybe your child did something to you. Maybe your spouse did something to you. These bags represent what may have occurred in our lives and the fact that we have yet to deal with those occurrences.

Can you imagine carrying all these bags around? Can you imagine what it would be like to put all these on your back, strap them on, and somehow walk through life? That is exactly what we do with the baggage of the past if we do not ever deal with it. And after awhile, the baggage really can accumulate, and before long it is so weighty, so heavy, that we cannot move forward at all. In fact, just to move forward takes our whole concentration. Forget hearing God. Forget knowing what a good future may be out there for us. Forget trying to initiate the relationship. We are still dragging the old stuff from the past with us. Why do we drag it? While we are weighted down by our bags, life rushes by, because life does not wait on the unforgiving, just like life does not wait on the wounded.

Now, what we need to do today is to find out how to take this big bag and get rid of it. Maybe this bag represents an issue of spiritual betrayal; a spiritual leader in your life has betrayed you. Maybe that one over there represents something entirely different, and yet, they are all the same. We have got to learn to deal with baggage and the way to do that is with this incredible term that I am going to introduce you to in just a moment: forgiveness. Please stand as we read the Word of God today, Matthew, chapter 18, beginning in verse 21—a very long passage that we will take the time to read in its entirety as we look at what Jesus says about forgiveness, prompted by a question by none other than Peter. Verse 21 says, "And Peter came to him and said, Lord, how often shall my brother sin against me, and I forgive him? Up to seven times?"

And I am sure Peter was thinking, you know, that is pretty noble of me to forgive someone seven times. In fact, after the first and second and third and fourth and fifth time, for me to have the patience and the character and the intestinal fortitude to say, "I forgive you, man," that is powerful. I am sure Peter was maybe just patting himself on the back just a little bit. And Jesus said to him something very unexpected, verse 22, "I do not say to you up to seven times, but up to seventy-times-seven." He goes on and begins to teach and here is what He says in verse 23.

> Therefore the Kingdom of Heaven is like a certain king who wanted to settle accounts with his servants. When he had begun to settle accounts, one was brought to him who owed him ten thousand talents. But as he was not able to pay, his master commanded that he be sold with his wife and children and all that he had and that payment be made. And the servant therefore fell down before him, saying, "Master, have patience with me and I will pay you all." Then the master of that servant was moved with compassion, released him, and forgave him the debt.

That is the verse that you need to keep in mind right there,

> But that servant went out and found one of the fellow servants, who owned him a hundred pence, and he laid hands on him, and took him by the throat, saying "Pay me what you owe." And his fellow servant fell down at

CHAPTER 13: CHURCH IN STRIFE

> his feet, and begged him saying "Have patience with me and I will pay you all."

Sounds familiar does it not? We have already heard that once.

> And he would not but went and threw him into prison until he should pay the debt. So when his fellow servants saw what had been done, they were very grieved and they came and told their master all that had been done. And then the master after he called him said to him, "You wicked servant, I forgave all that debt because you begged me. Should you not also have had compassion on your fellow servant, just as I have pity on you." And his master was angry and delivered him to the torturers until he should pay all that was due to him.

And then this is the clincher . . .

> So My Heavenly Father also will do to you if each of you from his heart does not forgive his brother his trespasses.

Powerful passage. In fact, if you read it correctly, the passage is frightening. Pray with me, "Father, thank You so much today for the opportunity we have to look at this passage, to look at Your words, literally from the mouth of Jesus Christ and learn what they mean to us. We ask this in Jesus' name. Amen." Please be seated.

We are going to take this passage, and although it is so long we cannot walk word-by-word through all of it, we are going to take three key aspects of this passage today, and we want to understand what Jesus is saying to Peter. Prompted by a question, what do we do about forgiveness? What do we do about those who offend us, not only those who have offended us once, but what do we do about those who have done something against us more than once—a repeated offense? What do we do about that? Peter asks, "Should I forgive my friend seven times? How many times do I need to do this?" Jesus begins right away speaking about the priority of forgiveness. That is the first thing that I want you to see today, the priority of forgiveness, the importance of forgiveness. Jesus says in verses 21 and verse 22, "I do not say to you up to seven times but up to seventy-times-seven."

Basically, Jesus said that forgiveness is more important than you can ever imagine, and it needs to be something engrained far more deeply in your life than you can ever imagine. It is not a matter of just saying, "Alright, he's offended me once, twice, three times. I can forgive that, and so I can do that three times, and I just say, 'You're forgiven', and go on, because I know there is a limit at some point, and at that point, I will say, 'No more! I'll draw the line.'" Peter was kind of drawing the line right there, and Jesus said, "Pick the line up. Do not draw the line." "I say to you, not seven times, but seventy-times-seven." Now for those of us who are mathematically minded, that equals 490 times. I want you to know that Jesus had no intention of anyone walking around with their little notepad in hand saying, "Let us see, that is 356. You have only got a few more to go. Then I cut you off." But that is the way we live life sometimes.

We begin to store things in this bag, "They did this to me, or somebody else did that to me, and I am adding that bag up, and it is getting heavier and heavier and at some point, it is going to be so heavy that I am just going to cut them off." But Jesus said, "No. You are not going to draw lines like that" for a number of reasons that we will look at in just a few moments. But, I am telling you the priority of forgiveness is such that you need to live a life of forgiveness. You need to be able to forgive again and again and again and again—not just seven times, not just 490 times. It is about living above all that. It is about understanding just how much you have been forgiven, and to the very depths of your forgiveness, being able to live out that saying, "I forgive you." Peter was not thinking that he might need a little forgiveness down the road, but he did, did he not? As we all do.

One of the most amazing pictures of forgiveness takes place in the life of Corrie Ten Boom. Corrie had been in a concentration camp in Nazi Germany, watched her sister die, and watched untold atrocities occur in her own life and the life of others. She tells a compelling story in her book on forgiveness. For the most part, I need to read the story just to capture what God does in the sense of forgiveness when He forgives us, giving us the capacity to forgive others and the importance of it. She writes,

> It was in a church in Munich when I was speaking in 1947 that I saw him. A balding, heavy set man in a gray overcoat, a brown felt hat clutched between his hands. One moment I saw the overcoat and the brown hat, the next I saw the blue uniform and visor cap with its skull and crossbones, which those Nazi soldiers wore. Memories of the concentration camp flooded back into my mind. This huge room with its harsh overhead lights, the pathetic pile of dresses and shoes in the center of the floor, the shame of walking naked past this

man. I could see my sister's frail form ahead of me, ribs sharp beneath the parchment of skin. Bethany and I had been arrested for concealing Jews in our home during the Nazi occupation of Holland. This man had been a guard at Ravensbrook Concentration Camp where we were sent and now he was standing in front of me. His hand was thrust out. He wanted to shake. I had just spoken on the issue of forgiveness and he was there. He said, "A fine message, fräulein. How good it is to know as you say that our sins are at the bottom of the sea." It was the first time since my release from camp that I'd been face to face with one of my captors and my blood froze.

"You mentioned Ravensbrook in your talk," he was saying, "I was a guard there, but since that time," he said, "I've become a Christian. I know that God has forgiven me for the cruel things I did there but I would like to hear it from your lips as well." Again, the hand came out. "Will you forgive me?" And I stood there, frozen—I could not. My sister, Bethany, had died in that place. Could he erase her slow terrible death just by the asking? It could have been many, many seconds when I stood there looking at his hand, but to me it seemed like an hour as I wrestled with the most difficult thing I'd ever done in my life, but I had to do it. I knew I did because I had been forgiven. I had to forgive him. The message that God forgives has a prior condition, that we forgive those who have injured us. "If you do not forgive men their trespasses Jesus said, neither will your Father in Heaven forgive your trespasses."

So, I stood there with coldness clutching my heart, but forgiveness is an act of the will and the will can function regardless of the temperature of the heart. "Jesus help me," I prayed. I can lift my hand. I can do that much. You supply the feeling and so, mechanically and woodenly, I stuck my hand out and he grabbed my hand and the moment I did that, the current started in my shoulder and raced through my arms, sprang into our joint hands and His healing warmth seemed to flood my whole being bringing tears to my eyes. "I forgive you, brother with all my heart." For a long moment we grasped each other's hands, a former guard and the former prisoner. I'd never known God's love so powerfully until that moment.[5]

Dear Friend, let me tell you something. When you walk in a spirit of forgiveness the way this woman was walking in the spirit of forgiveness, willing to forgive no matter how many offenses someone has committed against you, no matter how deeply they have hurt you, no matter how deeply they have wounded you, God meets you in that place of obedience. Even when you do not feel it in your heart, but when you are willing, by an act of the will to say, "I choose to forgive you whatever it is that you have done against me, no matter how repeatedly you've done that, I choose in the name of Jesus because of his forgiveness of me, I, by faith, forgive you and release you." That is when we begin to know the priority of forgiveness in our lives and the power of God at work.

The priority of forgiveness, Jesus begins with that, but He does not stop there. He gives us a picture of forgiveness. He wants us to see exactly what forgiveness looks like, and we have this incredible story that He tells, beginning in verse 23. It is a parable. But I want you to move down to verse 27 as Jesus zeros in on the very act of forgiveness, and I want you to focus on this, along with focusing on the worst thing that someone has ever done to you. Notice what Jesus says about forgiveness, "Then the master of that servant was moved with compassion, released him, and forgave him the debt."

You need to highlight that verse. You need to underline it. You need to put an asterisk next to it, because three words in that verse tell us the three incredible aspects of forgiveness that you and I need to walk out of here with today. We need to see that manifold picture of what forgiveness really is. Again, "Then the master of that servant was moved with compassion, released him, and forgave him the debt." Now what does forgiveness look like? What does it feel like? What does forgiveness really do when it unfolds?

Those three terms help us. First of all, we look at the phrase, "moved with compassion." The master was "moved with compassion." The phrase means to feel deeply with great pity and to act. I like to call this "compassion and action," because you never find this word "compassion" without some action taking place with it at the same time. You find it a number of times in the Gospels, and every time in reference to Jesus Christ. As Jesus was "moved

---

5. Corrie ten Boom, *The Hiding Place* (Washington, CT: Chosen Books, 1971), 215-16.

with compassion," He acted as a result of that. That is really what forgiveness is about—God being moved in compassion toward us and acting always with action. This kind of compassion that Jesus Christ had always requires action.

For example, let us look in Matthew, chapter 14. Turn your pages back—just a few pages to Matthew, chapter 14 and verse 14. Here the five thousand are sitting before Jesus, listening to him teach, and it says in verse 14, "When Jesus went out, He saw a great multitude, and He was moved with compassion for them and healed their sick." Not only did He have compassion in His heart, but action came as a result of that compassion. Turn one more page over to Matthew, chapter 15. This time in verse 32, "Jesus called His disciples to Himself and said, 'I have compassion on the multitude because they have now continued with Me three days and have had nothing to eat; and I do not want to send them away hungry lest they fall or faint on the way.'" And so, He sustained them. It is compassion with action, but you need to understand today that when you came to Christ, and He forgave you of your sin, and He gave you eternal life, you experienced compassion in action, not just that God felt pity on us, not just that God was grieved because of the circumstances and the situations of sin, but that He was moved to do something about it. What He did was send His son, Jesus Christ to die on a cross to pay for our sin. Compassion in action! And that's what He calls us to have.

A second word is in that verse, verse 27, and that is the word "released." "Then the master of that servant was moved with compassion, released him." Boy, this is a great word, because this word is a word that describes "to declare someone free." Listen to this—the decision to dismiss and to acquit of a crime. It means actually to declare it; to make the statement, "You are forgiven" is to make the statement, "You are released." In Luke, chapter 13, verse 12, a woman comes to Jesus and she is bent over with a spirit of infirmity the Bible says, and Jesus looks at her, and he says, "You are loose, you are released." And then He brings His hands upon her, prays for her, and she actually walks away whole. First comes the declaration; then comes the healing, and the declaration is incredibly important. It is saying this about sin. To say, I release you from that sin. I acquit you of that sin. It is very similar to a judge banging his gavel with a verdict, "Not guilty!" And that is what He does with us, because Jesus Christ has paid for our sins on the cross. God Himself says, "I release you, not guilty anymore."

Then there is a third word. That word is "forgave." Again, in verse 27, "The master of the servant was moved with compassion, released him, and forgave him the debt." It is a word that means to send forth, to release, to let go. It means, and this is so important, to abandon the issue, to let go from the obligation for which one is responsible. I have news for you. I am really, really glad I was forgiven that way. Can you imagine what it would be like if God were to bring up our sins over and over and over again, even though He says we have been forgiven? To drag those and parade those through our eyes and through our lives and through our dreams and anything else—are you not glad that God says, "When I forgive you, I forgive you completely and I release you from that? I declare that you have been cleansed and washed free and I abandon that whole issue, you are no longer under obligation. That sin is completely removed out of your life."

You see, that is what we have gotten in life, and I for one am very, very glad of that. I can sit here today and tell you all the sin that I have committed in my life, and you would look at that list and say, "That's too long for a preacher." I could look at your life and say, "That's too long for you as a believer." But aren't you glad that when Jesus Christ embraces us, and we embrace Him—after Jesus Christ has gone to the cross and paid for our sin that these three things take place in our life—God is moved with compassion, He releases us, and He forgives us. That is why He says in 1st John, chapter 1, verse 9—and you may want to turn to that because it is so important in relation to your sin and my sin. Look at what John says in 1st John, chapter 1, verse 9—look at that passage.

This is something that you need to experience today, because what I am going to tell you in a minute, lets you know, that the reason that you do not often forgive others is because you do not understand what I am speaking of right here. You do not fully grasp it. It says in 1st John 1:9, "If we confess our sins, he is faithful and just to forgive us our sins (the same word) and cleanse us from all unrighteousness." Turn the page, 1st John, chapter 2, verse 12. In that verse it says this: "I write unto you little children because your sins are forgiven you for His name's sake." Remember what it means to be forgiven? It means to abandon the cause against someone, to remove the obligation from someone because of their sin. And what that means is, when we come to Christ, that has all been removed. God no longer holds us responsible for the sins of our past.

Martin Luther was said to have had a dream, and that dream involved Satan standing in front of him unrolling a scroll with the details, the sins of his life. And the devil unrolled the scrolls and said, "Martin, these are your sins." And then he unrolled a second scroll and laid it out and said, "Martin, these are your sins as well." And then he did the same thing with the third, and he unrolled it, and he said, "These are your sins, Martin, what do you think about that?" And in the dream Martin says, "Well, you have left one thing out." And the devil said, "What is that?" He said, "You have forgotten to add at the bottom of it all that the blood of Jesus Christ has cleansed me from all those sins." Dear friend, that is what we need to keep in mind. Are you glad about that today? That the blood of Jesus Christ has forgiven us of all that. You need to keep in mind, I need to keep in mind that we have had that kind of forgiveness in our lives. Now, this parable is not about salvation. This parable deals with the issue of forgiveness and tells us who have been forgiven to forgive others.

But, I want to share with you, if you have never received forgiveness, you can never grant it. And I really believe with all my heart that one of the reasons that we do not forgive others more quickly, more readily, one of the reasons that we do not walk in a spirit of forgiveness toward those who will in the future offend us is because we have never understood God's forgiveness of us wholly.

A number of years ago, I heard a man preaching, and he really spoke to me in a powerful way. He was preaching about the Lord's Prayer, which has a line in it that says, ". . . forgive us our trespasses as we forgive those who trespass against us," and he was talking about the fact that people will offend us every day of our lives. We know it is going to happen. We know that there is always potential for harm and for grief and for injury or insult, and he says, "You need to learn the spirit of forgiveness." And what he said that day I have never forgotten, and I have lived by it since that time.

Here is the principle that he gave me. He said, "Since you know that God has forgiven you of your sins, since you know that someone else will at some point in the day say or do or insinuate something that will offend you, why don't you walk in the spirit of forgiveness, determining in advance that you will forgive them even before they say it or do it or insinuate it." He said, "Why don't you learn to walk in the spirit of forgiveness?" And it goes something like this: "Lord, I understand how much that you have forgiven me. I understand that if I sin in the future, that as I come to You, You will forgive me again and again and again, because Your blood is sufficient completely to forgive me of past, present, and future sins. And so because of that, I determine in my heart that when someone says whatever they will say or does whatever they will do against me, I determine that I will forgive them before it ever takes place."

I tell you, it really saves you on decision-making time. "Shall I forgive them? Should I not? Should I? Should I not?" You are going to forgive them at some point, because God will not leave you alone until you do. And so, how important is it to walk in the spirit of forgiveness? Say, "I understand what I have been forgiven of, and so I'm gonna walk in the same way toward you." I think I could do that seven times, what about 490? What about a lifestyle of forgiveness? Do you want to live a transformed life? Do you want to be transforming in the relationship in which you are involved? Walk in a spirit of forgiveness. Learn what it means to be forgiven, and forgive in the same way.

Now, how do you receive forgiveness? Let me give you six basic steps of forgiveness this morning. First of all, agree with God. That is the word, confession. First John 1:9, "If we confess our sins, He is faithful and just to forgive us of our sins and to cleanse us from all unrighteousness." First of all, agree with God. The word "confession" is a word that means to say the same as. If I want to receive forgiveness, then I need to confess my sins to God. I need to say, "God, I acknowledge what I've done is wrong, what I've said is wrong, and You have convicted me of that or shown me in Your Word that it is wrong. I acknowledge that. I agree with that and I agree with You." You cannot argue with God and walk in harmony with God. You have to be in agreement with God. It begins there.

Number Two. Assume your responsibility. James, chapter 4, verse 17 says, "To him who knows to do good, and doeth it not, to him it is sin." Assume your responsibility. You know that my sin is a result of my own doing and that nobody else can be blamed for that. When you have got six kids in the house and they sometimes argue with one another, you know the all-too-popular blame line, the word that they use, "My sister made me do it. My brother made me do it." And, we still do that when we are adults. We are driving down the road, and somebody cuts us off, and we are just trying to get to work. We are trying innocently to get to work. Somebody cuts us off, makes us slam on the brake, and we hit our fist on the steering wheel, and we say, "They made me mad." That is kind of juvenile reasoning, is it not? They really did not do that. You chose to respond the way you wanted to respond, and forgiveness is all about agreeing with God—not only what we did, but who is responsible for it? I am responsible for my sin. I am responsible for how I respond to anyone else.

Third, amend your action. Jesus in Matthew, chapter 5 talks about the fact that ways may exist to make amends. In fact, He says to one that is worshiping, "Leave your gift at the altar, get up and go reconcile with your brother and then come back and then make your offering to the Lord. Be reconciled." The whole idea behind that is make sure that you do all you can do to take care of those relationships. Like we spoke of last week, do all you can do.

Number Four. Accept your forgiveness. You know it is hard to believe that we can be forgiven. We just need to learn to accept forgiveness by faith. Paul said to Romans, chapter 5, verse 20, "Where sin abounded, grace abounded all the more." Wait a minute. You do not know how big my sin is. I mean, my sin is huge. I could not possibly be even able to put it in that food cup. It is so huge, but we are seeing "abound"—grace abounds all the more—much more, much more. How big your sin is does not matter. God's grace is far bigger than your sin, and so we must come to a place by faith where we say, "Lord, I accept your forgiveness, even though I cannot fathom with my mind how you can do this—I believe you have, because you have said you did and I accept that." Sometimes, friends we have got to remember that God has forgiven us so that we can get up and go on. We have to remember over and over not to sin, but the forgiveness of that sin is available when we do.

Number Five. Acknowledge your release. Acknowledge your release. Romans, chapter 8, verse 1 says, "Therefore, there is now, no condemnation for those who are in Christ Jesus." Now, I know this to be a fact. I know that many of us walk through life with a wave of guilt and condemnation. I think the best of us walk around with this stuff. I think the best of us tread with that. In fact, the reason I think that some of those who really want to walk with the Lord struggle faithfully with that, is because they cannot believe in their zeal to walk with God; they actually committed that sin. "I cannot believe I did that. I cannot believe that I actually let myself do what I did, and I know that God has forgiven me, but man, man, was I horrible to do that?" And, we walk with a measure of guilt, and we walk with a measure of condemnation, and it flavors everything we do—even how we respond to other people. We need to be able to say, "God's Word is true, whether I feel that it is true or not, whether I can sense that it is true, it is just true, and no condemnation exists now for those who are in Christ Jesus." I want to tell you, some things I never again want to remember about my life. I never again want it to be brought back up, but the only way that is possible is to know that I have been forgiven and cleansed and released. God no longer holds me accountable for that. Praise God!

The next one, not only do we acknowledge our release, but we seek to break the pattern. What I mean by that is found in Galatians, chapter 5, verse 16, where it tells us that if we walk by the Spirit, we will in no way carry out the lust of the flesh or fulfill the lust of the flesh. Simply, what I am saying is that as we come to God for forgiveness and confess our sin and acknowledge His power and to acknowledge His act of forgiveness and to walk without condemnation, without guilt. We then ask him, "Lord, fill me with your power so that I can follow you with a whole heart, never giving into sin on a daily basis like I once did. I want to walk in your power." And until you do that and walk in that, you have never understood what it means to receive forgiveness fully. Now, why are you focusing on this? I thought it was about forgiving other people. Well, it is, but it begins with this. Watch me.

If you never understand what it means to be forgiven fully by God, you will never be able to grant to someone else what God tells you to give him in the sense of being forgiven fully. Here is what Kay Arthur said in her book, *Lord, Heal My Hurts*. She said, "If you do not understand or receive the forgiveness of God, you will find it almost impossible to forgive those who have hurt you deeply or who have failed to be to you what they should have been to you as a mate, a mother, a father, a sister, a brother, a child or a friend. So, we begin by being forgiven. And once we understand the grace of that, once we understand the freedom of that, once we understand the release of that and the fact that we have been declared free and that is no longer held over us, then we can say, "As I have received it, so I can give it. As I have received it, so I can give it." "Wait a minute," you say. "People have done some pretty despicable things to me, and they intended to do that. I never intended to do that toward God. I never intended to fall that deeply into sin. I was not railing my fist and shouting at God what people have done toward me."

Oh, friend, you have. You have. No matter what we have done, it is all the same, it all condemns us, it all separates us from God, until we receive the forgiveness of Jesus Christ. That forgiveness is so complete, so thorough, so full, that when we receive His forgiveness, we will then know how to forgive someone else. I want to tell you that if you have been loved by God, you can love others. If you have been forgiven by God, you can forgive others, and you are called to do it.

Jesus ends this in really a frightening verse, because not only does he talk about the priority of forgiveness and the picture of forgiveness, He ends it with the price of unforgiveness. This is disturbing, because this passage tells me that God is very serious about the business of forgiveness, first toward us and then for us to forgive others. Look at verse 34. This is not something I am making up, nor if I had a choice would I make it up. This is God's Word. Here is what He says, verse 34, "His master was very angry and delivered him to the torturers until he should pay all that was due to him." At first, we have a tendency to think, "That was a parable. Every detail does not fall into place like you might think." But, then it says in verse 35, "So my Heavenly Father also will do to you if each of you from his heart does not forgive his brother his trespasses." You know what Jesus would say about this parable, which typically has one core truth. He says, this is the core truth right here, "You must forgive your brother, you must."

You see, not forgiving our brother or sister has a price attached to it. According to these verses here, there is the price of initiating the anger of God. Literally, if we have been forgiven, all that we have and we refuse to forgive our brother or sister, then we are initiating the anger of God. It says in verse 34, "And his master was very angry." The *New American Standard Version* says, "He was moved to anger." We find the direct opposite in verse 27, where he is "moved with compassion." Now, he is moved with a different kind of perspective. Instead of compassion, it is anger, and the reason that God would be angry with us—the reason that would violate His sense of character, is because He is a forgiving God. Whenever we have experienced the forgiveness of God, and do not give that to other people, we violate the very principle by which we have a right relationship with God. We are saying, "I want that forgiveness in my life. I am not willing to give it to anyone else. I want only what I can get. I am not concerned about anyone else experiencing Your love, Your forgiveness. I am not interested in them experiencing any freedom from what they have done in their past."

In *Ephesians*, chapter 4, verse 32, Paul makes an important statement for all believers, and this, by the way, was a letter that was sent throughout all the churches. Look at this verse with me for just a moment. Verse 32 of *Ephesians*, chapter 4 says, "And be kind to one another, tenderhearted, forgiving one another, even as God in Christ forgave you." That is pointed. "You mean, I am supposed to forgive others in the same way that God forgave me?" You got it! Absolutely right. "You mean, no matter what they do, how many times they do it, no matter how deep the offense, I still need to forgive them no matter what they do." You got it! That is right. Because you will be so full of having known the grace of God and the forgiveness of God and the release of God and the fact that God does not hold you responsible for the sins of your past, you will be so full of that grace, if you have really received it, that you have got plenty to pour out into people's lives. And not to do that is to violate the very thing that God has done in our lives—to violate His very character.

You see at the heart of it all, the reason God has forgiven us of our sins is so that His Son, Jesus, can live through us. By refusing to forgive, we cancel the possibility of Him living in fullness in our lives. But not only do we initiate the anger of God, we invite the consequences of sin. We are literally giving an invitation for things that we do not want to experience. Verse 34, "His master was angry and delivered him to the torturers (literally the gatekeepers) until he should pay all that was due to him." That word "torturer" literally means to vex or to torture as a prisonkeeper tortures. The consequence—he is right back in prison.

The consequence is that the world's worst prison is the prison of the unforgiving heart, that when we refuse to forgive, we box our lives in, and we do not have the opportunity to walk with God as we did before. We do not have the opportunity to experience all He wants us to experience. In fact, we experience all the things that we do not want to experience. We are weighed down by an incredible weight of baggage.

Carl Menninger, the famed psychiatrist, once said that if he could convince the patients in psychiatric hospitals that they had forgiveness for their sins, 75 percent of them would walk out the next day. I have known people who have physical illnesses, because they continue to hold on and play over time and time again in their minds, the crimes people have committed against them in the past. Mentally, they are moved away from stability. They are physically hurting. They are emotionally dragged down, because they have not released those who have hurt them in the past. Spiritual pain may be present. Anguish may be present in your life. The heavens may go silent if we do not forgive others, because God has called us to do that.

Let me read to you what David said in *Psalms*, chapter 32, in the first few verses, David is telling us what it is like not to forgive, not to confess, not to have forgiveness. He said, "Blessed is he whose transgression is forgiven, whose sin is covered. Blessed is the man to whom the Lord does not impute iniquity and whose spirit there is no deceit." Verse 3, "When I kept silent (David said), my bones grew old. Through my groaning all the day long, for day and night, your hand was heavy upon me; my vitality was turned into the drought of summer." He says in verse 5, "I acknowledge my sin to you and mine iniquity I have not hidden. I said I will confess my transgressions to the Lord; and you forgave the iniquity of my sin." He said, "I was vexed from every side. I was weighed down, because I was not doing what I needed to do, but then I forgave, as You forgave." That is what it is like to hold unforgiveness in our lives. You may miss the opportunity that God has for you in the future. You may walk weighed down in life.

A number of years ago, back in 1999, my wife and I were faced with a circumstance that we really never had been faced with before. We were faced with having to forgive someone of something that really hurt us, and we struggled with it. We struggled with it, because of the circumstances of it. Without going into detail, I can just say that my wife and I prayed about this for a number of months, and finally one day we said, "Not only do we need to forgive them, but we need to write a letter of forgiveness, and we need to send it to them, and until we do that, we really will not be absolved of the matter. We need to release them and all that they have done against us, and we just need to do it now."

And so, I remember very vividly on January 20th, 1999, we wrote a letter, put it in the mail. The next day we got a phone call that I believe was a life-changing consequence in our lives. I believe a significance existed in the matter of time between the day we finally dealt with that issue of forgiveness, wrote it down, declared it, put it away, and the next day getting a phone call that literally changed our lives with regard to our calling. In evaluating what God was doing in those days, I realize that I can often delay what God really wants to do in my life simply because I am holding onto unforgiveness, bitterness, and holding something against someone else. I would never want you to experience the holding back of all God's blessing in your life, and yet we have this incredible responsibility today to forgive.

I want you, for just a moment, to close your eyes and bow your heads for just a brief moment, and I want to ask you today what it is that you are holding back, that you are refusing to release about somebody else? I cannot possibly know who that might be. I cannot possibly know exactly what the circumstances are, but you know. In fact, you know it all too well. It may be that you played that over in your mind, over-and-over again, and now it is coming up again today, and the very mention of this passage is really giving you a fit in your heart. You feel the piercing of the Holy Spirit; you recognize the need this morning to respond to God.[6]

Lessons

One of the greatest lessons of this situation is what John Meador will not share. The sermon he preached was highly effective to move the church along the road to recovery. In visiting about concepts and sermons, Pastor Meador gave extraordinary insights. When asked about this situation in particular, Meador said that this crisis in his church was a church family matter. He said it is important that for in-house crises in church, the churches should keep the details internally and away from publication to guard the church as it moves to what God wants it to be. This is a noble lesson for every pastor. Though this book is based on learning from things pastors have shared, in some areas of conflict, the pastor would do well to address such privately, find forgiveness, and aid the church in forgetting the past mistakes just as Christians long for our Lord to forget ours.

Jerrien Gunnink took a church that was strife-torn. In fact, he wrote a book on the subject. He said that preaching is a way to bring a church back to life after strife. He did not come to his church saying, "I have a plan here." He knew his gift was preaching and that was the gift he used. After eleven years in the pulpit, leading his church to recovery, he went back over his sermons to see which books he preached the most. He was surprised to see that he had preached more from First and Second Corinthians than any other books. Gunnink says preaching from the Corinthians was not deliberate; it was just where God led him to preach in that church. He said the Spirit of God heals, and He will lead the preachers to the passages that are most appropriate since only God knows the hearts.[7]

No better illustration exists of what a preacher should be in a strife-torn church than the picture of Jesus with a towel over His shoulder and a basin of water in His hands, washing feet. Jesus called the pastor to do likewise. Preaching to a strife-torn church requires patience like a cut on the hand,

---

6. John Meador, senior pastor, Euless, Texas, "Life Won't Wait on the Unforgiving (Matt 18:21-35)," October 8, 2006.

7. Gunnink, interview.

which has to be washed, sterilized, and wrapped by a Band-Aid or gauze. Over time, a scab forms, and eventually the wrapping is discarded. Without seeing it, healing takes place slowly, but surely. The wound becomes smaller until the scab eventually falls off, leaving a scar hardly noticeable. That is the way the Holy Spirit will bring healing to such a church using the preaching of God's Word along the way.[8]

---

8. Gunnink, *Preaching for Recovery*, 37-38.

Chapter 14: **The Culture**

Picture in your mind the floor of the United States House of Representatives. The time was the mid-1800s. The room was stuffy. The debate was heated. The issue was slavery. Texas had just been annexed, balancing the slave states with the free states, but now the issue of adding the territory of Oregon into the union as a free state troubled most slave supporters. The imbalance would benefit the abolitionists.

It was at that time, that the former president of the United States, who had in recent years become a member of the House of Representatives, John Quincy Adams, took to the floor to weigh-in with his opinion. He was a staunch, vocal abolitionist who spent the majority of his life fighting slavery. Adams pointed to the Bible that always lay on the table in front of the Speaker of the House and asked the clerk to read Genesis 1:26-28. He said, in essence, this passage provides the foundation of the United States' right to the territory of Oregon. The clerk read,

> Then God said, "Let Us make man in Our image, according to Our likeness; and let them rule over the fish of the sea and over the birds of the sky and over the cattle and over all the earth, and over every creeping thing that creeps on the earth." God created man in His own image, in the image of God He created him; male and female He created them. God blessed them; and God said to them, " Be fruitful and multiply, and fill the earth, and subdue it; and rule over the fish of the sea and over the birds of the sky and over every living thing that moves on the earth."

John Quincy Adams, who read five chapters per day of the Bible his entire life, said there in that Book was "the foundation of all territorial rights. . . . There, sir, in my judgment is the foundation not only of our title to Oregon, but the foundation of all human title to all possessions."

Adams did not stop there with his Bible lesson for his colleagues. He told the clerk to read the eighth verse from the second chapter of Psalms. The clerk read, "Ask of Me, and I will surely give the nations as Your inheritance, And the very ends of the earth as Your possession". Then with excitement, Adams told the clerk to turn back a couple of verses and see to whom it was said that He would give them. The clerk read, "'But as for Me, I have installed My King Upon Zion, My holy mountain'. I will surely tell of the decree of the Lord: He said to Me, 'You are My Son, Today I have begotten You'".[1]

Amazing that on the floor of the House of Representatives, a great Christian man is using the Word of God to handle a national crisis. John Quincy Adams, like his dad John Adams, knew the power of God's Word for life and for life's crises. He leaned on the first chapter of Psalms during his tumultuous times as president, and many other verses at the death of a son and other relatives. Lincoln said of the Bible, "In regard to this great book, I have but to say, it is the best gift God has given to me. All the good Savior gave to the world was communicated through this Book. But for it, we could not know right from wrong. All things most desirable for man's welfare, here and hereafter, are found to be portrayed in it."[2]

On the Left—The Culture

Contemporary culture is no longer very interested in history. For many college degrees, history is no longer a requirement. The world rotates, based on people's attitudes and personal experiences or the projected cultural experience. It sees no objective truth on which to rely or follow. Religious faiths of all sorts are looked upon as equally valid. Mandates and the declaration that there is one way to Heaven (or even one way to do anything) are deemed pre-historic. Tradition is viewed as too binding as culture's desire to break free from what was valued in the past grows.[3]

What is the result? More sex on television, less marriages by percentile, more divorces, more unwanted or abused children, more depraved alternative lifestyles, which bring misery and shortened lifespans. More acceptance of drug use prevails, more laughing at the instances of drunkenness, more tolerance of obscene language in homes, schools, and on major television networks. More instances occur of children abusing and disrespecting adults. Contracts and bank notes are no longer binding. The government is looked to as the parent-figure to rescue its children, its citizens. No cause is considered worthy for giving one's life.

1. Marie B. Hecht, *John Quincy Adams: A Personal History of an Independent Man* (Newtown, CT: American Political Biography Press, 1972), 618-19.
2. John Donald Hawkins, *Famous Statements, Speeches and Stories of Abraham Lincoln* (Palm Beach Gardens, FL: Heathcote Publications, 1991), 16.
3. James Earl Massey, "The Preacher as God's Steward," *Preaching* 21, no. 5 (March/April 2006): 15.

The culture has renamed its sins. Abortion is referred to as a choice. American Greeting Cards has a line of cards for expectant mothers. The majority of these cards read, "Congratulations on your baby-to-be!" This pushes the agenda that until the baby is born, it is not a baby. It is just a baby-to-be if the mother chooses to carry it. Homosexuality is called an alternative lifestyle. Husbands and wives are called "partners," allowing cohabitating couples and gay couples to be elevated to equal footing.

Tolerance is declared for all religions, but apparently, Christianity is left in the cold, because it is the religion perceived to be guilty of acts of cruelty and oppression. Islam can be taught in the schools under the auspices of cultural education. But, a Bible course has to go through both houses of Congress, the judiciary, and overcome the veto threat of the executive branch. Evolution and global warming are seen as good science, while Creationism is seen as a superstitious myth held by the uneducated. To speak Jesus' name is to offend practically all within ear-shy. To close a prayer in Jesus' name is seen as a marked form of aggression against all that is civil.

In the Middle—The Church in Culture

The Church was called to be a city on a hill, the salt of the earth. Paul called upon the believers in Philippi to be pure and blameless. This little Philippian church stood in the middle of a godless time and was intimidated constantly by the adversaries of Christ. Those who came to Christ in that era were considered a dishonor to their families and a disruption to the cohesion of society.[4] Paul's letter initially addressed to the pre-Christian era, now applies to the post-Christian era of today. The Christian confession of "Jesus is Lord" was just as much a political quandary then as it is today.[5] Unfortunately, many who consider persecution or social discomfort as being distasteful, have retreated from firm beliefs in any eternal truths.

In many ways, the Church appears to have lost its saltiness. It no longer sets the example for society. It has actually become a reflection of society. Christians have become quite confused in recent days on issues of right and wrong. The majority of Christians now do not believe that the Bible is the literal Word of God, nor do the majority of Christians believe only one way to Heaven exists.[6] They attend church less frequently, and those who attend less frequently are more likely to embrace abortion, homosexuality,

---

4. Thompson, "Preaching to the Philippians," 299.

5. Ibid., 300.

6. Pew Research Group, "U.S. Religious Landscape Survey," *Houston Chronicle*, June 24, 2008, A1.

and sexual promiscuity.[7] No wonder schisms exist in the Episcopal, Presbyterian, and Methodist churches on the issue of homosexuality, homosexual membership, and homosexual clergy. Battles are brewing over the same issues in the other denominations such as Baptist and Catholic. In practice, no notable difference exists in divorce rates of Christians compared to non-Christians.

Leaning Left—Biblical Illiteracy

A big cause of the problems in the United States and its Christian churches can be credited to Biblical illiteracy. When Wade Hodges took over as teaching pastor at Garnett Church of Christ in Tulsa, Oklahoma, he took a church that had been in decline. During his first six months, he visited with his leadership team about doing a series on one of the Gospels. One of his leaders said, "I think we've got the Gospels figured out. Let's figure out a way to move the ball downfield." Hodges knew at that moment that he had a problem in his church.[8]

Unfortunately, that leader's opinion is a prevalent attitude in today's churches. Today's preachers often look at God's Word as dated material, which needs his apologies of where it has biases and shortcomings. He can approach the Bible as if it is an "uncouth childhood friend who is difficult and embarrassing, but must be tolerated."[9] To diminish the role of the Bible, and to draw big crowds, some preachers resort to challenging sermons like "Fifteen Reasons to Get up Tomorrow" and "Thirty Ways to Get Over a Headache." A belief exists that truth must be given out in small doses, be positive, and do a little pop psychology so everyone feels good about themselves.[10] Sadly, such preaching that is less intensive and less demanding brings better offerings.[11] The people are being served milk instead of meat. Perhaps it was in anticipation of this that caused Paul to write Timothy in 2 Timothy 4:3-4 and say, "For the time will come when they will not endure sound doctrine; but wanting to have their ears tickled, they will accumulate for themselves teachers in accordance to their own desires, and will turn away their ears from the truth and will turn aside to myths".

7. Ibid., A12.
8. Wade Hodges and Greg Taylor, "We Can't Do Megachurch Anymore," *Leadership* 28, no. 1 (Winter 2007): 50.
9. Anthony B. Robinson, "Courage to Preach," *Christian Century* (September 18, 2007): 36.
10. Brunson and Caner, *Why Churches Die*, 174.
11. Ibid., 178.

To answer the question, which came first the "lite" sermon preacher or the "itching-ear" Christian, one would have to flip a coin to decide. When the pastor says, "Open your Bibles and turn to Mark, chapter 12," no rustling of pages is heard as in times past. Few even carry their Bibles to church. What is more shocking, most Christians have no knowledge of even the most familiar Bible stories. To help explain some divine truth, the pastor may refer back to what he would think is a familiar Old Testament account, just to find the church giving him a blank stare of confusion. Today's church member is likely to look at God's Word as the "Double U"—Unknown and Unnecessary. They have no basic understanding of its words, nor do they find Biblical restraints and disciplines appealing. They like Jesus a lot, but sports, shopping, fun, and making money seem a lot more exhilarating.[12]

One Presidential candidate recently communicated that opinion on the campaign trail, questioning the Bible's credibility because of its call for adherence to all its dietary restrictions and because of what he calls its "promotion of slavery." Such statements demonstrate the Biblical ignorance of the day. A billboard on Interstate 45 in Houston was placed to promote a vegetarian lifestyle. It had a picture of Jesus, and it said, "Jesus was a vegetarian." Sadly, most would see that billboard and assume that He must have been. The reason many fall for the first cult that comes along is that they do not know God's Truth. Jesus said that man cannot live by bread alone, but by "every word that proceeds out of the mouth of God" (Matthew 4:4). The majority of Christians are stumbling through life malnourished. This is not Jesus' intent.

On the Right—The Bible

Christians need to take another look at the Bible. Author James Qualben gives the perfect imagery of the Bible. He says it is like a jewel whose worth is seen in how many brilliant lights radiate from it—the more lights, the more valuable a text. As one moves through life and around that jewel, new lights radiate from it—lights never seen before. The source of that light is God. He is also the Giver of light and revelation.[13] The Bible is a living book with a vital living message from a living author.[14] It is authoritative, because it comes from the mouth of God by the Spirit of God moving the hands of men. Other evidences attest to the authority of the Bible. It has proven historically ac-

---

12. Gordon MacDonald, "Behind the Curtain: When Things Get Ugly," *Leadership Magazine*, (Spring 2007): 52.

13. Qualben, *Peace in the Parish*, 147-48.

14. Bisagno, *Letters to Timothy*, 155.

curate and internally consistent. Its prophecies, written hundreds of years before, have seen their foretold events come to pass. It has influenced the course of human history more than any other book, continuing to change the lives of millions of individuals reaching back to history and reaching forward to the future. Through the Bible, people have come to find salvation. The Bible has majestic beauty and profound depth, providing teaching unrivaled by any other book. The Bible does not hide the fact that it is God's Word, nor does it leave it for someone else to say. The Bible proclaims hundreds of times over that it is the very words of God.[15]

The Bible is the full, complete record from God for life; no one part should be excluded. The Bible is able to mold the Christian through its stories and lessons into the people that God wants them to be. Too many churches have neglected the Old Testament. They have relied on a distorted view of the New Covenant.[16] As a result, no awe of holiness is present. No call against sin is present. No realization of the tremendous price that had to be paid is present. Further, by ignoring the Old Testament, the Christian misses the commentary on contemporary culture where everyone does what is right in his or her own eyes. Jeremiah said it is like a hammer that breaks rocks into pieces. In the prophet's mouth, it becomes a fire that devours people like wood. Isaiah said it brings light upon Israel, and the entire nation reels under its impact. Hosea said it hews like a sword. Amos said that when God Almighty lifts His voice and roars, the pastures and forests of Carmel wither.[17]

It is the Bible—all-sufficient, for no other thing needs to be added or taken away. The Bible needs no "new thing." This narrows the focus for Christians to the Bible in finding what God has to say. Such sufficiency is shown by the strength of a simple noun. The Bible is not simply true. It is truth. Jesus affirmed as much when He prayed in John 17:17, "Sanctify them in the truth; Your word is truth". He did not say that God's words were true, but that God's Words are truth itself.[18] The only tool necessary is to distinguish between right and wrong, truth and error.[19]

Dietrich Bonhoeffer said that one does not need to make the Bible relevant. Its relevance is self-evident. God's Word will prove true every time

---

15. Grudem, *Systematic Theology*, 78.

16. James Armstrong, *Telling the Truth: The Foolishness of Preaching in a Real World* (Waco, TX: Word Books, 1977), 84.

17. Ibid., 95.

18. Grudem, *Systematic Theology*, 128.

19. Brunson and Caner, *Why Churches Die*, 177.

one follows it.[20] The Bible is balanced, providing a balanced dietary plan for Christians, giving them all that they need for daily living, for overcoming darkness, for leading people into the light, and for assurance in times of fear and doubt. Paul said it best in 2 Timothy 3:16-17, "All Scripture is inspired by God and profitable for teaching, for reproof, for correction, for training in righteousness; 17 so that the man of God may be adequate, equipped for every good work".

In the Gap—The Preaching

What did God say through Paul concerning this Word? He said in 2 Timothy 4:2, "Preach the word; be ready in season and out of season; reprove, rebuke, exhort, with great patience and instruction". The Bible is for teaching, rebuking, correcting, and training. Paul says, in essence, "then use it to teach, rebuke, correct, and train." God calls for the foolishness of preaching by a human instrument to apply the Word to the people. David Jeremiah said he spent the first part of his ministry learning what God's Word said and explaining it to the people. Then he realized that this was incomplete preaching. The preacher must apply what the Scripture means to the person's individual life. It is not that the Bible is not relevant. It is that many fail to show its relevance.[21]

The word "crisis" is used appropriately, for what the preacher faces today. The Chinese character representing "crisis" means both danger and opportunity.[22] Crisis is defined as: "the turning point for better or worse in an acute disease" or "an unstable state of affairs in which a decisive change is impending."[23] Preaching is the change agent, which God has deemed necessary. When John the Baptist stepped onto the pages of history, Matthew records, "Now in those days John the Baptist came, preaching" (Matthew 3:1). The time had come, the crisis of all history—the sins of humanity facing the judgment of Holy God, and John the Baptist came preaching. People responded with repentance, the way was made straight for the Author of Salvation to bridge the gap between God and man. That is what preaching does. An old term for church officials was the word "pontifex," which means "bridge-builder."[24] That is the preacher's role.

20. MacDonald, "Speaking into the Crisis," 44.
21. Jeremiah, "Preaching Through Pain," 20.
22. Muse, "Clergy in Crisis," 183.
23. Philip Babcock Gove, ed., *Webster's Third New International Dictionary* (New York: G. & C. Merriam Co. Publishers, 1961), 537.
24. Willimon, *Preaching About Conflict*, 34.

To the culture, the preacher proclaims Romans 10:13, "Whoever will call on the name of the Lord will be saved". To the culture, he shows from God's Word that the accepted lifestyles and sins of the day are detrimental to one's health. For years, people thought smoking was good for their health. If someone discovered it was detrimental and kept silent, people would continue smoking until, hopefully, the hard facts would dawn on them. The health organizations did not leave it to intellectual dawning; they launched an all-out blitz warning everyone of the danger. Their work has saved thousands-upon- thousands of people. Many still smoke, but they do so by ignoring all the warnings. The preacher warns that the wages of sin is death, ending in eternal punishment. The listener can respond or ignore. Nothing should excite a preacher more than to hear that a lost person in church needs to be saved.[25] That puts grease on the preaching skid.

Thankfully, the Word of God preached is persuasive, capable of melting even the hardest of hearts. Augustine saw that in his life, as did John Newton and millions of others. Paul faced the Roman governor Felix, and through sharing the Word of God by the power of the Holy Spirit, even hard Felix was almost persuaded. When a lady in a church was angry about how the youth dressed for church, a preacher shared a sermon from Acts 15 called "Freedom Worth Fighting For." In this sermon, he extolled the virtue and benefit of Christian freedom. After the sermon, the lady of the church came forward with tears streaming down her eyes confessing her sinful attitude and actions.[26]

The preacher has more to say. He is to stand up and speak against sex outside of marriage, adultery, gambling, abortion, homosexual rights, racism, and murder. If the preacher will not address these issues, who will? Many fear how the congregation will respond, or if such stands will affect his job security. One who truly believes the Lord and loves Him, trusts Him with the consequences. For Brian Newman to stand behind his pulpit in Amsterdam, of all places, and speak against sex took a lot of courage.[27] But, he did, and many in his church came forward, repented, and are seeking to be what God wants them to be. How great it would be to see Las Vegas preachers speak against gambling, or Washington D.C. preachers speak against congressional perks!

In our little town of my first church, I spoke against the three bars in the city where so much crime and violence were being launched. We prayed that God might shut them down. That sermon was carried on the

---

25. Burton, *Prince of the Pulpit*, 58.
26. Preston, *Pastors in Pain*, 78.
27. Newman, "License to Thrill," 48.

local radio channel as was each Sunday's service. No threats came thankfully; but amazingly, two of the three bars closed in that year. Please do not misunderstand, these vices can never be overcome through one's willpower. The preacher only exposes the sin and its harm so that the listener can be led to the saving and redemptive work of Jesus Christ in His love.[28]

Adam Hamilton of the United Methodist Church of the Resurrection in Leawood, Kansas, had an interesting approach. He announced to the worshippers and the community that they would be covering a series of sermons on: Separation of Church and State, Evolution in the Public Schools, the Death Penalty, Euthanasia, Prayer in Public Schools, Abortion, and Homosexuality. Each Sunday's attendance was one thousand people over the normal attendance. In those sermons, he took the Biblical stand. They lost some people, but many new people began attending. People in the community were thankful that a church would deal with these hot issues respectfully, yet truthfully.[29]

The preacher must have the backbone to speak against societal, cultural, national, and international injustices. Dietrich Bonhoeffer said a preacher must "speak up for those who cannot speak for themselves, for the rights of those who are destitute." He was urging Christians to speak up for the victims of Hitler, particularly the Jewish people.[30] Bonhoeffer paid the price, but his rewards he enjoys eternally. His counterpart, Helmut Thielicke grew tired of the persecution for his stand, and sought time away, out of the line of fire. Not long into his rest, he returned to the "bombs, the damage, and the suffering for there he found reality, courage, and community which became his seedbed for preaching."[31] Preaching will never make one comfortable, because it is disruptive by nature and threatens everyone in sight.[32] Nonetheless, the man of God must have the confidence in Scripture, the courage to preach it, and the willingness to put themselves at risk.[33]

The preacher has a word for the church and the Christian. Preaching instructs in the ways of righteousness, it corrects and rebukes the Body of Christ, and unites them in doctrine and love. The preacher stands before them willing to speak what God's Word says, even when it is painful, but he makes sure it is God who speaks and not he, himself. Spurgeon said that the

---

28. Shelley and Miller, "Fundamentally One," 19.

29. Hamilton, "Opening Closed Minds," 38.

30. Philip Yancey and Tim Stafford, eds., *NIV Student Bible* (Grand Rapids: Zondervan, 1986), 691.

31. MacDonald, "Speaking into Crisis," 46.

32. Robinson, *Biblical Sermons*, 36.

33. Ibid., 37.

Bible is sharper than any two-edged sword. It needs no help from the preacher in the cutting.[34] The preacher provides serious study that is sometimes unachievable by the congregation, due to their secular vocations. Therefore, they attend every Sunday to understand more of God.

They come to hear a word from God as they face their struggles and personal crises. From the pulpit, God's servants bring clarity for the church in realizing its identity, its purpose, its mission, and its future.[35] Bible preaching is great counsel. David Lino, a pastor in Houston, says that he will not counsel anyone privately, if he or she refuses his corporate counseling every Sunday morning. He makes a good point. When the pastor preaches Scripture, the Holy Spirit works through that instrument to do divine surgery on the listener. If the person places so little value on God's Word preached, what good will a man's counsel do? W. A. Criswell said that preaching expositionally from the pulpit will decrease the pastor's counseling load, because he is counseling them from the Word of God.[36]

The Insulating Balm, The Dessert

God is amazing in giving the preacher the words that he needs to speak at the moment he needs to speak them. So much of this writing has dealt with the reactive approach guided by God's hand to bring a congregation through a storm and help a pastor weather the storm. One last thing is of the utmost importance. It is last, not due to priority, but last in an effort to send the preacher out with a take-home message to be engraved upon his heart and mind. The message is to preach God's Word in total through Biblical books, not selecting Scripture randomly, and not as to meet one's fancy. Many will never preach through the whole Bible. As a result, many treasures will remain buried and hidden through a random approach of exposition.

Unfortunately, often, the best method of dealing with storms is overlooked. Design exists in how God ordered His Word. One cannot look at the cell without seeing design and order established for the fullest functionality. Looking up to the heavens, the solar system, the stars, and their constancy, the optimal, perfect design must be observed, and the exclamation must report, "No better way existed to do that!" With that in mind, the Bible is opened, and the books are ordered by God for optimal effect. The chapters of each book are ordered to bring about the biggest impact. God gave the Bible to aid the preacher and the Christian through every issue in life—either

34. Spurgeon, *Lectures to My Students*, 88.
35. Willimon, *Preaching About Conflict*, 33.
36. Patterson, interview.

specifically, or in principle. As a result, preaching through a book in the Bible, or preaching through the Bible in general allows the pastor to deal with any and every issue that will come down the pike in his church.

The best way to deal with a crisis is to address it before it occurs. The best way to assist a people to deal Biblically with crises is to condition them beforehand in a Godly way. Dr. Paige Patterson has stated that no better way exists to deal with conflict than to head it off before it starts. When a huge fight arises concerning a deacon, the best time to preach on the qualifications of a deacon may not be then. It can be done, and often in crisis, it must be done. However, the better approach is to have taught the congregation about the deacon office and deacon life when going through the Biblical book of Second Timothy.[37]

Or, God's spokesperson could preach the book of Acts systematically. When he gets to the sixth chapter of Acts, a natural exposition of the purpose of the deacon's position is in God's design. At this point, an open heart exists to the teaching of God's Word for church function. The church knows that the topic has come through the normal reading of God's Word. They will know that the preacher is not selecting something out- of-hand to expound on some pet-peeve of his. The congregation knows where the preacher preached last week. The congregation knows where he will be preaching the following week. As a result, they are not prone to question, nor do they have evidence to question, why the pastor covered what he did when he did.

Preaching through the books of the Bible is a proactive approach to inoculate the church against a virus that may in the future threaten its health.[38] This works the same for doctrinal issues. If the preacher of the church waits until the issue comes to the surface, it may be too late to give the church an objective lesson on the issue in question. At that point, the opportunity for a split is already at hand, especially when people infiltrate the church, pushing their favorite theological wedge. In waiting around for an issue to surface, the infiltrator will have already exposed and enlisted many in his or her camp for some "new" truth he or she is espousing. How much better to have preached faithfully through the books of the Word of God, and to have been proactive in dealing with every issue that God brings to bear in this manner. When preaching God's Word through, the preacher might choose to skip some issues due to the explosive nature present in some passages. But, if the preacher will bring boldly the full Word by the Power of the Holy Spirit, he will fare much better in the day of challenge.

37. Ibid.
38. Gunnink, interview.

One benefit of this method is that it removes the emotion that will encompass the preacher in any conflict. God works through the personality of the preacher. He is to be steel-cloaked in velvet.[39] Unfortunately, the foolishness of preaching resides more in the preacher than the word preached. That steel can often push through the velvet, and expose the raw steel with raw emotion. The preacher is a sinner saved by grace, called by God to teach His truths, not to taint them by his fleshly input. Even when preaching through a book this can happen, so caution must be taken any time a preacher preaches in crisis.

Lastly, God uses preaching through the books to help the pastor prepare for something in his own life. Dr. Mac Brunson preached about Paul's shipwreck in Acts 27-28. He called the sermon, "Sailing Through the Storms of Your Life." That night he got out of the pulpit, and a mom of a girl his son dates, ran to tell him his son was in the emergency room. He imagined the worst. The whole way to the hospital, he kept remembering that God is in control of the storm. His son made it fine. Another Sunday, he preached Romans 8 about how God works all things together for good. As soon as he was through preaching, a man came to tell him his wife was in the hospital losing lots of blood. He was told to get to the hospital immediately. Again, as he headed for the hospital in horrible fear and grief, he kept thinking of God's Word in Romans 8, God works all things together for good.[40] And, God did.

---

39. Patterson, interview.
40. Brunson, interview.

Chapter 15: **The Charge**

The late Peter Marshall was an eloquent speaker, and for several years, he served as the chaplain of the United States Senate. You may be familiar with a story he loved to tell, it was entitled "The Keeper of the Spring". It told about a quiet forest dweller who lived high above an Austrian village along the eastern slope of the Alps.

The old gentleman had been hired many years earlier by a young town councilman to clear away the debris from the pools of water up in the mountain crevices that fed the lovely spring flowing through their town. With faithful, silent regularity, he patrolled the hills, removed the leaves and branches, and wiped away the silt that would otherwise have choked and contaminated the fresh flow of water. The village soon became a popular attraction for vacationers. Graceful swans floated along the crystal clear spring, the mill wheels of various businesses located near the water turned day and night, farmlands were naturally irrigated, and the view from restaurants was picturesque beyond description.

Years passed. One evening the town council met for its semi-annual meeting. As they reviewed the budget, one man's eye caught the salary figure being paid to the obscure keeper of the spring. Said the keeper of the purse, "Who is the old man? Why do we keep him on year after year? No one ever sees him. For all we know, the strange ranger of the hills is doing us no good. He isn't necessary any longer." By a unanimous vote, they dispensed with the old man's services.

For several weeks, nothing changed. By early autumn, the trees began to shed their leaves. Small branches snapped off and fell into the pools, hindering the rushing flow of sparkling water. One afternoon someone noticed a slight yellowish-brown tint in the spring. A few days later, the water was much darker. Within another week, a slimy film covered sections of the water along the banks, and a foul odor was soon detected. The mill wheels moved more slowly, some finally ground to a halt. Swans left, as did the tourists. Clammy fingers of disease and sickness reached deeply into the village.

Quickly, the embarrassed council called a special meeting. Realizing their gross error in judgment, they rehired the old keeper of the spring, and within a few weeks, the veritable river of life began to clear up. The wheels started to turn, and new life returned to the hamlet in the Alps once again.[1]

Some days, you are going to feel like quitting. Days will come when people will want you to quit. But, you cannot. Moses wanted to quit many times, but God would not let him. Moses, resisting the temptation of his free will, stayed at the helm. During the Civil War, when his generals were hesitant to engage the enemy and the losses of Union lives were mounting up, to assume that President Lincoln considered quitting, either the office or the cause is natural, but he did neither. He said, "God selects His own instruments and sometimes they are queer ones. For instance, He chose me to steer the ship through a great crisis."[2] Jesus told the disciples, "You did not choose Me, but I chose you." Jesus has chosen you to steer your church's ship in the crisis it faces. Do not quit. You are the keeper of the spring. God has called you to keep his living stream clean, useful, functional, and beautiful. You are the one who removes the moss branches of heresy, the leaves of discontentment, and the silt of laziness, so that the fresh flow of God's Words may refresh, rejuvenate, and enliven His children in a dry and weary world. The minute you quit preaching God's Word, or quit altogether, the whole Body of Christ will suffer.

Paul says, "Stand firm therefore." He has equipped you well. Ephesians 6:14-18:

> Stand firm therefore, having girded your loins with truth, and having put on the breastplate of righteousness, and having shod your feet with the preparation of the gospel of peace; in addition to all, taking up the shield of faith with which you will be able to extinguish all the flaming arrows of the evil one. 17 And take the helmet of salvation, and the sword of the Spirit, which is the word of God. With all prayer and petition, pray at all times in the Spirit, and with this in view, be on the alert with all perseverance and petition for all the saints.

You have the only weapon you need in His Word, and you are filled with power unfathomable in His Holy Spirit. The biggest things you need

---

1. Peter Marshall, *Keeper of the Spring, Stories from the Heart*, comp. Alice Gray (Sisters, OR: Multnomah Books Publisher, 1996), 97.

2. Hawkins, *Famous Statements*, 45.

to bring to the table are: your gifts (which God has given also), your resolve to persevere, and a soft, clean heart through which He can do marvelous things. Servants of God may find themselves in the journey cast down, but God best uses those who have been emptied of self-reliance. The whole purpose of this book is to allow you to know that, contrary to what others may tell you, no matter what you face, you CAN preach your way out of this mess!

Early in this journey, we revisited the dawn of ministry, the excitement, the mission of making a difference as God's instrument, and the vision of what lay ahead. Now, we look forward to the sunset of ministry. May it be said of us, as was said of Truett at the end of his life, "The world cannot do without such preaching as was done by George W. Truett. Dark, dark would be the day. We knew then, that his lips were closed forever, that his appeal to higher living no longer challenged men's hearts; that his call to repentance no longer pointed the way to salvation and life."[3]

I have to quit writing now. We are trying to build a church. Our first builder misled us, so we let him go. The second builder took $86,000 from our church and has not performed, and now hardly returns our calls. Another crisis is always around the bend. Let there never be a time when the preacher seeks to remove his preaching from the crisis. To do so is to imply that the Bible is irrelevant for the church today.[4] I have a sermon to prepare as our church faces this new crisis. Can one sermon make a difference in church? Ask Ezra. Can one sermon make a difference in our culture? Ask Jonah. As Paul exhorted Timothy, so I will, "Preach the Word."

---

3. Burton, *Prince of the Pulpit*, 20.
4. Willimon, *Preaching About Conflict*, 9.

Bibliography

Books

Adam, Peter. *Speaking God's Words: A Practical Theology of Preaching*. Vancouver, BC: Regent College Publishing 1996.

Armstrong, James. *Telling Truth: The Foolishness of Preaching in a Real World*. Waco, TX: Word Books, 1977.

Ayres, Alex. *The Wit and Wisdom of Abraham Lincoln*. New York: Penguin Books, 1992.

Barna, George, and Mark Hatch. *Boiling Point*. Ventura, CA: Regal Books, 2001.

Bell, B. Clayton. "Preaching and Conflict." In *Handbook of Contemporary Preaching*, ed. Michael Duduit, 530-35. Nashville: Broadman Press, 1992.

Bell, James S., Jr. *The D. L. Moody Collection*. Chicago: Moody Press, 1997.

Bell, Roy D. *Biblical Models of Handling Conflict*. Burlington, ON: Welch Publishing Co., 1987.

Bisagno, John R. *Inside Information: Worship Wars, Calvinism, Elder Rule & Much More*. Longwood, FL: Xulon Press, 2007.

———. *Letters to Timothy*. Nashville: Broadman & Holman Publishers, 2001.

Brunson, Mac, and Ergun Caner. *Why Churches Die: Diagnosing Lethal Poisons in the Body of Christ*. Nashville: Broadman & Holman Publishers, 2005.

Burton, Joe W. *Prince of the Pulpit: A Pen Picture of George W. Truett at Work*. Grand Rapids: Zondervan Publishing House, 1946.

Criswell, W. A. *Expository Sermons on Revelation*. Grand Rapids: Zondervan Publishing House, 1962.

Cymbala, Jim. *Fresh Wind, Fresh Fire*. Grand Rapids: Zondervan Publishing House, 1997.

Duduit, Michael. *Handbook of Contemporary Preaching*. Nashville: Broadman Press, 1992.

Fee, Gordon D. *1 and 2 Timothy, Titus*. New International Biblical Commentary. Peabody, MA: Hendrickson Publishers, 1984.

Gangel, Kenneth O., and Samuel L. Canine. *Communication and Conflict Management in Churches and Christian Organizations*. Nashville: Broadman Press, 1992.

Garrett, James Leo, Jr. *Systematic Theology: Biblical, Historical and Evangelical*. North Richland Hills, TX: BIBAL Press, 2000.

Gray, Alice. *Stories for the Heart: Over 100 Stories to Encourage Your Soul*. Sisters, OR: Multnomah Books, 1996.

Grudem, Wayne. *Systematic Theology: An Introduction to Biblical Doctrine*. Grand Rapids: Zondervan Publishing House, 1994.

Gunnink, Jerrien. *Preaching for Recovery in a Strife-Torn Church*. Grand Rapids: Zondervan Publishing House, 1989.

Halverstadt, Hugh F. *Managing Church Conflict*. Louisville, KY: Westminster/John Knox Press, 1991.

Hawkins, John Donald. *Famous Statements, Speeches and Stories of Abraham Lincoln*. Palm Beach Gardens, FL: Heathcote Publications, 1991.

Hecht, Marie B. *John Quincy Adams: A Personal History of an Independent Man*. Newtown, CT: American Political Biography Press, 1972.

Hicks, H. Beecher, Jr. *Preaching Through a Storm*. Grand Rapids: Zondervan Publishing House, 1987.

Hoge, Dean R. and Wenger, Jacqueline E. *Pastors in Transition: Why Clergy Leave Local Church Ministry*. Grand Rapids: William B. Eerdmans Publishing Co., 2005.

Kemp, Charles F. *Pastoral Preaching*. St. Louis: Bethany Press, 1963.

Leas, Speed, and Kittlaus, Paul. *Church Fights: Managing Conflict in the Local Church*. Philadelphia: Westminster Press, 1973.

Linn, Edmund Holt. *Preaching as Counseling: The Unique Method of Harry Emerson Fosdick*. Valley Forge, PA: Judson Press, 1966.

Lloyd-Jones, D. Martyn. *Preaching and Preachers*. Grand Rapids: Zondervan Publishing House, 1971.

MacDonald, Gordon. "Speaking into the Crisis." In *Great Preaching—Practical Advice from Powerful Preachers*, ed. Paul Woods, 43-49. Loveland, CO: Group Publishing, 2003.

Marshall, Catherine. *A Man Called Peter*. Grand Rapids: Chosen Books, 1951.

———. *Mr. Jones Meet the Master: Sermons and Prayers of Peter Marshall*. London: Fleming H. Revell Co., 1949.

Marshall, Peter. *Keeper of the Spring, Stories from the Heart*. Comp. Alice Gray Sisters, OR: Multnomah Books Publisher, 1996.

Mathews, Kenneth A. *Genesis 1-11:26*. New American Commentary. Nashville: Broadman & Holman, 1996.

———. *Genesis 11:27-50:26*. New American Commentary. Nashville: Broadman & Holman, 2005.

McGee, J. Vernon. *Genesis-Deuteronomy*. Thru the Bible. Nashville: Thomas Nelson, 1981.

———. *Joshua-Psalms*. Thru the Bible. Nashville: Thomas Nelson, 1982.

Nixon, David F. *Leading the Comeback Church*. Kansas City, MO: Beacon Hill Press 2004.

Nohl, Frederick. *Luther: Biography of a Reformer*. St. Louis: Concordia Publishing House, 2003.

Phillips, Donald T. *Lincoln on Leadership: Executive Strategies for Tough Times*. New York: Warner Books, 1992.

Phillips, John. *Exploring Genesis*. Grand Rapids: Kregel Publications, 1980.

Powell, Paul W. *Basic Bible Sermons on Handling Conflict*. Nashville: Broadman Press, 1992.

Preston, Gary. *Pastors in Pain: How to Grow in Times of Conflict*. Grand Rapids: Baker Books, 2005.

Proctor, Samuel D. *Preaching About Crises in the Community*. Philadelphia: Westminster Press, 1988.

Qualben, James. *Peace in the Parish: How to Use Conflict Redemption, Principles, and Process*. San Antonio: Lang Marc Publishing, 1991.

Rediger, G. Lloyd. *Clergy Killers: Guidance for Pastors and Congregations Under Attack.* Louisville, KY: Westminster/John Knox Press, 1997.

Robinson, Haddon W. *Biblical Sermons: How Twelve Preachers Apply the Principles of Biblical Preaching.* Grand Rapids: Baker Book House, 1989.

Rogers, Cleon L., Jr., and Cleon L. Rogers III. *The New Linguistic and Exegetical Key to the Greek New Testament.* Grand Rapids: Zondervan Publishing House, 1998.

Rogers, Joyce. *Love Worth Finding: The Life of Adrian Rogers and His Philosophy of Preaching.* Nashville: Broadman & Holman Publishers, 2005.

Russert, Tim. *Big Russ and Me.* New York: Miramax Books/Hyperion, 2005.

Spence, H. D. M., and Joseph S. Exell, eds. *Genesis-Exodus.* Pulpit Commentary. Peabody, MA: Hendrickson Publishers, 1950.

———., eds. *Ezra-Job.* Pulpit Commentary. Peabody, MA: Hendrickson Publishers, 1950.

Spurgeon, Charles Haddon. *Lectures to My Students.* Grand Rapids: Zondervan Publishing House, 1954.

Strang, Stephen E. *Solving the Ministry's Toughest Problems.* Altamonte Springs, FL: Strang Communications Co., 1984.

Swetland, Kenneth L. *Facing Messy Stuff in the Church: Case Studies for Pastors and Congregations.* Grand Rapids: Kregel Publications, 2005.

Teikmanis, Arthur L. *Preaching and Pastoral Care.* Philadelphia: Fortress Press, 1968.

ten Boom, Corrie. *The Hiding Place.* Washington, CT: Chosen Books, 1971.

Towner, Philip H. *1-2 Timothy & Titus.* IVP New Testament Commentary Series. Downers Grove, IL: InterVarsity Press, 1994.

Tucker, Austin B. *A Primer for Pastors.* Grand Rapids: Kregel Publications, 2004.

Vines, Jerry, and Jim Shaddix. *Power in the Pulpit: How to Prepare and Deliver Expository Sermons.* Chicago: Moody Press, 1999.

Wagner, E. Glenn. "Preaching from Down Under." In *Great Preaching—Practical Advice from Powerful Preachers,* ed. Paul Woods, 131-47. Loveland, CO: Group Publishing, 2003.

Wallace, Daniel B. *Greek Grammar: Beyond the Basics.* Grand Rapids: Zondervan, 1996.

Wenham, Gordon J. *Genesis 1-15.* Word Biblical Commentary. Nashville: Thomas Nelson, 1987.

———. *Genesis 16-50.* Word Biblical Commentary. Nashville: Thomas Nelson, 1994.

Wiersbe, Warren W. *Be Authentic, Genesis 25-50.* Colorado Springs: Victor Books, 1997.

———. *Be Basic, Genesis 1-11.* Colorado Springs: Victor Books, 1998.

———. *Be Obedient, Genesis 12-24.* Colorado Springs: Victor Books, 1991.

Willimon, William H. *Preaching About Conflict in the Local Church.* Philadelphia: Westminster Press, 1987.

Woods, Paul. *Great Preaching: Practical Advice from Powerful Preachers.* Loveland, CO: Group Publishing, 2003.

Yancey, Philip, and Stafford, Tim, eds. *NIV Student Bible.* Grand Rapids: Zondervan, 1986.

Articles

Berkley, Jim. "Have I Come to the WRONG Church?" *Leadership* 7, no. 2 (Spring 1986): 50-53.

Burrows, William R. "Things to Keep in Mind When Preaching 'Mission.'" *Living Pulpit* 12, no. 2 (July-September 2007): 8-12.

Chapell, Bryan. "The Fallen-Condition Focus and the Purpose of the Sermon." *Preaching* 20, no. 6 (May/June 2005): 29-33.

Clark, Charles. "The Suicide of a Church." *Preaching* 15, no. 4 (January/February 2000): 29-31.

Dorrien, Gary. "American Liberal Theology: Crisis, Irony, Decline, Renewal, Ambiguity." *Crosscurrents* 55, no. 6 (Winter 2006): 456-81.

Duduit, Michael, ed. "Expository Preaching in a Narrative World: An Interview with Haddon Robinson." *Preaching* (July/August 2001): 4-13.

———. "Purpose-Driven Preaching: An Interview with Rick Warren." *Preaching* 17, no. 2 (September/October 2001): 6-17.

Ford, Leighton. "Evangelistic Preaching in the Twenty-First Century." *Journal for Preachers* 30, no. 4 (Pentecost 2007): 25-36.

Hamilton, Adam. "Opening Closed Minds." 25, no. 2 *Leadership* (Spring 2004): 37-41.

Hodges, Wade, and Taylor, Greg. "We Can't Do Megachurch Anymore." *Leadership* 28, no. 1 (Winter 2007): 49-51.

Jeremiah, David. "Preaching Through Pain." *Preaching* 18, no. 5 (March/April 2003): 15-21.

Karkabi, Barbara. "On God, Religion and . . . Texas." *Houston Chronicle*, 24 June 2008, 1 (A).

Keever, Jeannie. "As Americans Change, So Does Their Religion." *Houston Chronicle*, 26 February 2008, 1 (A).

Labberton, Mark. "Our Daunting Hope: Can Preaching Really Change Anyone?" *Leadership* 26, no. 3 (Summer 2005): 30-34.

Lotz, Louis. "Preaching on Controversial Issues: Keeping the Peace vs. Keeping the Purity." *Preaching* 16, no. 2 (September/October 2000): 40-41.

MacDonald, Gordon. "What's a Leader to Do When Followers are Revolting?" *Leadership* 28, no. 2 (Spring 2007): 50-54.

———. "Behind the Curtain: When Things Get Ugly." *Leadership Magazine*, (Spring 2007): 52.

Massey, James Earl. "The Preacher as God's Steward." *Preaching* 21, no. 5 (March/April 2006): 14-18.

Milton, Michael. "Hit by Friendly Fire: What to Do When Christians Hurt You." *Preaching* 21, no. 1 (July/August 2005): 36-41.

Mohler, R. Albert, Jr. "The Preacher as Servant of the Word." *Preaching Magazine* (September 2002): 9.

Morgenthaler, Sally "Does Ministry Fuel Addictive Behavior?" *Leadership* (Winter 2006): 58-65.

Muse, Stephen. "Clergy in Crisis: When Human Strength Isn't Enough." *Journal of Pastoral Care and Counseling* 61, no. 3 (Fall 2007): 183-95.

Newman, Brian. "License to Thrill." *Leadership* 27, no. 1 (Winter 2006): 48.

O'Day, Gail. "Preaching in Ordinary Time." *Journal for Preachers* 30, no. 4 (Pentecost 2007): 45-51.

Pearson, Calvin. "Sheep, Serpents and Doves: Using Argumentation Theory in a World Hostile to Truth." *Preaching* 42, no. 1 (July/August 2008): 14-17.

Pew Research Group. "U.S. Religious Landscape Survey." *Houston Chronicle*, June 24, 2008, p. A1.

Reed, Eric. "Restoring Fallen Pastors." *Leadership* 27, no. 1 (Winter 2006): 21-25.

Robinson, Anthony B. "Courage to Preach." *Christian Century* (September 18, 2007): 36-38.

Shelley, Marshall, and Kevin Miller. "Fundamentally One: An Interview with Truman Dollar." *Leadership* 7, no. 4 (Fall 1986): 12-20.

Thompson, James W. "Preaching to Philippians." *Interpretation Magazine* (July 2007): 298-309.

Warren, Rick. "It's OK to Preach Repentance." *Leadership* 25, no. 1 (Winter 2004): 59.

Work, Telford. "Messianic Showdown." *Christian Century* 124 (June 26, 2007): 28-31.

Doctor of Ministry Projects

Buchanan, William F. "Proclamation and Catharsis for Crisis Ministry: Preaching and Lay Pastoral Care." D. Min. proj., United Theological Seminary, 1995.

Liles, Jesse R. "Creating Attitudinal Change Regarding Worship Styles Through a Study of Selected Biblical and Historical Models." D.Min. proj., Southwestern Baptist Theological Seminary, 1998.

Molone, Leonard. "Equipping Church Leadership in Developing Conflict Management Skills." D.Min. proj., Southwestern Baptist Theological Seminary, 1993.

Sanchez, Peter, Jr. "Equipping Church Leaders to Address Congregational Conflict Through an Expository Preaching Class." D.Min. proj., Southwestern Baptist Theological Seminary, 2007.

Watson, Tracy. "Equipping Leaders from the Double-Mountain Baptist Area in Conflict Management Skills." D.Min. proj., Southwestern Baptist Theological Seminary, 1998.

Williamson, Robert A. "Avoiding Forced Termination of Pastors: A Win-Win Possibility Through Polarity Management of Conflict." D.Min. proj., Southwestern Baptist Theological Seminary, 2003.

Internet Websites

Barna Update. "Pastors Rate Themselves Highly, Especially as Teachers" (January 7, 2002) [on-line]. Accessed 27 July 2008; available from http://www.barna.org/FlexPage.aspx?Page=BarnaUpdate&BarnaUpdateID=104; Internet.

Barna Update. "Americans Draw Theological Beliefs from Diverse Points of View" (October 8, 2002) [on-line]. Accessed 27 July 2008; available from http:// www.barna.org/FlexPage.aspx?Page=BarnaUpdate&BarnaUpdateID=122; Internet.

Franklin, Rebecca. "Traditional French Palate Cleansers." About.com [on-line]. Accessed 29 August 2008; available from frenchfood.about.com/od/explore/frenchfood/a/palatecleanser.htm; Internet.

New York Avenue Presbyterian Church, Washington D.C. [on-line]. Accessed 18 August 2008; available from www.nyapc.org; Internet.

Sande, Ken. "What Are Three Ways Leaders Can Deal with Difficult Congregants?" BuildingChurchLeaders.com (2008) [on-line]. Accessed 18 August 2008; available from http://www. buildingchurchleaders.com/help/asktheexperts/ken sande/q1.html; Internet.

"Sorrowful Time: Falcons' Robinson Gives Postgame Apology." *Sports Illustrated* (February 1, 1999) [on-line]. Accessed 28 July 2008; available from http://sportsillustrated.cnn.com/football/nfl/1998/playoffs/news/1999/01/30/robinsonarrested/index.html; Internet.

U.S. Department of Energy. "A Consumer's Guide to Energy Efficiency and Renewable Energy: Landscape Shading" (September 12, 2005) [on-line]; accessed 28 July 2008; available from http://www.eere.energy.gov/consumer/yourhome/landscaping/index.cfm/mytopic=11940; Internet.

Sermons

Bisagno, John. Retired senior pastor, First Baptist Church, Houston, TX. "The Unity of Faith." Sermon archives, First Baptist Church, Houston, TX.

Criswell, W. A. "The Church of the Open Door (Revelation 3:7-8)." Preached 9 June 1968. Criswell Sermon Library [on-line]. Accessed 8 August 2008; available from http://www.wacriswell.com/index.cfm/FuseAction/Search.Transcripts/sermon/1589.cfm; Internet.

Jackson, James F. Senior pastor, Chapelwood Methodist Church, Houston, Texas. "The High Cost of Spiritual Self-Deception (Judges 17:1-13)." 30 December 2007.

────. Senior pastor, Chapelwood Methodist Church, Houston, Texas. "The Promise of Light." From the Series "Naming the Darkness, Seeing the Light (Isaiah 9:1-7; Matthew 4:12-17; John 3:19-2)," 23 December 2007.

Meador, John. Senior pastor, Euless, Texas. "Life Won't Wait on the Unforgiving (Matt 18:21-35)," October 8, 2006.

Robertson, Mike. Senior pastor, Wichita Falls, Texas. "Valley of Trouble (Joshua 7)," September 23, 2007.

Swindoll, Charles R. "Setting the Stage for Disaster (Job 1:1-12)." Insight for Living. Plano, Texas, 2002.

Teague, Johnny. Senior pastor, Church at the Cross, Houston, TX. "Things a Son Would Do (Genesis 37)," January 20, 2008.

────. Senior pastor, Church at the Cross, Houston, TX. "What a Dad! (Job 1:1-6)," June 11, 2006.

────. Senior pastor, Church at the Cross, Houston, TX. "When We Go Where God Leads (Genesis 26)," October 28, 2007.

Vines, Jerry. Senior pastor, Jacksonville, FL. "The Woeful World of Uz (Job 1-3)." July 24, 1996.

Wells, Bruce. Senior pastor, Liberty City, Texas. "State of the Church Address (Gal 6:1-2)," September 9, 2007.

Interviews, Lectures, and Movie

Allen, David. Dean of the School of Theology, Southwestern Baptist Theological Seminary, 2008 Expository Preaching Workshop lecture, Fort Worth, Texas, 2008.

Bisagno, John R. Retired pastor of First Baptist Church, Houston, TX. Lecture in Pastoral Leadership class, Southwestern Baptist Theological Seminary, Houston, TX, Fall 2005.

BIBLIOGRAPHY

Brown, Byron. Senior Pastor of a Texas Baptist church. Interview with project leader via e-mail, March 30, 2008.

Brunson, Mac. Senior pastor, First Baptist Church, Jacksonville, FL. Telephone interview with writer, April 22, 2008.

Bryant, James. Senior Professor of Pastoral Theology. Criswell College, Dallas, TX. Personal phone interview with project leader, April 21, 2008.

Fraser, George. Titus Task Force. Personal phone interview with project leader, May 28, 2008.

Goss, John. Senior pastor, Central Baptist Church, Crockett, TX. Personal interview with project leader, February 13, 2008.

Gunnink, Jerrien. Former pastor and author. Personal phone interview with project leader, May 27, 2008.

Hunt, Johnny. Pesident, Southern Baptist Convention. Interview via e-mail to writer. June 27, 2008.

Jackson, James F. Pastor of Chapelwood Methodist Church, Houston, TX. Personal interview by project leader, June 11, 2008.

"A Man Called Peter." 20th Century Fox, 1955.

Meador, John. Senior pastor, First Baptist Church Euless, Texas. Personal interview by project leader, March 27, 2008.

Patterson, Paige. President, Southwestern Baptist Theological Seminary, Fort Worth, Texas. Personal interview by project leader, April 22, 2008.

Schibler, Bill. Pastor. Personal interview by project leader, Hico, TX, March 10, 2008.

Vines, Jerry. Retired pastor, First Baptist Church Jacksonville. Personal interview by project leader.

2008 Expository Preaching Workshop. Southwestern Baptist Theological Seminary, Fort Worth, TX, 2008.

Wells, Bruce. Senior pastor, Liberty City, Texas. Personal phone interview with project leader, May 27, 2008.

www.ingramcontent.com/pod-product-compliance
Lightning Source LLC
Chambersburg PA
CBHW070737160426
43192CB00009B/1475